Laughter from Land's End

Laughter from Land's End

Of the first edition, 500 copies have been printed.

This copy is number: 478

LAUGHTER FROM LAND'S END

by

ARTHUR CADDICK

Edited by Rod Humphries

For Sheila,

all very best wishes

Happy Birthday!

again, Rod.

5/7/17.

The manuscript of *Laughter from Land's End*

is by courtesy of

The University of Exeter, Special Collections

Laughter from Land's End

The Madrigal of Mead (illustration, Appendix VII)
Marsden Prophet for the Cornish Mead Company

Cover Photographs
front: *Arthur Caddick* : photographer unknown,
kindly supplied by Simon Parker of the
Western Morning News
back: *Rod Humphries* : Tobi Carver

Design & Composition: Tobi & Toni Carver
Printed & Published by:
St Ives Printing & Publishing Company,
High Street, St Ives, Cornwall TR26 1RS, UK

ISBN 0 948385 39 1

Laughter from Land's End, a vibrant account of an extraordinary life. In his own words Arthur Caddick brings alive the person behind the poetry.

Stimulated by the illusive mystery of Cornwall, his genius flowered in the unique post-war period that brought painters and writers together to share the bohemian life-style. A time that will never come again.

We, his family, rejoice that in publishing *Laughter from Land's End*, Rod Humphries has begun the journey of restoring him to his rightful place in Cornwall's literary tradition.

Diana Caddick

Northam, Devon.

March 2004

"In my view Arthur Caddick is Cornwall's forgotten poet, equal to importance in the area as Thomas Hardy was to Dorset."

Dr. Catherine Brace

University of Exeter

On the arrival of Caddick's papers at Exeter University.

Quoted from the Cornishman 4th December 1997.

CONTENTS

ILLUSTRATIONS

ACKNOWLEDGEMENTS

None of this would have been possible without the backing, unfailing patience and kindness to me of Diana Calvert née Caddick, her husband, Ken, David Caddick and his wife Ann. My special thanks to Ann for her sustained effort at making this a much better book through her dedicated proof reading. My thanks for the help they gave cannot be measured. And of course, Peggy Caddick.

Lists of 'thank yous' are always difficult since the risk of leaving out someone is very real. My humble apologies to anyone not included, it is my oversight, not a slight. I should like to thank the following who have contributed in a variety of ways: loan of materials, energy, ideas, information, support, advice, research, skill and, especially friendship. I greatly appreciate all of you. In simply alphabetical order:

Michael Bridge
Peter & Maureen Caldwell
Castle Inn, St. Ives
Dr Catherine Brace
Express Newspapers
Hywel Gillard
John & Ruth Greenaway
Harbour Bookshop, St. Ives
Nick Hayes
House of Lords Record Office
Maureen Humphries
Roger Humphries
Roland Humphries
Colin T. Johnson
Glenys Kent
Morrab Library, Penzance
Barbara Pallett
Simon Parker
Punch Ltd
Radio Cornwall
Les Rowe
Frank Ruhrmund
St Ives Library
St Ives Reminiscence Project
St Ives Printing & Publishing Company
The University of Exeter, Special Collections
Martin Val Baker
Paul Vibert
Helen Walasek – Punch Cartoon Library
David Wilkinson

THANKS ARE ALSO OWED to those kind people who pre-ordered copies... And waited! Again in alphabetical order:

Bob Acton
Brian and Marion Atkins
Edna Berryman
E. Boyns
Justin Brooke
Clyde Brush
S W Cocking
Paul Colbourne
Ivan and Heather Corbett
Marcus Cotterell
Joyce H Crawford
Julie Curtis
C. E. Daniel & David Daniel
John Dayman
Jack & Win Doswell
Edwin J. D. Eddy
Eric Ellis
Michael Grist
Sue Halliday
Wendy Hill
Keith & Sue Hodge
Christopher S Hogg
Max & Brigitte Huber
Mrs P.K. Hugo
Patricia Kazan
Glenys Kent
Harding Laity
Sheila Lanyon
Dr Lavern and Kathryn Herman
Sonia Martin
Doreen Monckton
Alan Neatby-Smith
Peggy Netcott
K. F. Northey
Eleanor O'Kelly
Marie O'Donaghue
Ken Olds
John Purchas
Dorothy Phillips
J. C. Perkin
Margaret Perry
Audrey Randle Pool
Frank Ruhrmund
M. E. Reed
P Reid
Les Rowe
Phil Saward
Pat & Ernie
Phillip Semmens
John Stevenson
E. Stubbings
Donald S. Swan
Charles Thomas
Sharon Thomas
Wendy Topsey
D Tredinnik
William Waters
M. F. Wilkins
J. Wiles
Barbara Williams
K. F. Worthy

Arthur Bruce Caddick

March 20th 1911 – April 10th 1987

ARTHUR CADDICK was born in Coatham, Yorkshire. Although he described himself as being: "Scotch, Welsh and English in judicious proportions".

He suffered from colitis for much of his childhood and was taken to clinics and hospitals around the country in search of a cure – which badly disrupted his schooling.

He was educated at Sir William Turner's, Sedbergh, and then at Wadham College, Oxford where he read Jurisprudence to please his father, although he wanted to read English – indeed he spent much of his time attending English Lectures![1]

After leaving Oxford he became General Secretary of the Faculty of Architects and Surveyors. He edited the architectural journal 'Portico' for a year.

In 1938 he married Peggy Thompson who was from what was then Southern Rhodesia, after a very brief courtship![2] They moved to live a somewhat Bohemian life in Brittany, returning to the UK. on the outbreak of war in 1939. During the war he worked as a censor at the War Office.

He was a very keen amateur dramatist even then and was a semi-professional member of a reparatory group, both acting and writing a number of short plays and sketches, during the war.

In 1945 came the family move to Cornwall, the occupation of 'Windswept' and his job at the Nancledra power sub-station. Caddick tends to trivialise his work there, but it was a highly responsible position. He received a severe injury on one occasion whilst dealing with an emergency.

His work with the electricity board finished in 1953 and, from then on he relied on his writing and the kindness of family and friends for a living.

Finally in March 1981 owing to his and Peggy's declining health, they moved from 'Windswept' to live in Fremington near Barnstable, Devon close to his daughter, Anne and family, it was here where he completed *Call of the West* in 1983. He suffered a stroke in 1985 which, while it did not totally disable him, it effectively stopped his writing.

Tragically Anne died in 1986. Arthur and Peggy then went to live at Newent in Gloucestershire with Diana and Ken while a bungalow was being built for them.

It was at this time his name was being considered for the post of Poet Laureate.[3]
Following a further stroke in 1987 he died in hospital in Gloucester on April 10th. He is buried, as he wished in Ludgvan Churchyard, not far from Nancledra.[4]

1> Jurisprudence: Science and philosophy of human law. 'Skill in Law' — see also Chapter I

2> For details of his and Peggy's courtship, see Appendix 1.

3> See Appendix II

4> See Appendix III

Preface

YOU CAN OF COURSE ignore this preamble and get stuck straight into *Laughter from Land's End*, no one reads this bit anyway. I know I don't! But for those who may be interested, read on!

I am not a biographer and many will say with justification, I am not a very good editor!. However this is how it all came about.

In August 1999 for reasons not relevant here I found myself in Nancledra. A friend had very generously placed a caravan at my disposal, on land he owned.

Nancledra, a wonderful name, we shall hear more of it and have reason to learn to love it. It is pronounced nan-kled-ra or traditionally 'cledry, pronounced kled-ri.

I was pleased to learn it meant Clodri's, or Rhodri's Valley.

As my eldest son's name is Rhodri it seemed a very good place for me to settle.

One very hot day busying myself cutting brambles, moving stones or both – a lady asked me if I knew where Arthur Caddick had lived. I can't remember her exact words but I totally got the wrong end of the stick – not unusual for me, but there we are.... I suggested she asked at the local post office, as I was new to the area!

She briefly explained that he was a poet and had lived nearby. Regretfully, I was unable to offer her any help. This was my initiation into the world of Caddick.

I was in the process of exploring the locality and had seen the name 'Windswept' but it meant nothing to me. Although I was to appreciate in later months how it obtained its name! I'd also seen a nearby building that I'd been told was either an old mining building or a former electricity sub-station – both as turned out!

I knew of some Cornish born poets mainly Jack Clemo and Charles Causley and others such as John Betjeman et al who'd written in, or about the county but Caddick?

My first port of call was, as ever in this position, the local library.

Here I obtained a copy of Eric Hirth's biography on Caddick, "Never Sit Down in the Digey!" which, incidentally, has an excellent foreword by Frank Ruhrmund. He fascinated me! What a character, what a poet! I followed up Hirth with Caddick's daughter, Diana's book, *I'll Raise The Wind Tomorrow*. I managed to obtain some of his books – all sadly out of print – from second hand bookshops and with the help of a friend, 'on the net'.

There was something about his style that jumped from the pages and grabbed me! – I can't explain it, why, I wondered, wasn't he better known?

Michael Williams in his *Curiosities of Cornwall* has the poem 'Top Person Talking' in full and describes meeting him. (See Chapter XXI) He appears in only one anthology of poetry, and that published this year.[1]

His friend Denys Val Baker refers to him in his book, *A View From Land's End* (1982) but, his earlier work, *The Spirit of Cornwall* (1980) which has a complete chapter on the poets and poetry of Cornwall ..... nothing. He is referred to astutely several times in Alison Oldham's *Everyone was Working* — see bibliography. Dr Catherine Brace wrote an excellent study in Cornish Studies No. 7 *Cornish Identity and Landscape in the Work of Arthur Caddick* — see Chapter XI and bibliography.

There I suppose matters would have rested, however, fate was to play a hand. St Ives has held a Festival for a number of years. A mixture of the arts: poetry, music, talks, walks, readings, studios would be open and so on.

Alongside the Festival ran the Fringe Festival, the brainchild of local poet and artist, Colin T Johnson.

The 2003 St. Ives Festival had to be cancelled, but Colin decided to hold a Fringe Festival. I went to one of the early planning meetings, where he was open to offers for fringe events.

Prior to this, my brother, Roland, had a vague plan to visit all the places in Cornwall, which featured in song, and to give performances of said songs in the actual locations.

I'd looked at the idea of visiting the pubs Caddick reviewed in *One Hundred Doors Are Open* and declaiming his poetry...... perhaps not a very good idea! The two ideas somehow gelled.

Colin's request for events led to me leading two walks 'n' talks through St Ives called: 'We Shall All Sit Down In The Digey'.

Originally I'd planned to look at the pubs as they were described by Caddick in *One Hundred Doors are Open* see how they had changed, read some of his work. This would have proved a little impractical so a stroll through the town was planned covering, very generally, his life through his poetry and prose. Before the walks were finalised, I wrote to Diana who kindly approved the idea.

The two walks took place during the St Ives Fringe Festival 2003. Diana had hoped to come but was unable. However, David and Ann Caddick turned up and we had a very enjoyable, and for me, informative talk later in The Castle.

This was followed by a visit to Exeter University Special Collection Library to see Caddick's papers.

I'd read the extracts of *Laughter at Land's End*, which had appeared in *The Cornish Review* – but to my surprise, I found in one of the boxes, what was to all extent and purposes, a complete manuscript of *Laughter from Land's End*. The staff at the library told me I'd need the permission of Peggy and Diana before this could be copied – this permission was quickly forthcoming. Barbara and I then spent a memorable week-end with Diana, her husband and of course, Peggy at their respective homes in Devon. It was here I learned that Arthur and Peggy called each other 'P' and 'T', short for Piglet and Tigger!

I shall make no mention about the monkey in the cinema ... Some facts you can't find in books!

The Manuscript

The first reference I know of the title, 'Laughter from Land's End', was in *Quiet Lutes and Laughter* (1955). The book is in 5 sections: Tilts at the Times, Songs of Love and Children, A Croft in Cornwall, Laughter from Land's End and Conclusions. Some sections from

Laughter From Land's End appeared in the Cornish Review entitled 'Laughter at Land's End', Spring 1966 and as 'More Laughter at Land's End', Summer 1967. Footnotes state that they are 'From an autobiographical work in progress.' Cornish Review No. 22 winter 1972 has a piece, 'Marks of Royal Favour.' Caddick makes no reference in a footnote to it being a part of his autobiography in progress either at of from Land's End.

However, Val Baker in his editor's commentary says: "Arthur Caddick contributes another amusing extract from what everyone will hope is one day his published autobiography, *Laughter at Land's End.*" Caddick presumably did not wish it to appear in the manuscript which is a pity as it is a very funny piece of writing — although, it does have a hint of darkness.

It is not an autobiography in the conventional sense, it is more a series of stories about the fortunes and misfortunes of Caddick. The manuscript is slightly unusual in that there is no mention of early childhood, schooldays or even his courtship of Peggy. He does include a description of his rather unpleasant treatment for colitis (see Chapter I.)

The manuscript as it stands was obviously intended for publication. It was written in 1961, and revised in 1975 – I have kept all revisions. I am sure Caddick would have carried out further alterations. Written on the title page in Caddick's hand is 'Complete First Draft' and the date 10/IX/75. Added by the University ('complete' draft) with reference EUL, MS, 124 (BOX 10). Most changes have been made in pen, others typed presumably using the backspace key during the original writing.

Some changes are very minor, e.g. Chapter IX was originally entitled, 'A happy issue out of all afflictions'. This was altered to 'A happy issue of all our afflictions – 'our' being penned in at some later date. Does it matter? I think not.

Other hand written changes are very extensive and very difficult to read. I have corrected some obvious typing errors – which he had not altered, other things I've left; eg. his use of 'alright' – I know 'alright' is acceptable but show me a dictionary with it in!

Interestingly he wrote Trencrom as two words – 'Tren Crom' – again does it matter? – No.

Some of his alterations in the manuscript, to me at least, are very difficult to read. Where this occurs there will be (......? ....) Where there is no ? or broken line the brackets are Caddick's. I have made a few comments in square brackets thus [Ed]

His command of English was superb, having a very extensive vocabulary. I needed to refer to my dictionary on more than one occasion! Eg. indehiscence, Chapter XV or fuscal, Chapter XVI. I would not like to have played Scrabble with him!

The task of transferring the manuscript to disc – no, it would not scan – fell to my former sister-in-law, Honor Humphries. She made two trips to St Ives, 'one to fetch, one to carry' completing the task at her home in Oxford.

She would return home from her 'proper job' to resume her self-imposed, task excited to find out, "What next?" It made her laugh aloud. She felt she actually came to know Caddick, his family and friends, they came to life for her. Her computer did complain about the length of sentences asking her, "Do you want a full stop?"!

It is, I think, easy reading – not in the sense of trivial or light, but superbly written.

Arguably, Chapters VII, VIII and IX are overly long and possibly contain too much irrelevant detail. That is purely a personal opinion, not a literary criticism.

As for my additions, I have added a few footnotes, and potted biographies of some of the people mentioned. At one stage, I became a little too enthusiastic – practically putting footnotes on footnotes ... and if I'd put details for all those mentioned! There was a danger of it becoming too much biography, and not enough autobiography.

Also there are some appendices, which, hopefully, may be of interest.

Toni Carver, proprietor of the St. Ives Printing & Publishing Company, made a comment to me about how much easier it would have been for Caddick if he'd had access to modern printing and publishing methods. (See Chapters XIII and XV).

I think his prose outlay using a word processor may have been much greater and also, more efficient. (see Chapter XII). More importantly, his unpublished novel, *Two Can Sleep Cheaper*, would not have been lost ... I'm sure it would have been a wonderful read. (See Chapter XIV).

His novel *Respectable Persons* (see Chapter V) is delightful – if a little dated – I dislike comparisons but it is a cross between Evelyn Waugh and P. G. Wodehouse.

He doesn't have the venom of Waugh – although he could be very caustic if he wanted, and it is, to me a step above the style of Wodehouse. I should add I enjoy the work of both these writers.

His novella, *The Tilting of the Scale* (1962) is a much darker piece, which he considered, and I agree, "...some of my best writing" (Chapter XXII).

I feel it is a shame Caddick never really developed his work as a writer of fiction, or would that have been detrimental to his talent as a poet? His poetry was often written quickly and spontaneously so his prose could have, arguably, existed alongside.

In my introduction to my festival walks, I said how Derek Tangye had said: "It is my belief that Arthur Caddick is the Dylan Thomas of Cornwall". (quoted by Diana in, *I'll raise the Wind Tomorrow*). I generally dislike comparisons that the press or critics tend to use during the careers of writers, sportsmen, actors etc.

We all have influences in our lives; be it a book, picture, piece of music or personal mentor, and of course one can learn or draw inspiration from them but I dislike the constant comparisons we tend to get from critics.

In all fairness, I think Tangye was suggesting that Caddick's name was synonymous with Cornwall as that of Thomas's is with Wales and not comparing their poetical talents. 'The Call of the West' (1983) in *About The Poet* has the following quotation, ". . . It is my belief that Arthur Caddick is the Dylan Thomas of Cornwall. Like Dylan Thomas he has the gift of touching our hearts."

Having said all that, back in September 2003, I made the comparison of Caddick with cartoonist, Ronald 'Carl' Giles.[2] Now, as far as I know, Giles wrote no poetry and Caddick did very little drawing.[3] However, both had very similar views on life.

They each had an eye for detail, an eye for the ridiculous and could create their own work on topical subjects – local and national. Both had a keen dislike for bureaucracy and for what they considered, the actions of small minded and pompous bureaucrats.

Caddick, like Giles was quick to satirise what he saw as ridiculous and pompous – sometimes seriously – but more often, not so seriously.

Both had strong views on modern art and it shows in their work. Caddick, like Giles was fiercely protective of the environment, they had a love of the country and animals. Giles was a farmer and hunting was close to his heart, which was contrary to Caddick's beliefs. They enjoyed the culture of the pub. Many of Giles' cartoons are set in pubs and refer to the cost of beer!

Caddick, like Giles, was fiercely protective of the environment. In the Summer of 1971 there was a huge outcry when the South West Electricity Board sought permission to erect an overhead line on 100 foot pylons, extending from Hayle to Penzance. The number of objections to the scheme was so great that the public enquiry held at the Guildhall in Penzance continued for two days, at the close of which Arthur Caddick rose to his feet, and to the delight of everyone present, voiced his objection in verse, which he had written specially for the occasion and called *A Plague of Wire-Worms*.

Here is one verse as quoted in Hirth.

> A Board, or something of the sort desires
> To gain, for Cornwall's sake extensive powers
> To beautify Mounts Bay with copper wires
> Festooned between skeletal Eiffel Towers

The Giles cartoon overleaf shows what Giles thought of pylons! Giles fought a similar campaign in Suffolk in the 1960's. Despite a fierce battle he lost and had to suffer a pylon 100 yards from his home.

Both had circles of close friends. But, to me when you think of Caddick and Giles, you think of families.

Caddick, of course, had his own family. Giles, although very happily married, had no children. However, he created one of the more memorable families, albeit in cartoon form. Both families had their ups and downs, boyfriend and girlfriend problems, culture clashes and pets galore! Through their families both found inspiration. But, above all, what came through to me from these pages of *Laughter from Land's End* was, despite everything, warmth, love and laughter.

Enough! Turn over and enjoy *LAUGHTER FROM LAND'S END.*

Rod Humphries

1 > The Dreamt Sea, An anthology of Anglo-Cornish Poetry. *Edited by Alan M Kent.*

2 > *Ronald 'Carl' Giles. 1916 — 1995*
Although he had no formal art training, he was probably one of Britain's most popular cartoonists.

His main work was for the Daily Express *Group, which he joined in 1943. He retired in 1989.*

He produced many thousands of cartoons covering a vast range of topics from the end of World War Two to the opening of the Channel Tunnel.

His Christmas cards drawn fro various charities were always popular — many were drawn for the RNLI, a charity very close to his heart. They are now collector's items along with other pieces of his work, such as the 1978 Guiness Calendar.

*He toured Cornwall in his vast self-designed/built caravan-cum-studio. "Apparently he holds the St. Ives, Cornwall, record for backing the monster uphill all the way out of the town resort in the height of the holiday season, leaving the entire town intact." (*Squib *magazine — December 1992/January 1993).*

3 > *For an example of Caddick's art, see appendix III*

"I hope this client knows what he's doing – giving us

a bob for every pylon we knock down on his farm."

Sunday Express, April 18th, 1965

Dedication

ARTHUR'S BOOKS WERE USUALLY dedicated to Peggy. Although no dedication is in the manuscript of *Laughter From Land's End*, I don't see why it should be different.

I therefore take and slightly amend the dedication from his last publication, *The Call of the West*

To Peggy,

With all my love, as ever, and to memories of Windswept, our granite Cornish home for over half our lives.

"He was difficult, but we loved each other." Peggy to Rod January 2004.

Also in memory of Anne Dubois Bruce Daniel née Caddick, 1940 — 1986.

For Rhodri, Gareth and Josie with love.

RLH

LAUGHTER FROM LAND'S END

by Arthur Caddick

I
Enter one Smudge-Faker

WHILE I WAS SHAVING for Tea on my fiftieth birthday, it came across my mind with the convulsive jump of a hiccup that I had all the happy things in life except an income. I gave myself a curt stare in the mirror. Yes, there I was! A successful failure! Why wasn't I an abysmal success like some of my friends? Why was I standing there, scraping my chin in a tiny hillside cottage in Cornwall, before sitting down with a wife and five children, all waiting for me to blow out the candle-tokens of half-a-century, which I would first light from the fire with a letter from the bank complaining about my "dormant overdraft"? A dormant overdraft, though tinged with melancholy, is, by its very nature, a small sign of triumph. Overdrafts are born dominant: they grow clamant: if they end up dormant, you've worn one bank manager down at least.

After my Fiftieth Anniversary Tea that day (how I hate those senescent syllables!), I began to brood, gently, over the possibility of writing this book. I intended it as a corrective discipline for my spirit. I begin to fear I have written a treatise on the art of organizing fiascos. I know there are many admirable citizens who organize their careers on a Time-and-Motion basis – the trouble is they look like it. They have the appearance of having been baptised with Dehydrated Water. I had a friend once who took himself seriously. One day he showed me a Schedule. I remember two items for the day. "3 o'clock: get hair cut (singe?)" and then the lapidary phrase, "6.15: write a poem." I never took him seriously again – and if you ever come across a sonnet that's being troubled with dandruff, it'll be his.

In 1936, when I was almost twenty-five, I took up my first paid employment, by becoming a Classics Master at a Preparatory School in a London suburb. My most important duty was to count the Latin Grammars at the end of Term, trace any losses to the proper culprits, and give the Headmaster's wife a list of the Extras to be charged to the respective parents. My Situation, as it was then styled, did not prove congenial, and I retired at the end of six months. This span of time, brief when reckoned against years of living on an allowance, nevertheless seemed to me eternal, and I succumbed to a chronic chagrin at the prospect of any employment other than the work you do on your own account. I don't even think of that, now, with much rapture, after twenty years of precarious free-lancing. I should like to be a peasant – with a private income. Poverty is only a jest to those who play at it.

Since 1936, therefore, I have been a Retired Schoolmaster, without rights of Pension, even, for my six months service. The School was not in the Private Superannuation class at all. Indeed, it did not take me very long to discover that it was in Queer Street, a phrase I use in the old-fangled sense to convey an absence of cash without sexual undertones.

One day, I had been doing the Term Reports, and I had come to a boy who could be particularly nasty without even trying to be. I had to report on him as his Form-Master. I was also the Gym Master, the Swimming Coach, though we never went swimming, and the Resident Experienced Honours Graduate shown in red on the prospectus. I considered the case of the nasty little boy, and wrote: "Illiterate always, often profane, punctual seldom, never polite." Thus do young innocents nurtured on the Isis rush to their doom!

I passed in my bundle of Reports that evening. After breakfast the next morning, when I was standing outside the latrines on duty as Bowel Invigilator, a prefect came haring up to me with a terse note, in a sealed envelope, from the Headmaster-Proprietor. It said: "You will kindly report on the boy you dubbed profane as follows – 'a high spirited scholar with unlimited prospects.'" I galloped towards catastrophe ventre a terre, and burst into the Prop's study with these words: "Mr. Headmaster, Sir, I must protest on principle. I am his Form-Master!" "I am sorry, Senior Master" – this was the pompous way he addressed me – "but his father is my Bank Manager!"

We parted company that end of Term; soon after he landed up in Carey Street. The Bank Manager must have known his son too well to be tempted to put the life-boat out.

I may now reveal that I am also a Retired Electrician, Law Tutor, Company Secretary, Editor, Censor, Fire-Watcher, Labour Manager,

Repertory Actor, Colliery Stores Clerk, and Parcels Sorter. All Retired. Hence my look of infinite withdrawal.

For one vivid afternoon I was also a Smudge-Faker. A Smudge-Faker is one of those Street-Photographers who economize on developing by not using any fixing materials at all. So they collect the cash for the snapshot and then whizz away like an electric hare. They have to. Since the snaps are not fixed, they start going black as soon as the customer holds them up to the light. This happens immediately the money changes hands. The prudent Smudge-Faker gives the shilling a good hard bite to see if it is counterfeit or not. If not, he beats it in double-quick time.

Long, long, ago, in a tavern near Kew Gardens, one radiant afternoon in June, I contracted, in a moment of indehiscence, with a flamboyant Cockney Smudge-Faker, to stand on the Green and solicit custom from an expected charabanc party of Lady Evangelists. My wages were agreed as five pints of beer in the evening at the Cricketers Arms.

How I steeled myself to accost twenty teetotal virgins in a public place I shall never know, but I did. And they fell like ninepins to my charms. Actually it was my accent that did the trick. I heard one of them whispering, in a voice that must have carried right to Richmond Hill, that I seemed a well-spoken man, almost a gentleman, and must have come down in the world. The Cockney snapped the lot in a burst of rapid shooting, whisked round his trilby for the lolly, and handed me the photographs to dish out. Then he disappeared as if he had never been. But he double-crossed me and never told me that I had about another forty seconds to do the same.

I shall never forget the next half hour, which is "photographically lined on the tablets of my mind, though the Yesterday has faded from its page." The general sense of the hen-party was crystallizing towards the calling of a cop, when I saved the day by stumping up a quid, and walking haughtily away. The same horrible voice whispering double-forte followed me with the words: "I am sure he's just out on a ticket-of-leave!" I bought my own beer that night.

So much for my industrial past. Work hard, young man, like I didn't, and we'll both get nowhere at all.

The problem now facing me is to get my family and myself firmly in print, and in Cornwall in 1945. I have already blurred the picture by starting with London in 1936. The difficulty is that I have very little sense of the passage of time. I brood on all the past and it is vivid, and it all becomes now, and happens again, all at the same time. This crowds true actuality out of my brain, with the present that is clamant and the now that is urgent, which the Americans heighten into as of now. Once you neglect the actual, instant, now, you are deadwood like the past itself. Friends have often accused me of neglecting the present. One among these, who has sporadically visited my Cornish cottage for seventeen years, in between wide travels of his own, said this to me last time he came. "I open your door. You're always here. It's like going back to a theatre to see the same play over and over again. Don't you get bored?"

No, I do not get bored. I am not watching the play. I am acting it out on my cerebral stage. Whether this has been an entirely laudable setting for a man with a wife and five children is another matter, which I approach obliquely.

Shortly after we were married, my wife and I went to live in Brittany, in the hamlet of Kerbournec, on the Quiberon peninsula. We found it by chance, when we sailed there across the bay from Carnac, where the stones are granite ghosts of pre-history. I was the only man then living in Kerbournec. All the others were drowned fishermen wrecked on the Savage Coast. Their widows scraped the carbon-copy of an existence by toiling in the unfertile fields. I had just had a novel accepted by Hutchinsons, and I was trying my hand at journalism for the French Press. We were wrapping our lives in a timeless idyll when war came. We crossed to Southampton as the panzers crossed into Poland. When we gave our Breton cook five pounds on leaving, she broke down. This was the sum she had struggled in vain to save, through widowed and threadbare years, for her daughter's dowry.

During the war, after I was made Medical Grade IV, no revision, we lived, during varied war-work, at Hampstead, Highbury, Chelsea, Solihull, Henley-in-Arden, Henley-on-Thames, Taunton, Bournemouth, Middlesborough, Shrewsbury and Little Dawley in Salop. We ended up in 1945 in a garden-flat opposite Holloway Jail. We were surrounded by a desolation of dirt and brick and noise and concrete and corruption. Our first three children were as much prisoners as the women locked up opposite them, in that monstrous Palace of Penal Insanity. I sometimes watched the wardresses knocking back gin in the Northern, the village inn of the penitentiary, the landlord of which used to send in cigars and champagne to the 18B internees before they went off to sully the Isle of Man.[1]

One morning in April, my wife, Peggy, and myself, came almost telepathically, at the same time, to the same conclusion about London after VE Day. We called on a dealer in Seven Sisters Road, and told him we wanted to sell up, lock-stock-and-barrel. He came and sniffed at our sticks. Then he gave us a cheque on the spot, in an all-time record, knock-down bargain, for him. We handed in the keys and went to Paddington, and booked our tickets for Cornwall. For Penzance, the last station in England, and the genial, healthy, happy centre of a peninsula where the air is clean, and the seas wash round, and the earth lies tranquil beneath the most intricate light in the kingdom.

No, I am not bored. Are my wife and children? I believe Cornwall has given them all something, weighed against which most material lacks are pennyweights. Jails have far more inmates than their roll-call of cold cells records. Cities can be jails. Their dwellers do not watch the seasons. The eight o'clock news tells them when it is Spring.

I had my own private reason for going to Cornwall. I wanted to make something of my writing, and I imagined Cornwall as an ideal environment to write in.

I have never wanted to do anything else, except to read; to read anything and everything in order to detect the writing that is nothing. I passed what is known as a sickly childhood, that to say that, between the ages of two and sixteen, I spent an aggregate of several years in bed. I was a chronic sufferer form colitis, which ravaged my youth. It is now recognized as an allergic complaint, and I have no reason to doubt this. It disappeared when I was sixteen, and for five rip snorting years I rioted in all sorts of excesses, in order to prove to myself, I suppose, that I had never been ill. I see now that this was a predictable reaction; I had spent four Christmas Days in bed, eating Benger's

Food; I had never been allowed to get my feet wet on country walks; I was denied brown bread, currants, unpeeled apples, because of the roughage. I had stayed, quite uncomplainingly, at Nursing Homes in Liverpool, Newcastle, Manchester, London and Harrogate. It is quite true that I never complained; perhaps because I was intelligent enough to realise that complaints don't cure colitis. I recall taking a detached interest in the succession of coloured ampoules our doctor brought round, at one time, for a course of hypodermic injections. As far as I know, all they did for me was to send my temperature sky-high every Sunday night. Each change of colour signalled a bigger dose of bugs, and the sequence of ascent was in thousands.

I have boasted that I did not complain; in the case of Harrogate, I did something else. I mutinied. I was taken there for another wonder-course which was, this time, dead-certain to cure my colitis. I am quite sure my father and mother never used the term "dead-certain" to me. They were far too tactful. Once, when I was eleven, I overheard a family friend remark "I never thought you'd rear that poor boy at all. You have a lot to be thankful for!" I took this as a mortal insult, which, in a sense it was. It rankled. When I was twenty-one, I even remembered not to invite the person to my party.

The specialist at Harrogate, similarly, wounded my pride, and he hurt something else, as well. I had gone there for something which I think was called the Plombiere Treatment; anyhow, it had something to do with plumbing. It involved my lying on my stomach while they inserted yards of rubber-tubing in the only opening available while you are in that position. Then they started to pump some ghastly mineral fluid into me. For the first session, which proved to be the last, the specialist, an assistant doctor, the matron of the Private Nursing Home (owned by the specialist) and a nurse, all stood round me to watch. I got fuller and fuller, and felt sicker and sicker. Then I jumped from the couch, trailing clouds of glory till the connection failed, and screamed my head off for my father. He was there; he was always there when you needed him. And he stood by me, and we went back home. The Stoic, or the worm, had turned.

I solaced all my childhood with books, more books, and still more books. First of all, the classics that all children love; then, for my sick-bed was a hot-house that forced my precocity as a reader, the books that are the backbone of our civilization. My father had bought and read books all his life, and digested them, too, for many of his volumes were annotated and cross-referenced. He read widely in Philosophy. In fiction, he admired Thomas Hardy, and had a collection of all his novels. He once walked with Thomas Hardy along the Embankment, near the old Adelphi, in a twenty minutes' stroll when they met by chance, taking the early morning air. The first book of poetry I remember possessing was Robert Louis Stevenson's "Child's Garden of Verses", given to me by my Uncle David, my father's eldest, bachelor, brother. Uncle David used to fly into my life on wings of mystery and romance, for he lived in a London Club, wrote books on Political Principles, and occasional leaders for the Spectator on Economics, and he had been gassed in the War, when he threw up a lucrative post as a Naval Architect to join the Artists Rifles as a Private. That wasn't romantic at all, really; the gas caused Bright's Disease, but he went on writing for nine doomed years till, inexorably, it killed him.

I created around me a world drawn from books, and made of words. Words are the main difference between men and monkeys. They are the precision-tools of the intellect. Gradually it became clear to me that I must write as well as read, and this is what I have been trying to do from the age of fifteen up to now.

It makes a deal of difference to a young writer how his first work is rejected. Miraculously, out of the debris of the years, I have somehow preserved the first verses I ever sent to a paper, and the letter with which they came back.

I was eighteen, and in my first year at Wadham, compulsorily reading Law when all my mind was set on reading English. The Lecture system at Oxford was remarkably free-and-easy in those days. Nobody checked on those who did not attend; equally, nobody was at all interested in those who did. So I went to English Lectures with my friends, as and when I liked.

I had just read the report of a characteristic tirade by George Bernard Shaw, in which he expressed the wish that Oxford and

Cambridge might be blown up and their ruins sown with salt. So I wrote the following, and sent it off to Punch.

Lines written to G.B.S.

A dreadful dream possessed me,
When deep I slept last night,
I dreamt I saw George Bernard Shaw,
Armed with some dynamite.

He was setting out for Oxford,
With Cambridge his first halt,
And on his back he had a sack
Of Cerebos Table Salt.

I stood in spellbound horror,
Too well I knew his plot,
For all his views are in the news –
He'd be cross if they were not.

I heard the first explosion,
I thought "That's Cambridge gone!"
I shed one tear then to my ear
Came the sound of a louder one.

Ah! Woe for Oxford's learning,
And woe for Cambridge old!
But woe still more for Bernard Shaw
With neither left to scold!

A few days later, my verses came back, but they were accompanied by a letter from Mr. Charles Graves, then Assistant Editor of Punch.

"Dear Sir,

I like your verses, and return them with regret, but we have already returned a contribution on somewhat similar lines, on the ground that the most effectual way of dealing with G. B. S's tirade is to take no notice of it whatever.

Yours very truly,

C. A. Graves

Assistant Editor"

Now a Chartered Accountant would say that this letter was a voucher for a deficit of three pence, in those days the cost of sending a poem to a paper, including return postage.

To me it was nothing of the kind. Charles Graves, son of a famous writer, Robert Perceval Graves, and brother of Robert Graves, a promising young man, actually liked my verses! Nay, more! I read the letter for the thirtieth time – the greatest comic paper in the world was privately informing me of its literary policy!

I hugged the letter to my heart, as a defaulting financier, boarding the plane to Tangier, might clutch his Bearer Bonds.

The letter was a promise of fame and fortune. It was only a question of time.

Actually, it was another six years before Punch put my first poem on its middle page, but you see how my mind worked. [2]

It is only a question of time. Thirty-five years ago, it was only a question of time. I must be on the right track. I attribute my longevity to not being dead.

Meanwhile, let me remind you that we are just boarding the train to Penzance, my wife and myself, with three children aged five, four, and one, the change from the dealer's cheque, one pushchair, three suitcases, and faith and hope and man's unconquerable mind.

[1] > I think Caddick is being a little unkind here. Holloway was a holding prison for internees before transfer to the Isle of Man. Ironically many political refugees including many German Jews who had fled persecution found themselves in Holloway.

Regulation 18 of the Emergency Powers Bill of 1939 gave the government power to detain anyone whom the Home Secretary believed to be of "hostile origin or associations", or to have committed acts "prejudicial to public safety or the defence of the realm"

In May 1940, amendment B gave the Home Secretary, the power to detain any member of any organisation, which he believed to be, "subject to foreign influence or control". Sir Oswald Moseley , leader of the British Union of Fascists and his wife were imprisoned under this amendment.

Interestingly, Winston Churchill felt it a breach of the Habeas Corpus Act of 1679, which he saw as being at the heart of the liberties Britain and Her allies were defending. I wonder what Caddick would think of today's legislation regarding internment?

[2>]See Appendix V.

II

Ridiculous Odyssey

AS PRUDENT TRAVELLERS, we were proceeding to Penzance, a destination of which we knew nothing, to sleep the night in a place we had not yet discovered, on the recommendation of friends we had still to identify. It was a hilarious journey. Neither my wife nor myself doubted for one moment that, as they say in the Theatre when a rehearsal looks the absolute end, it would be alright on the night. Because we were in high spirits, the three children thought the millennium had come, though not in so many words. "Nice Puff-Puff, Daddy! Wanna, wanna, wee-wee!" This was the refrain for most of the journey. I believe it was the call of the corridor not the kidney that prompted most of the peremptory demands.

On the suitcases and the pushchair we kept the eyes of lynxes and the watch of hawks. All these things were battered and nor worth stealing at all; but we were conscientiously being wise after another event. In 1940, we changed trains during an air-raid, and the Guard bustled us in and said all our baggage would be quite alright. An hour later, we discovered that it had all been stolen – two hat boxes, a trunk, and three suitcases, all solid leather, with the palmy look of former opulence. They contained all our portable wedding presents, prized relics such as my long-dead father's dress-studs and cuff-links, and a fantastic layette of silk and Breton lace my wife had collected in Morbihan and Paris, ready for the arrival of her first baby. They were not insured, and never traced. At Shrewsbury Station, in 1941, a Railway Solicitor handed me a cheque for £16, as an ex gratia payment.

Now that we had so little to lose we became strict custodians of it, and our threadbare paraphernalia reached Penzance, not intact, for two of the suitcases kept bursting open and shedding oddments like socks and napkins, but certainly untouched by felonious hands.

When we reached Penzance I discovered it was Whit Saturday, so everybody we met kept assuming we were tourists, not immigrants. This meant that they kept directing me to expensive hotels (the luggage was in the Cloakroom, otherwise they would have started lower in the social scale). I stood outside several and tried to work out the nightly rate for two adults, and three children (if they took children) and my arithmetic kept furnishing such nightmarish answers that I stayed outside. Then I had a brain-wave. I crossed the threshold of my first tavern in Cornwall, the old Turk's Head, and before my pint was down I was fixed up with an address. We moved into a pleasant, unpretentious, and very clean little lodging-house, in the premises later occupied by the Penzance Sailing Club.

We bedded down the bairns and slept like two logs and three faggots.

Spring in Cornwall seemed so warm and pleasant to us, that year, after our last winter in London, in the middle of an acute fuel shortage when Local Authorities were driven to stripping the timber from bombed houses at breakneck speed so that they could sell it on the spot as an emergency supply to householders, that it suggested to us a stop-gap solution to our private housing problem. We rented an agreeable holiday chalet, at Marazion, right opposite St. Michael's Mount, for a singularly unmercenary sum.

It was free-and-easy, and like a camping holiday, and we all enjoyed it, for a spell. We were busy looking for a furnished cottage. Meanwhile, the sun shone, the sands were near, and the year approached its' high-noon. I heard a nightingale one night in early June, but nobody believed me, at the time. A few weeks later, letters appeared in the local Press from others who had heard it. This confirmed in my resolve to hear nightingales whenever I felt like it.

Then I had a most bizarre experience. We were living just near the marshes that skirt the shore of the bay, between the bridge and Marazion. I am not sure whether they are below sea-level or not; certainly they are very low lying. A warm mist had settled over the bay, and the ramparts of the Mount were swathed in Celtic cotton-wool.

I have told you that I was released from one allergic complaint when I was sixteen. When I was twenty-one, the old trouble re-appeared, transformed to asthma, which has been my faithful companion ever since. Much of my sporadic moving of house and home during the war was prompted by a desperate search for a climate I could breathe in.

All of a sudden, at Marazion, I started with the ultimate apogee of all asthma-attacks. It went on and on, for three days and three nights, and the doctor could find no way of relieving it at all. On the fourth day I was looking like a candidate for the hereafter. I just to say remember being carried out on a stretcher. Then there is a blank. They rushed me to hospital and revived me with oxygen.

I remember lying on a bed in a maze, or a haze, or a daze, trying to sort out where I was. Then I heard voices which seemed to be trying to tell me where I was. This is exactly what I heard.

> "E's gorn, I tell you!"
> "Not 'im! 'is missus is waiting outside for 'im to pass on!"
> "E's gorn, I tell you!"
> "E's just going!"
> "E's gorn! I 'eard the death-rattle!"

I sat up in bed and gasped "Damn you!" Then I fell back, exhausted with this flow of oratory. Then my wife came in with the doctor, and I stopped worrying.

They had placed me, in emergency, in the only space available, a small room where two incredibly old Cockney gaffers were being housed, as evacuees, even at this date, because nobody knew where to put them, and they had no earthly ideas on it themselves. They evidently had heavenly ideas on me.

It did not take me long to convince them that I was still with them, but I am sure I never convinced them that I had acted entirely honourably by looking so finished and then starting again. I felt as if I had begrudged two children a treat. [1]

After I left the hospital, our fortunes took a turn for the better. I obtained a post as a Temporary Civil Servant, in a Government Department in Penzance, and we found a furnished cottage, at Trenowin Downs, Nancledra, which was one of an attached pair of cottages owned by a farmer up there. He had let both to an old lady, who lived in one, and sub-let the other, furnished. Trenowin Downs are 500 feet above sea level, and they face Tren Crom to the East, and behind them, to the West, runs the least spoilt part of Cornwall, the strange hinterland before Land's End and the Atlantic. It was a fine altitude for breathing in, after the marshes of Marazion, and I would not care to live elsewhere. From the window of the furnished cottage, I first noticed, down across some rough croft, tangled with bracken and furze, and fragrant with heath and wild thyme, the cottage we have made our home for the last nineteen years. This cottage was called Windswept, and stood by the side of the ancient bridle-path from Marazion to Zennor, down which the pack-mules trod with tin through ages whose history is now as indecipherable as the contours of St. Michael's Mount when the clinging wraiths of mist drift past its ancient shore. It also stood near an up-ended granite oblong, which was to play a considerable part in my life in Cornwall, a sub-station erected in 1925 by the Cornwall Electric Power Company. When I first saw it, I was only mildly curious as to what it was doing on the croft, and did not guess that, to me, it was to become a twentieth century Lorenzo Di Medici, handing out bread and butter to a minor poet in major difficulties.

For the moment, however, I was a daily commuter from Trenowin Downs to Penzance, where I followed my occupation as a Temporary Pen-Pusher, Grade III, Scale Z, a sort of amoeba in the zoological hierarchy of bureaucracy. I used to walk along the rough lane for twenty minutes each morning, to catch the bus on the main road, at Fingar's Point. Fingar is a Cornish Saint, and I don't think much of his choice of a bus-stop. It was wide open to the gales and the rain, strategically chosen to deter people from wanting to stop a bus or from thinking of anything but a wild jump down the nearest mine-shaft.

When we took this cottage and I started commuting, we did not possess anything in the way of a time-piece at all, nor did we bother to get a wireless set. There is an intense pleasure to be derived from not listening to the radio, particularly when you have been glued to it for years to catch the calamities and catastrophes of Total War. Indeed, I often used to think, in the weeks leading up to VE Day, that Peace would, by definition, include the silencing of all broadcasting. I have long ago turned traitor to this Trappist faith, and I have done several broadcasts myself during the last few years. I now maintain Peace means not watching Television. But, again, I have done three BBC Television programmes recently, so perhaps I am not consistent at all. I think that must be the answer. I had an aunt who was always consistent and it killed her in her prime.

For several months I managed to leave the cottage at the same time every morning, without looking at a clock or listening to a radio. I would wake with the dawn, as soon as its first light flooded through the uncurtained window on to my eyelids. Then I would shave, dress, eat, and wait for the explosion. This reverberated promptly at the same time each day – eight o'clock – as the quarry at Newlyn blasted still more granite out of Cornwall, from its workings near Mousehole. Some mornings the blast was peremptory and staccato, when sound was carrying well; at other times it was muffled and remote, as when the coast was heavy with mist and all the acoustics of West Penwith became unpredicatable. These variations in the strength of distant sound invariably interest me; on some still New Year's Eves, I have stood outside the door, armed with coal, salt, bread, for my traditional Northcountry entry as Firstfoot, and waited for the sirens of coasters at Hayle, Newlyn, and sometimes at St. Ives, to give the authentic signal for the start of another year. These have been the infrequent clear nights when December was dying, and the air was passing sound along crisply. Usually New Year's Eve at Nancledra is warm and misty, and there is a honeyed smell of furze and no lights roundabout to signal Hogmanay.

While I was going daily over the downs to Fingar's Point, the use of the quarry as a knocker-up, or rather as a kicker-out, became more and more difficult as the year declined to darker days. Daylight began to be delayed nearer to eight o'clock. By November, I was going to bed in a state of speculative and macabre neurosis. Would the dawn or the dynamite wake me first? If the latter, I knew I would be doomed to a panting gallop towards a rendezvous with my unspeakably humdrum duties, unshaven, with no fast broken. Then my wife had a brain-wave and a windfall of two pounds, at the same time, and with the simplicity of genius she went out and paid hard cash for an alarm clock. It had luminous spooky hands and I loathed it. Aurora should have rose tipped fingers.

I cancel the last sentence, and leave it in as a stark example of how I used to write when I was fuddled by the study of creeps like Ralph Waldo Emerson, and the flatulent scribes whose work the hacks used to collect as "Fifty Plums of English Prose."

Dawn is an attitude of mind. When I was broadening my mind and enlarging my liver in a flat at Earl's Court, I loved to lie abed. After a few weeks on the hills of West Penwith, I caught the glittering excitement of early mornings when the clouds cling to contours and the silks of spiders are radiant with dew. That is the time to walk the croft, and watch the world wake up, when the earth seems simpler and life looks cleaner.

It was about five o'clock on a brilliant morning in June that I met Wotan Gruntz, on the west side of Tren Crom. He was living in sin and a hen-house, with the niece of an Abyssinian nobleman, and I struck up an acquaintance with him, and he took me back to his dwelling to show me his Well-Tempered Waking Clock.

This was how he described it to me. [The poem is set out in the manuscript as depicted here. Ed]

The Well-Tempered Waking-Clock

Of Wotan Gruntz

Of ersatz glass her outer case is made
And therefore so her inwards are displayed.
We turn my clock and con her bright behind-
Ach! See the Gruntz Control-Knob! Him we wind.
We set the Gruntz Alarm and lie for sleep
Safe in my Waking-Clock's well-tempered keep.
Be postulate our rising-wish as Nine!
So! Now to explicate my great design!

Is bad for man to frighten at awake-
Is good for man the stages Gruntz can make
First, Clock is plonk along the slumber-bed,
One metre distant from the slumber-head.
Our rising-wish is Nine. Lo, dawn has blushed!
For some shall shave be blood, and sausage rushed!
Not so my slumber-head! His wake is Plan!
Behold the easy-stages waking-man!

At seven-house-click! – my Gruntz protrudes a spring –
Up wobbles female-lark and starts her sing!
She chirps pianissimo, this cute hen-bird,
A coma-obligato dumbly-heard.

She percolates the slumber-dream with glee-
Our object man grunts chuckles, happy he!
Till seven-fifty hours he dotes the charms
Of lark-song rending Mendelsohn unt Brahms.

But now is eight! The Duty-Motif comes!
The Gruntz Control-Chord groans out muffled drums.
Then – pouf! Out pops a rod, out walks a hand-
He is the anti-Sloth Herr Gruntz has planned!
He pokes the slumber-rib with mirthful vim
And scientifically tickles him.
Auf Wiedersehn to swoons of maidens sweet!
The anti-Sloth plucks bleakly at the sheet.

Ho! Pluck pluck pluck! The waking-man is bare!
His stance is upright-bolt while bugles blare!
But still from sleep subconscious lark-notes trill!
Our mirthful waker gulps his rising-pill –
His dawn is Tops – his Ego is sublime;
He up gets gleely at our project-time!
You, too, can wake with larks and Brahms and me
And morning-joy – and can send C.O.D.

Throughout the reverberations of the technical discourse, the dusky love of Wotan Gruntz, all eighteen stone of her, lay still, like a delivery of cooking fat, and punctuated his words with sow-like snores, which shook the hide-out of their illicit amours.

[We don't come across Wotan again, but a Siegfried Gruntz raises his head twice in *Broadsides from Bohemia*, where we meet his friends, D. Smooch and W. Bindweed — Blight!]

1> This part of the chapter appeared in the Cornish Review 2nd series No.1, Spring 1966

Further extracts from this Cornish Review are spread out over a number of chapters, mainly: Chapters III, V, VI, XI , XV and XXII

III
Windswept

ALTHOUGH WE did not live in it during 1945, I share with all my family the belief that our Cornish life did not properly start until we moved into Windswept Cottage, Nancledra in 1946. For the two youngest of my children, this is the literal truth They both began here. We moved into Windswept in August, 1946. My third daughter was born on a radiant day in August, 1947; my second son blew in upon a gusty Trafalgar Day in 1948; this prompted our cheerful village grocer to nickname him Nelson.

I daresay that none but the feckless and the shiftless would have behaved as we did, moving into a four-roomed cottage with three young children and then proceed practically to double its density of infant population in the span of two years. We did so, quite contentedly, and have had no regrets at all. All the same, as the years galloped by, we sometimes stared blankly at each other, by the fire at nights, and wondered why the cottage seemed to be shrinking every day, and at twice the diminution rate in the winter. The light of summer magnifies space, but winter darkness makes it dwindle. This is a discovery much older than Einstein, and may be expressed as the Law of the Seasonal Relativity of Relatives. It sometimes crossed my mind that I had more than two sons clumping round me on a wet day. However we managed not to suffocate each other, by reason of running our family as a democracy-tempered by a dictatorship. I do not believe in letting children tell parents what to do, well not me anyhow, and life in a small space is impossible for a large family unless there is a system of manners, and Pa has the veto and the casting vote.

I acquired Windswept as our family home by moving into it as a service-tenant of the old Cornwall Electric Power Company. The cottage went with the keys and custody of an oblong block of cement. This was the Sub-station, and it serviced, among other places, the pumps at Geevor Mine, and the Land's End Radio Station. Consequently, it had always to be attended by somebody on the spot, who could be summoned to the phone inside it by a titanic alarm-bell in the bedroom. This bell , its thunderous tocsin shook the cottage with its clamour, much as the hunchback shook the belfry of Notre Dame. I would switch it off and then hare like hell over the croft to the substation, and peer at a massive array of dials until I discovered what had blown up and where. Then I rang Control at Hayle Power Station and told them the worst. Usually, I then had to isolate sections of the line, with meticulous safety precautions, while the gang of linesman went out on to the hills to find the fault. They would climb the poles in darkness, sometimes with a seventy-mile-an-hour gale lashing torrential rain at them, and they might have to patrol and climb all night and all the next day until the service was restored. And they asked my wife to heat for them some of the toughest and most lethal Cornish pasties I have ever seen. All these linesmen were Cornishmen, and I am proud to have been their friend. The toughest and most loyal men I have ever worked with.

I suppose the substation might be described as a glorified fuse-box, where something blew when an Earth or Overhead Fault developed. I contracted with the Power Company to be available at all times of the day and night, including Bank Holidays and Sundays, and never to leave my cottage or its' three-quarter of an acre of ground without getting prior permission by phone from the Control Officer in Hayle. For a whole year, I contented myself with going out for a drink every eighth Saturday only. This saved money and restored my liver, and I tilled my land like mad and learnt to use my hands for the first time in my life.

Officially, my certificate on leaving, of seven years satisfactory service at all times describes me as an "Isolator of Bus-Bars.! Yes, I isolated Bus-Bars for seven years, and I still don't quite know what Bus-Bars are. But I did as I was told and never argued, and learned to be useful, and the Bus-Bar dutifully isolated themselves. There might be nothing to do for five weeks; then pandemonium might break out in the bedroom in the small hours and I might find myself doing a hectic twelve-hour stretch of switching and phoning, when a major breakdown occurred. Often, trouble was caused by lightning. Then the nightmare that haunted us all was the exposed telephone lines to the substation. Very often, the lightning blew the phone, and I had to trot up and down to the village phone-box, taking instructions from

Control until the Post Office mechanic restored the phone. Often, the phone would be blown three or four times in the same thunder-storm, and life became hectic.

I remember one night when I was trying to close a switch on a fault, and the mechanic suddenly told me he would rather go outside and watch the proceedings from a safe distance. I laughed like a demented person and watched him retreat. Then I banged in the switch and it blew up, and a hail of fragments of porcelain insulators hit the walls all round me. Luckily, they missed my eyes, but it took the maintenance men forty-eight hours to put the damage right. I only had one accident in this job; I injured my right hand on a faulty switch and years later paralysis started and I had to have it operated on. At the time, I had my arm in plaster for two months, and then on the Christmas Eve of that year I got a cheque for £99.10.00 in settlement of my claim for personal injury. Yuletide became a floating paradise of toys and rum, clothes and candies, and useless gewgaws that enthralled us.[1]

I remember rushing to the village to phone one tempestuous summer night, when all the hills around us kept flashing out white in the sizzles of lightning. When I got to the village I found lights on all over, and men outside the police station. A fine, young, village lad had been drowned on the treacherous North coast of Cornwall, and the grim tidings had just reached the village. That desolate night still haunts me when I see summer lightning.

I had, of course, got myself hired as a Bus-Bar Isolator, because the job seemed ideal for a writer. A service-tenancy, a modest weekly sum; these seemed made for my need, and counterbalanced the decrepit earth-closet in a shed in the garden. It was in this inconvenience that I saw my first adder in Cornwall. The month we moved in, I was seated alone in glory when a twenty inch long viper insinuated itself under the door. I jumped on to the lid, abandoned my trousers, grabbed a spade in the corner and cut off the head of the snake. I have never needed an aperient since that serpent wriggled its last. Adders in Cornwall don't die till sundown you know, so this one must have spent several hours of life without a head.

Having got my service-tenancy, I now had to rack my brains for some method of making an extra income at home to bring my weekly wage up to the bread-and-butter level. Clearly, writing would not be reliable for some considerable time. I was lucky. I obtained a position as Postal Tutor in Common Law with a large Correspondence College, and for the next seven years I corrected papers for Bar and Law Society pupils from all over the Empire as well as from all parts of Great Britain. I found some of the Africans students' papers a nightmare; I first had to learn the knack of fathoming what they were trying to say before proceeding to check whether what they were trying to say was good law. When the work got very tedious (it required speed to make it a paying proposition, and intense concentration) I invented little diversions, to cheer me up in the middle of the night, when I usually did the correcting. For instance, I would sort out all the clean papers, without reading the addresses, in one bunch, and all the dirty ones in another. Uncannily, the clean ones would be ninety per cent from Scotland, the dirty ones would be the same from Wales. I can't really believe there is a word in Welsh for blotting-paper at all.[2] Most of the Welsh papers seemed to have been put through a spin-drier.

So, then, when we started life at Windswept, I had split up my personality into four parts; I was a cut-price postal egg-head; a Bus-Bar Isolator, intermittently attending to 10,000 volts when they misbehaved; a part-time peasant scratching three-quarters of an acre of rich, black, Cornish soil to grow vegetables; and I was working hard at writing. My wife, as usual, was working very hard at being my wife.

One evening, she was reading a weekly paper which gave expert advice on everything from rabbits to radishes, and told you how to grow mushrooms in a grandfather's clock.

"Fancy!" she exclaimed. "They can get Red Mite!"

"What can? Beetroot?"

"No, no, not Beetroot, though I haven't got as far as the Beetroot column yet. Hens can! Our hens can – at least they will be able to when we get some! And listen to this! They are prone to liver trouble! Shall I read you the symptoms?"

"You can skip them!"

"Anyhow, you're looking much better," said my wife obliquely.

"Gracious! They have a pecking order! And they get egg-bound! And listen to this! Boredom drives them to cannibalism! Well, I'd never have dreamed of that. Hens look so respectable, but cannibalism!"

David, aged five, made a dramatic announcement."Mummy, Daddy! Fowl Pest is a crime!"

"What on earth do you mean?"

"If you don't tell the policeman, he locks you up!"

"Who told you that?" asked Anne, who was six, with all the aloofness of the family first-born.

"Boy at school!" said David, crushingly.

"Well then, we'd better not get any hens, after all" I said. "I don't want to do three years on Dartmoor for Red Mite, or whatever you said it was."

"Hygiene's the secret," said my wife, calmly. "Plenty of Jeyes!" Then she looked thoughtfully at David's boots and cried "Get those filthy boots off at once!"

Then all conversation died abruptly as an unearthly wail made a rent in the heavens.

"Only Diana!" said Anne, casually.

It was indeed only Diana; but Diana's screams when she was a baby in London had often filled air-raid shelters in split seconds when the flying-bombs were falling. Diana was born during the London raids of 1944, not long before the doodle-bugs. When she started her screaming, we used to be quite proud and say it was because the V-bombs had made her highly-strung. But she went on with her screams long after VE-Day, and right past VJ-Day too, and we started to lose our proud pity for the child. She would close her eyes tight, go heliotrope all over, open her mouth wide, and then this concentrated high-frequency jet of discord would wail out, and men who had won the George Cross would turn white and run.

We even took her to a hospital for it once. But the scream-specialist examined her and just said: "Perfect little girl! Very robust! Wonderful thorax!" And that was that. I only wish he had heard her in full throttle.

Now, in her second year in Cornwall, Diana, though a little less frequently, still gave her imitation of Florence Foster-Jenkin going all out at Carnegie Hall, and we trembled till it was over.

We never knew what started her off. We never knew what stopped her. All of a sudden, the world would become beautifully still, and the air would be a harmony of silence and her sweet little face would turn again to boiled pink, and order was restored.

She stopped suddenly now.

"Wanna chucky-egg!" she gurgled.

"That child's quick," said her mother. "It will calm her when we get baby-chicks for her to watch."

"You'd better get chicks that are immune to screams" I replied. "Perhaps we could invest in Rhode Island Deafs?"

"Chickens get Wobbles," murmured Anne darkly.

"Warbles!" grunted David.

"Wobbles!"

"Warbles!"

"Stop all these quibbles!" I cried, to make peace.

"Quibbles or Warbles or Wobbles!" said their mother. "They'll get none of these on balancer-meal!"

"Tell you what!" shouted David.

"What?"

David had just started the village school, so we guessed what was coming, or at least where it was coming from.

"A big boy at school promised if I'd give him tuppence he'd show me – guess what!"

"What?" I breathed amazedly.

"A cockerel he's got at their farm that keeps laying eggs!"

"And what did you do?"

"I went and bought two penny liquorice laces instead."

"Sensible boy!" purred his mother.

"Then what d'ye think?"

"What?"

"The big boy said he'd show me for one liquorice lace! So I went! Wasn't he silly? He lost a whole penny!"

"Er – what did this cockerel look like?" I asked.

"Coo!" David crooned. "Honestly Daddy, you'd never believe! It looked just like a hen!"

At this moment, Diana, who had been sleeping in her cot in the corner, work up and shrieked."Wanna sweetie! Di-Di wanna sweetie!"

We all turned and stared.

"Wanna nice sweetie!" she shrieked. Then she left her mouth open, and her cheeks went bright red.

"She's going to scream!" I whispered.

"David," asked his mother quickly, "have you any liquorice left?"

"Might have," said David cautiously.

"Well, give some to Di at once, like a good, kind, boy. Look! Here's tuppence for you!"

David put the coins if his left trouser pocket and trotted over to Diana. From his right pocket he fished a grubby handkerchief. Then he unrolled from it a juicy, treacly, straggle of liquorice lace, and before anyone could move, popped it into Diana's mouth which was still wide open.

"Nice sweetie!" she cooed, her lips trickling black. "Nice Day-Day! Di-Di luv Day-Day!" she added, and went straight back to sleep. Diana already had something of the time-and-motion study air about her.

"Was it clean?" demanded their mother, catching her breath.

"Specially clean!" replied David. "I washed it in the spring on the way home from school. Day-Day clever!"

By the side of this spring stands a notice saying "This water is unfit for Human Consumption. By Order." Cows drink there daily.

"I broke a teeny-weeny bit off for the tadpoles, and they smelt it!" added David, proud of such an attentive audience.

"I didn't eat any dirty liquorice!" said Anne, looking smug and trying to look noble.

"I never asked her!" bellowed David. "So there!"

1> *See Chapter XVI*

2> *The Welsh for blotting paper is papur smotyn – so there!*

IV

Two Cornish Towns

IN MY FIRST weeks in Penzance, a butcher in the town made a remark to me I have always remembered. He was Garfield Harvey, whom I came to like and respect. Now alas, he is dead untimely, after a long illness caused by injuries he got when felling a tree one Sunday. What Garfield Harvey said to me, when we were standing in the doorway of his shop talking about the town was: "You'll find most of us in Penzance very comfortable people, Cap'n."

"Comfortable!" Yes, he was right. Penzance is an unworried sort of town, where even the quarrels on the Council don't seem to get so acrimonious as in other places. Perhaps it is the mild and gentle air, or the barricades of brackened hills that run round its boundaries, so that what is good is contained and what is bad does not too easily creep in. Perhaps it is its' mellowed antiquity. It has seen many things come and go, and remained a pleasant place. After the Knights Hospitallers had attended a service in the Holy Land to celebrate the capture of Jerusalem in the Fifth Crusade, they trooped straight back to Penzance and commemorated again at Madron, where the ancient baptistery still remains. What if Madron were a corruption of Mater, and this was the Mother Church of all England? It would not surprise me a whit if some scholar one day proved this. Down on the wharf still stands the Dolphin Inn, where Sir John Hawkins gave Cornish Captains their battle orders when the Armada was sighted. From the waters of Mount's Bay, hailed from a frigate hastening to Portsmouth, came England's first tidings that Trafalgar was won, and Lord Nelson lying dead. They stopped the music and the dancing at the assembly in the Union Hotel, in Chapel Street, to break the double-edged news of glory and its' companion, grief.

For two or three years after the war, Penzance seemed to me a high-spirited town on Market Day. The main Penzance Market Day is Thursday, and I am told by those learned in Old Cornish that the name of its' main street, Market Jew Street, means in the ancient native dialect, "Market Thursday Street." They also tell me that Marazion means the same thing, and that neither of the two has any connection with Jewry.

On Thursdays in Penzance the inns are wide open – high, wide, and proper-handsome open – until four of the afternoon, a princely time for drinking to, a trysting hour for Bacchus. I swear I have seen Bacchus reincarnated in the form of a rotund and laughing farmer, emerging from his temple not too promptly after four, and rolling down the Terrace before cutting up the steps on the left to find his jiggle and cob at the cattle market. On the road to Marazion I once came across a jiggle tilted into the blackthorn hedge. One shaft was snapped. The other pointed in a carefree semaphore to the western sky. At the back, I found two objects; the one was a broken gin bottle; the other a lady's left, black satin, high-heel shoe. This ensemble still haunts me. What was it? Ravishment? Robbery? Rum? Shout a question to the south-west wind, and make what you will of the answer!

I only celebrated one or two Market Days during my second year in Cornwall. Faithful to my new career as a Bus-Bar Isolator, I only went into Penzance on every eighth Saturday. This was the only day of the week on which there was a bus back to Nancledra at the decadent hour of 10.15 pm! O Troc! O Café Royal! And O you Shepherds' Market! I lingered in the Farmers Arms and thought all three well lost.

As I saw them so infrequently, that friends I quickly made in Penzance became in some measure dearer to me than those of frequent encounter. To enter the same inn, at the same time, at two-monthly intervals, and find the same man at the same bar, taking the self-same tipple, gives one a sense of perpetuity. Ah! I would think to myself, here is an established order in my world at last, where continuity presides and all things have their season. This feeling grew quickly weaker when my two-monthly friends started dying off. Alas, many of them did so. I think they went on celebrating too long after D Day. Celebrations should be intense and fierce, but not protracted. I hold the same of orgies. Orgies should be scarcer than celebrations; their flames should lick you hotly and then be quickly damped. Goats are welcome guests in bedrooms for brief weekends; after that they stink.

Where had I got to? Yes! Catching the 10.15 pm bus in Market Jew Street on a drizzly night, and going upstairs to sing jolly songs with farming folk over four cheerful miles of twisting road. I would then wander up the lane to Windswept, fragrant with the scents of furze and wild thyme, and remember to ring up my ghostly masters at Control, and not to hiccup as the Bus-Bar Isolator reported that he would be on duty, ready for all emergencies, prompt at midnight, then sat down and drank black coffee, and prayed for a silent night.

I remember a glowing example of the comfortableness that enwraps the citizens of Penzance. I was asked to be on a Brains Trust at the Penzance Society of Arts. The chairman was an august friend of mine, Bouverie Hoyton, Rome Scholar, and the Principal of the Art School. Among the other members of the team were the late Canon R. H. S. Buckley, Vicar of Gulval, and John Cable, Penzance Borough Librarian. Canon Buckley was a well-loved and most efficient priest, who adhered to mirth and vintage port. John Cable's Library has put to shame every other Public Library in Cornwall, by the wealth and discrimination of its' volumes, and the admirable care it takes of the studious.

Just before the session, we were all invited to step into a back room and inspect a resplendent new Borough Coat of Arms, beautifully emblazoned and wrought in copper by a fine local craftsman. We stood back and looked. I could hardly keep back a guffaw. I glanced to either side of me; my companions were in attitudes of respectful admiration. So I pointed out delicately that, out of the five Latin words making up the Motto, one had been changed to a monstrous abortion, unknown to Cicero, and even to the barbarians. It should have read:"Quod improbum terret probo prodest"; instead, the copper letters brazenly ran "Quod improbum terret probo probest." [1]

"Arthur won't say anything," said Canon Buckly comfortably.

"Soon get that changed," said John Cable comfortably.

"The light's very bad," said Bouverie Hoyton comfortably.

I said I would keep silent, and I have kept my vow till now. It was a relative vow, with casuistic reservations. What an uncomfortable day it will be for England if Oxford abandons Latin as the official tongue of ceremony! The Admen, not the College of Arms, will be composing the new Armorial Mottoes, and all surviving craftsmen in copper will be prudent if they provide proofs in plastic metal, plus a classical dictionary, before they start beating.

To reach St. Ives from Penzance, you don't have to go round the bend, but you certainly need to travel beyond the fringe of normality. St. Ives has acute municipal schizophrenia. By long centuries of tradition, St. Ives is a stronghold of Puritan disapproval, where the Town Council instinctively says "No!" to everything, on principle. It has a multiplicity of sects and schisms, ranging from Plymouth Brethren to the Countess of Huntingdon's Connexion, and there are always martyrs who spend their Sabbaths by keeping watch for scoundrels trying to buy or sell postcards on Sundays. Moreover, until fairly recently, many of its' burgesses were excessively inbred. The harbour at St. Ives is the last small refuge for craft on the treacherous north coast of Cornwall, and its' seamen have not the familiarity of those of Penzance with traffic on the great arterial seaways of the world. In the days of Pitt and Nelson, naval vessels of the smaller draughts could try to reach Penzance if they were too crippled to reach Falmouth, and I have mentioned its' close association with the Armada. All these things have made Penzance outward-looking, tolerant, and much more easy-going. It was the pathetic lesser vessels of the sea that foundered on the terrible shores round St. Ives, and more often than not their drowned crews were natives of this little port. These facts have tended to drive St. Ives inwards upon itself. There is, of course, always to be remembered the macabre destiny of a Tudor Mayor of St. Ives. The King's Commissioner wined and dined his Worship one night, then hanged him next day on gallows they had both watched being erected in the market place. I am sure present day Mayors of St. Ives tend to brood, subconsciously, on this. They suspect, in their hearts, that all furriners are looking for high-class gibbet sites. [2]

As if all this burden of misery were not enough, St. Ives has for years now been trying to reconcile its ascetic soul to the melancholy destiny of having become an aesthetic shrine. It can cope, with a shudder, with tourists. You may hate the tourists' guts and love the tourists' money, and love will find a way. But Artists! No! What had St Eia done to be delivered to the heathen? There is a sad dichotomy here, and a shattering contrast between the container and the contained. St. Ives may be the Athens of the West, but the City Fathers simply refuse to become Ancient Greeks.

Nevertheless, the artists have pitched their tents and there is no sign of their folding them and of silently stealing away. Some of the liveliest spirits of our times live there, and to the end of my life I shall be grateful that many of them have become my friends. Of the closest of them, I shall celebrate the virtues later on.

When I began to know St. Ives, in the first few years after the war, it was a far pleasanter town than it is now. There was a tumultuous release of hope and energy among the handful of fine painters who formed the great founding nucleus of the Penwith Society of Arts in Cornwall. All Societies of Arts with the authentic fire of talent in them progress by a process of nuclear fission. The elements are centrifugal; they split apart, with the gigantic bang of controversy. I was lucky enough to become involved with some of these superb brouhahas, and I exulted in them. I used to run through the streets of St. Ives with Peter Lanyon, machine-gunning the ideas of others. And we were often caught in cross-fire.

These were the positive vitalities that made it an exhilarating town to be in. But there was a negative virtue, the absence of something else. The hitch-hiking hordes of Art's hangers-on had not yet come down like the locusts, to waste the substance of endeavour, and turn St. Ives into the Clapham Junction of the beatnik world.

I have never understood why dirt is now popularly thought to be innate in the creative worker. A work of art, in any sphere, it seems to me, is a sublimation of order out of chaos, a coalescence of particles rescued by the creator out of anarchy, and placed tidily and sublimely in the strength of a centre. The great function of the artist is to tidy up. Why then do his hangers-on look, by caprice or perpetual accident, as if they had bedded down for years in obsolete garbage-bins? Why do they smell like a horse someone has neglected to rub down after a gallop? And, above all, why does their unspeakable hair seem to teem with as much primeval life as the Amatonga Forest?

It is purgatory to be in the same bar with them; to sit near to them is hell. Why do these men spread like impetigo on the face of Cornwall? The women are worse. The Beat-Wench-Stench would knock a Sandow or a Bob Fitzsimmons for six. The first manufacturer to market drain-pipe trousers proofed with high power Carbolic will surely be given the Freedom of St. Ives – if he does it before the town loses its' Charter.

[1] *Instead of reading, "For the Reward of the good and the dread and terror of the bad". It read, "For the Reward of the good and the dread and good of the bad".*

[2] *The same fate is said to have befallen the Mayor of Bodmin. Many Cornish had taken part in the 'Prayer Book Rebellion' of 1549. The rebels wanted the restoration of the Latin Prayer Book – some say that as Cornish speakers they could not understand the English service but were familiar with the traditional Latin – see also Chapter XI.*

V
Lyrics from Nancledra

MY SATIRICAL NOVEL, *Respectable Persons*, was accepted in 1939, and published in 1940. It conflicted in public interest with the fall of France, and lost the contest. It received, however, warm mention from reviewers such as Milward Kennedy, and M. L. A. Gompertz (who wrote engaging adventure stories under the nom de plume "Ganpat"), and a positively glowing surge of enthusiasm from Miss Pamela Hansford-Johnson, in *Books of To-day*. Then it tottered away into oblivion.

This was disenchanting. Moreover, I had been forced to revise some of my earlier dreams about the rewards of authorship. This is the letter with which Messrs. Hutchinsons made an offer for my first novel:

"Hutchinson & co. (Publishers) Ltd — 34-5-6 Paternoster Row
Publishers & Exporters. — London EC4
Walter Hutchinson (Chairman)
Telegraphic Address — 8th May 1939
Literarius London
Telephone: City 3200 (10 lines)
Arthur B. Caddick Esq.
11 Chancellor's Road
Hammersmith, W.6

Dear Mr. Caddick

We have given very careful consideration to your short humorous novel entitled *Respectable Persons*, which you kindly sent us in January last.

Generally speaking humorous novels are rather difficult to sell but we are prepared to make you an offer of £30, outright for Copyright, and include it in our forthcoming list for the Autumn.

We should be glad to hear from you at your earliest convenience, and trust that you will see your way to accept this offer.

Yours very truly,

HUTCHINSONS & CO. (PUBLISHERS) LTD

My folly in accepting this offer has irked me through long years; my conscience has troubled me too – was I, by my avarice, putting too great a strain on this noble house, whose Chairman, later, was to give the nation the "National Gallery of Sporting Prints", and then hastily take it back again, on orders from accountants?

I shall never know. All I do know is that when the time came to sign the contract it included an option on my next novel. A year or two later, I called at these publishers, by then I think in Kensington, and suggested an advance on a half-finished second novel. The answer I got was an interview with Mr. Coffin.

I had come down to Cornwall determined to live the simple life, and write. Simple life, in Cornwall, is very complicated. If you come to the wilderness with three children to find solitude in a small cottage, it is not prudent to populate the wilderness. We did, and have never regretted it.

Slowly, over a period of two years, I started writing again, in an hilarious whirl of babies, Bus-Bars, beds of beetroot in the garden, agonized legal queries about Mayhem from African students, with names like Akkosioke-Benunar-Gulluba, and sporadic carousals in the taverns of Penzance and St. Ives.

But I did not start writing a novel, as I had planned, at least not in those early days. I started writing pastoral and lyrical poetry, and by 1949 I had enough to make the sort of small volume that, I suppose, I might have published as an undergraduate, except for one or two poems that, a priori, an undergraduate would not have written. I recall an epigram about my daughter, Diana.

Far recompense

I picked my child some rosemary: for thanks
There flashed, in insubstantial flight, as dips
A darting bird between a river's banks,
My long-dead father's smile across her lips.

The small volume was *Lyrics from Nancledra*. It was published by the Fortune Press, that useful and mysterious firm, that has brought out the first volumes of so many poets, and the second of so few.

I will leave *Lyrics from Nancledra* by quoting the epitaph on it I have liked most. It is from a broadcast by Mr. V. C. Clinton-Baddeley, when he reviewed it for the BBC.

"It isn't easy to criticize a book of poems in three hundred words. But it takes only one word to say 'welcome', and I think Arthur Caddick's *Lyrics from Nancledra* should be welcome to many people. I like them for three reasons, first of which is their clarity. I do not mean that they are facile, or simple, or comfortably shallow. On the contrary, they are like a reflection on clean deep water. The picture on the surface is plain and shining, but there are other things, too, below the surface, unobscure though in a darker light. Tangled words, weeds in the water, have long been esteemed as a cloak for nakedness. Mr. Caddick has no use for these disguises and no need for the subterfuges of an empty head.

Clarity is one quality in these poems: manliness is another: poems of love or poems of policy, they are all pungently masculine. The third characteristic which pleases me is the obvious affinity of Mr. Caddick's mind with a graceful and far distant age. He does not despise the modern idiom. He will use words like Geiger counter and Amp, and writes about atomic weapons and Sartre: he writes well about Cornwall, he has affectionate memories of Oxford and London, but I guess his heart is really far away, in the sunny country of Mythology, on the bright shores of Ancient Greece".

'O world too old for lyrics will you hear
An elegy on those who used to sing,
And will you now remember with a tear
The music that a poet's laughter made?
Dead are the garlands they were wont to bring
In sweet spontaneous offering,

Forever stilled are all those eager cries,
Save when, from some dim murmur from a shade,
The half-heard notes of an ancient longing rise
To haunt the modern ear.'

Yes! I was early welded to the embrace of dead languages, but, even in their eternal grip, I sometimes have enough breath to protest against the tyrannies of their love.

Scholars rate no dollars

That saturnine chauffeur, who sits there and waits
At the Ministry Door, has a Second in Greats.
He drives for a man with a Tripos in Stinks,
And chews on a relighted Woodbine and thinks:
"Not in kind but Degree does he differ from us –
Hallelujah! I'm an accusative bas.

I have by now made it clear that I was not one of the school of obscure womb-doom-tomb poets. Nor was I enamoured of some of the aspects of modern art I began to study in St. Ives. Much of the sculpture left me as cold as the stone it was hacked from, and I wrote an epigram about it.

An ultra-modern sculptor

All his concepts were too rarified for matter
So he crushed a chunk of marble into dust,
And dispatched it on a complicated platter
To a gallery with a label as a bust.

All the critics gaze with ecstasy unfailing
At this whole without a sole coherent part,
And on windy days they stand in groups inhaling
Little puffs of airborne particles of Art.

During 1949, Lord Dunsany had awarded me First Prize for a poem at the Inter-Celtic Festival, at St. Ives. He had said of it that it was "profound truth, clothed in very fine words," and, after I had written to thank him for his interest, we exchanged letters for a time. I sent him "An ultra-modern sculptor", and got the following letter back:

Hotel St. Petersburg
33 Rue De
Caumartin
Paris
May 16 1949

Dear Mr. Caddick,

Many thanks for your letter and for the kind things you were generous enough to say about my letter to Mrs. Lethbridge. I like your poem about the ultra-modern sculptor very much. Such things need to be said, so that people may come to understand once more that the sun is not square, and that bicycle wheels form no part of a woman's face. As for publication of poetry, I am very glad to read that you see a turn of the popular tide. Certainly all through the war there was a large public for poetry, and it was easy enough to write it then, for the air was full of the materials of it. So it is only for 3 or 4 years that it has been out of favour, due, as I have guessed, to people having read too much without melody, metre, or sense, and being afraid to say it is nonsense by saying instead "I know it is fine but I am not clever enough to understand it properly." Then they get the idea that all poetry must be beyond them, and think that they would not be able to understand:

On either side the river lie
Long fields of barley and rye,

or that if they can, it is not poetry. And the publishers are frightened and short of paper and even literary agents won't handle any poetry whatever, or at least mine won't.

Why don't you send your poem about the sculptor to Punch? I think they might like it, and though I don't imagine it would be much use telling them so, by all means do so if you like. They would of course consider the poem on its' merits, but I think these are quite good enough. And they pay quite well.

Yours sincerely

Dunsany"

[It was duly published in Punch. Ed]

Now, in spite of my reservations about the value of a great deal of post-war modern art, the painters who became close friends of mind in Cornwall were all MODERN ARTISTS in enormous capital letters, if you follow my meaning. They were gay generous vivid vital and passionately sincere, as different from the genteel school of English Landseer-scapers and Marine Scene Storemen as the old ham actors were from the electric eels of the Royal Court Theatre.

From about 1949, and onwards, I became involved in the aesthetic skullduggeries of St. Ives, the blood feuds, the crises, the manifestoes, the fiascoes, and shed ten years off my mentality in the process. St. Ives was brilliant, in the spring, with anemones and violets and cubists, and June in Cornwall was a feast of new potatoes, and a pandemonium of still newer painters. "Bliss was it in that dawn to be alive, and to be young was very heaven."

I first got to know many of the painters by making a friend of the extraordinary man who printed the best of their catalogues. He was Guido Morris[1], inimitable, irreplaceable, and, I fear, often a little irresponsible about meeting orders for printing which bored him. He had the Latin Press, at the top of the steep stone steps on the Island. There, he printed consummately in English, Latin, Hebrew and Greek; and if somebody had ever told him that gross and net income were not the same thing, I am quite sure he would be there still, to the adornment of all the public notices in St. Ives, and the delight of his stalwart supporters. You had to be his stalwart supporter, because disgruntled businessmen who saw you with him would buttonhole you and snarl "Capun! You ask that there Guy-Doh Murrace about my letterheads!" and all you could do would be to answer offhandedly "Mr. Morris is handprinting the whole of the Odyssey this week. I will mention your little matter to him – say, after the second Sunday in Advent." This last touch was to fit in with Guido's imposing description of himself, in the Cornish Review, "Born 1910, when the sun was in Cancer: son, grandson and great grandson of clergy."

It was said of Alexander Pope that he took tea with a stratagem. Guido Morris could look like the General of the Jesuits even when he was ordering our sixth pint of Bass. We floated our friendship in Bass, and it has never gone into liquidation. True to his ecclesiastical background, Guido went with us to Towednack Church one Sunday, when we had saved up three children to be christened en bloc, and had the water specially laid on, and stood as Sponsor to my daughter, Diana. I vividly recall arriving at the Church, and searching anxiously for Duncan's promised Godfather, David Haughton. We found him lying on a secluded tombstone asleep in the sun, but he woke up with meticulous courtesy, and he and Guido manfully renounced the world, the flesh, and the Devil, on behalf of their respective children in God, and, that night, we all walked down to Crowlas together and serenaded Cecil Green, the landlord of the Star Inn, and steeled ourselves against the pomps and vanities of the flesh with tots of rum. This Inn is the only place I have ever had a drink with a Water Diviner, a wonderful old man, with wicked eyes, who dowsed with twigs of ash. Happily, none of them pointed to the landlord's barrels.

Guido introduced me to Peter Lanyon[2]. I set down Peter's name on these pages with a sigh; he crashed his glider in 1964, and died at Taunton, after having been given only forty-six years for all that he planned to do. Peter was about thirty when I first knew him, and I was about thirty-eight; there was a spontaneous surge of liking between us, from both sides, and for several years we were very close together in many things. He had a mercurial mind, and he always wanted to know; he had a compelling desire to find out the core of things; he would take endless pains to get his facts right; he was interested in the new and he respected the old. With a generous, gentle, impulsive and a kindly heart, he harboured acute suspicions as to the motives of other painters, and he would take a fine mental scalpel to dissect the acts. And he always suffered from a foreboding that, somehow or other, Cornwall and the Cornish would inevitably be cheated. He glowed with love for his native St. Ives, and this Cornishness was the mainspring of his magnificent landscapes of Cornwall. He had absorbed the colours of the croft and the sea and the sky, and they permeated his canvasses. I remember, once, when Peter took me to see Godolphin, that splendid mansion where his sister now lives. I was engrossed in the eighteenth century memories it housed; the great desk of Sydney Godolphin, the Lord Treasurer who put through the Act of Union of England with Scotland; Wooton's portraits of the Godolphin Arabian, now restored to its' first home; the melancholy fatality that this tremendous family now had no heirs-male at all. Peter was excited about something quite different. What fired his mind was the vision of this mansion as the great dynamo that drove the Godolphin tin-mining ventures; the fact that it had once controlled the destinies of so many hard-worked, short-lived, Cornish miners, who honeycombed the acres all round with adamant blows from their picks. Peter saw the history of Cornwall as the lives of all the people who had gone before. I am sure that this was the reason why the St. Ives fishermen, and the men who had been miners long ago, and the smallholders at their struggling farms, and the old family tradesmen, respected him with an intensity that was really love.

Peter Lanyon's funeral in the sunlight at Lelant was the most heartbreaking hour I have ever lived through. I have never before seen so many sad young faces. And I sensed that many of the mourners there were also in the grip of an insensate anger that this was how he had found his end.

Through Peter, and Guido, I came to know Bryan Wynter[3]. Bryan is the epitome of the sardonic romantic; astringent, yet passionate, gay and melancholy, sensitive and sensuous, with a steel lining of loyalty. The first of his pictures that attracted me to him was 'Birds disturbing a Town'. When I mentioned this to him, years later, he laughed; so one of us may be wrong about it.

I also, gradually, came to know John Wells[4] a little, and to like him a lot. The trouble with him is that he has the gift of evading our amiabilities. His first defence is the rampart of an intense reserve; his final retreat is behind the barrier reef of his complete dedication to his painting. It was one of his paintings that first led me to realize what the new painters were doing. I went to an Exhibition and saw his 'Sacre du Printemps'. It is a hymn to Persephone sung in geometry, with the feet of Terpsichore flashing out of Euclid.

In 1949, also, Guido took me to see Bernard Leach[5], the great potter. I found a man of goodwill, with an infinite courtesy. I treasure a memory of my daughter, Caroline, when she was about five, taking tea with Bernard at my cottage. We had given youth and age a little separate table. It was an agreeable sight. Bernard behaved towards her with the meticulous polish of a Mandarin, and she had the grace to respond like a miniature Lady Teazle. Suddenly, over the barriers of the years, we heard the authentic cadence of antique ceremony. That was twelve years ago. If Bernard comes to tea again on a Sunday, I am quite certain he will mask his unutterable anguish, and smile the smile of a thousand blossoms, when Caroline, as she is bound to do, turns on the Pick of the Pops and asks him if he likes the Mindbenders' backing.

[1] *For more information on Guido Morris, see biographies*

[2] *Peter Lanyon, see biographies*

[3] *Bryan Wynter see biographies*

[4] *John Wells see biographies*

[5] *Bernard Leach see biographies*

VI
Anguish in Arcady

The oldest established Society of Artists in St. Ives is, as seems fitting, the St. Ives Society of Artists. In the first years after the war, it lived in the diffuse glow of the glory of its' past. This was not enough of a hot-house to nurture the talents of the ardent, experimental, energetic, and ambitious young men who started painting in St. Ives in the first years of peace. The Penwith Society of Artists in Cornwall was the meteor thrown up in the sky by an explosion in the old Society.

The Penwith Society seemed all set for calm, if avant-garde, seas, and a prosperous voyage, provided any buyers arrived down on the Land's End peninsula. Alas, the peace was illusory; there were wild conflicts of will and tumultuous cross-currents of ambition to shake the vessel almost as soon as it left port.

The climax came when it was proposed to subdivide the Penwith Society into two separate categories; whether sheep and goats, or goats and sheep, I have never been able to make out. The division was by means of a rule cutting representational artists apart from abstract artists, under the lettering A and B. As is well known, representational artists paint what they see without thinking about it; abstract artists paint what they are thinking about without seeing it. No doubt there were valid aesthetic motives behind those who engineered the separation, but many of the younger members saw it as a political move concerned with control and influence.

So there was another explosion. Led by Peter Lanyon and Guido Morris, ten or so artists went out into the wilderness again, among them Segal[1], John Wells and Isobel Heath. These were all friends of mine, so naturally I realized that an injustice was being plotted against them. When Guido arrived at my cottage one Sunday morning, with a wad of papers and the father and mother of hangovers, I let him unbosom the torments of his spirit, and, then, to soothe him, grabbed his papers, ran quickly through them, and wrote out the following letter (it was my birthday, so I rushed at it like a two year old):

"The Editor
The Western Morning News
Plymouth

Windswept Cottage
Nancledra
Penzance
March 20th 1950

Sir,

I have been so intrigued by reports in your columns of the controversy amongst the St. Ives artists, and by the letters printed from some of the protagonists themselves, that I decided recently to pay the sum of five shillings [25pence] and become a lay member of the Penwith Society myself, so that I might gain first-hand knowledge of the issues involved. I now find that I have bought the right to engage in an intellectual civil war conducted in one enormous vacuum.

The vacuum exists by reason of the fact that the dispute is being waged over rules and over bye-laws made by a committee, under non-existent powers, deriving from a constitution that has not yet effectively come into force. In so far as is revealed by the notices convening general meetings and assemblies, produced to me by a working member, after a most careful search among all the records available to him, only six out of the eighteen constitutional rules of the Society appear, prima facie, so far to have been legally adopted at all. Solely in the cases of Rules 2, 3, 6, 10, 18, and part of Rule 7 does it appear that all the formalities necessary to the proper adoption of a rule constituting the basis of the Society have been correctly and in toto followed.

Omissions are startling. The Society has no name. It is the anonymous Society of Artists in Nowhere. The Society has no Government. No rule providing for such has been legally adopted. It is therefore not an anonymous society but an anonymous anarchy. A mythical body has been making imaginary rules under powers derived from fairyland.

Surely, Sir, in order to put their affairs into some sort of working order, these fiery particles of a quasi-Society should be forthwith coalesced? This can still, and certainly ought to, be done by convening a constituent general meeting to adopt some workable and coherent constitution, and give to airy nothings a local habitation and a name. Surely this time the notices of meeting need not be written in invisible ink?

It is particularly urgent that this should be effected without delay, lest Mr. Philip James, Director of Fine Arts, Arts Council of Great Britain, should arrive in St. Ives, on April 1st, to meet a Society, and should find himself face to face with a metaphysical concept. Had, in fact, the purported rules of this Society, in their present draft, received proper sanction from the members, they would have still been open to perhaps the gravest objection that any artist in any libertarian society could have advanced against the Society's constitution.

The objection is that the purported constitution, whilst declaring that its' fundamental rules could only be altered by two successful general meetings, and were, to this extent, sacrosanct yet at the same time gave its' committee power to make bye-laws capable of basically altering and even of violating the fundamental rules. In other words, the Committee are forbidden to commit manslaughter, but licensed to do murder.

I am, Sir,
Your obedient servant,
Arthur Caddick"

When Guido read this, his hangover melted away like snow off a dyke. He jumped on his bicycle and pedalled like Mercury to the Engine Inn, and brought back six pints of draught Devenish. We sank it in agreeable communion, ate our Sunday dinner, then I sat down to make three fair copies of the letter. These Guido pedalled back with to St. Ives G.P.O. and the *Western Morning News*, the *Cornishman* and the *West Briton*, all splashed them the same week. The *Cornish Evening Herald* even ran an enormous headline: "Paid Five Shillings and joined Society of Artists in Nowhere."

The effect on my friends, the resigning rebels, was electric. From indignation, they passed to the sublime heights of martyrdom. They could afford to walk through St. Ives like Saints disdaining lions. As for the lions themselves, they roared, some in print, most in pubs. But, of course, they could make no effective answer. They had imposed a controversial rule on an easy-going fraternity, without doing their legalistic homework first. You should not start juggling with rules unless you can keep all the balls in the air at the same time.

The rebels who resigned did themselves no harm at all. They had all made their protests, and some of them went on to make their names.

I do not know whether it was the beneficial effect on the liver of digging my garden or congenital frivolity, but, from this time onwards, I found there was a hilarious audience for comic verse in West Cornwall. In the old days in London, I had often woken up reflecting: "Something's wrong with me – I'm feeling well!" Now, I found myself waking up feeling so high-spirited that I knew I was going to write a satire.

I remember Guido sending me a most distinguished piece of printing he had done for Peter Lanyon, a Catalogue for a one-man show, printed in an ink that had the sheen of orange you sometimes find in rust, on hand-made paper of a warm, buff, colour, and composed in the Aldine Bembo type, in the use of which Guido was an acknowledged master. [see footnote I Ch XIV]

These were the delights on the cover of *Paintings from Penwith,* as the Exhibition was entitled. Inside, there were rarer delights still. I quote two extracts.

> "To see Cornwall as a Cornishman sees it, it is necessary not merely to have been born and brought up in the county, but to come from Cornish stock.
>
> Mr. Ronald Bottrall
> Director of Education
> British Council"
>
> and,
>
> " – the work of a true Cornishman, born and bred in West Penwith, not one of the cuckoo orphans come down to claim

the home where the rightful heirs belong to be . . . Peter Lanyon's work has a backbone of granite underneath its charm; when this trips up the foreigner there is a chuckle of laughter on the Downs, from knockers deep beneath the soil and ghosts, never laid, that haunt the Lanyon Quoit. You take risks here, Stranger.
Miss R. Glynn Grylls"

I took a paper knife and carefully slit the sides of Guido's thick ivory envelope, so that I had a long strip for writing. Then I started writing, and this is what emerged, in the first draft, with hardly any revisions at all:

Cuckoo Song

O Auntie! Fetch the family tree!
Have I any Cornish blood in me?
Did my forebears ever rove
Somewhere round by Lanyon Cove?
Did they chase the fairies in
The mystic darkness of the glynn?
Did they live on Bodmin's hills
Roasting goats for Celtic grylls?
O Auntie! Fetch our pedigree!
If I'm not a proper Celt,
Do I hit below the belt
If I say that, now and then,
I've seen the little whimsy men,
Leaping on the Bottrall Downs,
Laughing like demented clowns?
The cuckoo calls! I must, I must
Become a Cornishman or bust.
Buy up scores of family trees,
Bottrallize me, Auntie please!
And then – O then! – no cuckoo, I
Shall sing canary-like on high
Fed on proper Celtic groundsel
From the Ancient British Council.

Polarthur Trebruce Pencaddick[2].

I posted a copy off to Guido, and returned to my treadmill of correcting papers in the Law. I recall that I was then helping out with a little Equity, including some Divorce, and that was the first day, for twenty years, or so, I had the pleasure of re-reading the "Non Omnibus Dormio" Rule. "I don't sleep with everybody." How very odd for our Puritan society!

The next day I got two telegrams, from which I gathered that my poem had miraculously been published. It had. Guido had wheedled our dear friend, Michael, the Landlord of the Castle Inn[3], and he had agreed to "publish" it on his walls. This was the copy that was said to have eventually been displayed on Sir John Rothenstein's desk at the Tate. I hope this is so; certainly, Sir John Rothenstein, in what seemed to me the last agonies of boredom at the Penwith Festival of Britain Exhibition, cheered up when I showed him another lampoon, and brightly ordered me to pin it up on the walls. I did. Agony stared at it; grief glanced at it, and turned away. But it stayed till closing time. Sir John had said so.

I have just unearthed a letter from my good friend William Redgrave, written in 1953, in which he told me that he had submitted a portrait of me, "far from abstract nicely framed in solid oak" to the Penwith, and that, after sitting in ponderous and horrified abstraction for a few seconds, they had thrown it and me out. I am very relieved to have avoided such glory; William Redgrave gave the portrait to my wife in 1961, and it hangs in the cottage. Someone might have bought it, to stick pins into.

After reading *Cuckoo Song*, a stupid man, who liked budgerigars, remarked to me: "Well, I am surprised! I thought Peter Lanyon was a friend of yours!" So he was, always. Peter loved it. Ronald Bottrall and Peggy and myself had an uproarious lunch in London, not long after. As for Miss Rosalie Glynn Grylls, who is Lady Mander by marriage, she arrived at my cottage one day, and her daughter, Loveday, frightened a herd of Friesians by declaiming *Cuckoo Song* to them, as she and her mother came up the lane. Nevertheless, there are a lot of very solemn souls about, and you never know how people are going to take things.

In my next three chapters, I will tell you the hair-raising tale of someone who Took Things the Wrong Way.

1> *Hyman Segal – see biographies.*

2> Quiet Lutes and Laughter, *1955*

3> *The Castle Inn and the Sloop Inn are both featured in Laughter From Land's End and played a large part in the art history of St Ives.*
Endell (Michael) Mitchell of the Castle and the Rogers family of the Sloop were very sympathetic to artists and writers, often exhibiting their work, extending credit and cashing cheques! Many artists would often exchange a picture for a pint in the Sloop. Caddick wrote much of his poetry in pubs – which was often dedicated to the landlord.
The only surviving example of which I know is in the Dock Inn, Penzance where landlord, Les Rowe, has it hanging today.

VII
The Worshipful Makers of Woad

From the east window of my room, which I think of as a study, and the family often dismiss as a dump, you can look across a ten acre field, then over the valley of the Cucurrian river, and see the western face of Tren Crom. There is a black clump of pines on the north side of the ridge below it, and through them you can see a cottage painted white. On dark days, when the sky of Cornwall suddenly shoots out arrows of crystal light, this cottage catches the radiance and flashes it back at you.

It is the Barn Cottage, on Lelant Downs, and, in 1949, there was living in it the celebrated Editor of the *Cornish Review*, Denys Val Baker[1]. Denys is the author of some very fine short stories, of novels, of volumes of reminiscences, of humorous books, and a great deal of pleasant ad hockery. The rows and rows of his own works under his own name are not the sum total of his labours. He has also written under several noms de plume, which he is rather coy about revealing. He is also an experienced Editor.

If Denys Val Baker had been merely the Editor of the *Cornish Review* it would probably have survived as long as himself. Alas, there was a dichotomy! He was the Publisher of it as well, and he shared with Guido Morris that inability to distinguish between gross and net income, which is the curse of the creator turned businessman. When I first learnt of this failing in my two friends, I used to be rather high-hat about it, and give them little logical lectures on arithmetic. Fortunately, our friendship survived it. When I became a publisher, on a microscopic scale, myself, I paid them the compliment of copying them, and fell into the same trap, for trap it is. This peculiar sort of mental arithmetic is not a fault, in the artist; it is a snare and a gin laid for him by the Eumenides.

It is so easy to muddle gross returns and profits. In fact, it sometimes seems inhuman not to. You publish, let us say, a wonderful little book, written by yourself, to retail at half-a-crown[12 1/2 pence]. It would be quite common for it to cost 10d [4 pence] to print. You then have to pass it on to the bookseller at 1/8d [nine pence][2] . The fatal thing is to be your own traveller.

Let us postulate a sunny day in May, when the first rustle of tourists is heard down the breeze.

"Alright!" says the local fancy goods man, who has suddenly started to smile after looking suicidal all the winter. "Alright! I'll try three dozen, at 1/8d – though I do wish you'd start writing something without so many long words."

"Terms are cash," you say, hastily.

"If there's an invoice," he replies.

This is another trap. Invoices are bits of paper which tell a tradesman who's buying your books that he is buying them. No artist ever has an invoice, so you buy a postcard of St. Michael's Mount by Moonlight, cash, no discount, and write the word "INVOICE" on it. Then you say: "This is a Receipt plus Invoice – I'm so sorry to say a printer's strike has delayed my letterheads."

"How much are they?" demands the buyer.

"Three dozen at 1/8d, as you said. That's . . . I say, have you a ready-reckoner handy?"

"I make it 60 shillings" [£3] is the reply.

You are absolutely delighted that this charming man makes it 60 shillings and you take it, thank him, and walk out of the shop opulently. This is where the trap starts to close.

Your net profit on that transaction is 30 shillings [£1.50p]. The other 30 shillings is due to the printer. You mutter this calculation resolutely to yourself, and decide to have just one pint, as business is so good.

You are just in the middle of this reward when a friend breezes in, and cries: "Ha! The Publisher! How's tricks?"

"Going like hot cakes, old man! I've made £3 this morning already."

"£3?" says the friend, very impressed.

"What's yours?"

You give him whatever he wants, gladly. You are a successful businessman now, not a downtrodden poet. Shall I turn myself into a Limited Company, you think blissfully. Arthur Caddick Limited – if there's an American Branch, Arthur Caddick Inc! How glorious to be Inc! And perhaps a subsidiary – Arthur Caddick Global Publications, Ltd and Inc! You know you have just made three quid, so you spend it. There ought to be a law against giving us cheque books.

I would not dare to suggest that Denys Val Baker spent the gross income from the *Cornish Review* on anything so sordid as booze, but whatever he did, he achieved the same result. He imperceptibly liquidated his gross profits. I am not telling tales out of school. Denys is disarmingly frank about such things, and tolerates his own weaknesses as much as he does those of others.

Denys Val Baker is a man with a large heart, incapable of cruelty – except perhaps to printers. He is a warm, generous, hospitable soul, and delights in the incalculable ways of men and women. He can even gossip about his friends without a whit of malice. It is his way of showing how much he loves them, to find out and retail their doings and their ups and downs, and help all he can in a crisis.

Denys is also an energetic and successful journalist, and some of his professional technique is original and diverting. He once sold a story to one Region of the BBC, and then, after a discreet lapse of time, got it accepted by another Region of the BBC, with a different title.

When Old Auntie Portland Place went up in smoke on discovering the second transaction, Denys blandly replied: "I didn't know you were both the same firm!" And they forgave him. He has had innumerable pleasant short stories on the Mid-Morning Light Programme – all virgin material, this time.

I first got to know Denys Val Baker when he was just starting the *Cornish Review*, and it was through him and his Quarterly that I became the Plaintiff, in the Penzance County Court, in an action I brought against the Worshipful Company of Mead-Makers as a result of what they did to a poem of mine.

In the ancient Parish of Gulval, towards the eastern boundaries of Penzance, there is a very spacious and lofty old mill, the wheel of which used to be turned by the small river which runs out to sea under the railway track at Chyandour. In 1947, it became the Mead Hall.

The Chairman of Mead Makers Ltd. was Lt. Col. G.R. Gayre, [1907 – 1996] and he had taken on the uphill task of converting a nation of beer drinkers to a country of Mead quaffers. Moreover, he had the technical task of producing enough Mead to keep his undercapitalised company going until the demand he hoped to stimulate became a fact, during the same period in which he was producing enough Mead to mature for a suitable time, so as to finish as a smooth liquor mellowing over long years. I am not clever enough to see the solution to both these supply problems. If Mead from the same source made at the same time is involved in both propositions, then one of them is a prior impossible, if there is not enough honey to keep the vats fermenting[3]

Col. Gayre was also something else. He was the Master of the Worshipful Company of Mead Makers, a mediaeval Guild restored to life by an act of faith, and gliding upon the Cornish scene with all the panoplies of Heraldry. The College of Arms had made to the Worshipful Company a Grant of Arms. I understand that the Grant cost somewhere around one hundred and fifty pounds, and the new struggling limited company paid these fees with a mystic bliss that must have baffled their accountancy.

Under the aegis of the resurrected Guild, West Cornwall was dragged forcibly backward through the long centuries to assist at the Mysteries of Mead Making. And, above all, of Mead Blessing. This was an annual benediction upon the year's vintage, held in August on the Feast of St. (? . . .), attended by cohorts of Anglican Clerks in Holy Orders. A symbolic stoupful of Mead was brought out for blessing by a Lady of the Chalice, and the ceremonies were conducted, partly in Latin, by Canon Buckley, the jovial Vicar of Gulval, who was the Chaplain to the (?. . .), in the presence of Their Worships the Mayors of Penzance, St. Ives, and Helston, and their Town Clerks, and their Beadles, with their Maces, each with platoons of local policemen to act as guards of honour. And all this was on licensed premises.

An insensitive clodhopper might have grumbled that it all boiled down to the retailing of hooch; but insensitive clodhoppers were not persona grata at the Mead Hall. On the contrary, the Board of Mead Makers Ltd. seemed to have a magnetic attraction for Well Connected Persons. As most of them seemed to leave as quickly as they joined, there was a to-and-fro of minor titles, and Second (? . . .) Field Ranks, who (? . . .) in Gulval almost the (? . . .) and the Army List. And all of them left Gulval a little poorer than they had arrived.

In August 1949, the *Cornishman* regaled its readers with profuse accounts in a whole page of all the pomp and publicity circumstance at the Annual Blessing of the Mead, and I subconsciously started to compose about it. In November, Denys Val Baker asked me for something comic for his Spring Number of the *Cornish Review*. So one misty November morning I sat down and wrote Denys my contribution. It was entitled 'The Worshipful Makers of Woad.'

[2 pages of the manuscript are missing, so here is the poem, which I suspect is on those 2 pages. Ed]

THE WORSHIPFUL MAKERS OF WOAD

In the land of surprising revivals,
Where legends drift in with the mist,
And the Bards go on seeking survivals
Of what did not really exist,
I announce, in the latest arrivals,
Trapped out in an old-fangled mode,
The Worshipful Company of Makers
And Warranted Mixers of Woad.
O indigo gloria
Isatis tinctoria,
O dye me and dip me in Woad!

They have taken an old habitation
And christened it Indigo Hall,
And grave beadles keep strict observation
on persons presuming to call,

And a Bishop pronounced an oration
On placing their Crest on its perch,
For the Worshipful Company of Makers
Is thicker than thieves with the Church.
Sit Domino gloria
Isatis tinctoria,
They're thicker than thieves with the Church!

Yes, the Church gave its grand benediction
In Latin and Olde Cornishe verse,
Then, in turn, to avoid any friction,
They blessed the whole business in Erse,
For they keep, with a pious restriction,
To rubrics in tongues which are old,
Since the Worshipful Company of Makers
Found Guilds had a value in gold.
In auro sit gloria
Isatis tinctoria,
Yes, Guilds have a value in gold!

While the tinctures are drawn by a siphon
To fuss-pots of Celtic design
(The Master has spent half his life on
Druidical details of line)
Lord High Stewards, whose names have a hyphen,
Sing hymns as the mixture is poured.
For the Worshipful Company of Makers
Has blue-blooded men on its Board.
O indigo gloria
The Waldorf-Astoria
Is frequently full of their Board!

But in what, you may ask, dwell the uses
At home, or abroad, of these dyes?
Do the lips of New York sport these juices
Or are they for Hollywood thighs?
What's the good of this Woad, which produces

A hue like some apes wear behind?
The Worshipful Company of Makers
Has secret instructions in mind.
Isatis tinctoria,
What chains of emporia
Will soon have your uses in mind!

When the mills and looms of Great Britain
Are silent, with nothing to weave.
And the hands of our friends, too oft bitten.
Are no longer stretched to relieve.
The Statutory Orders are written
That, when our last garments are gone,
The Worshipful Company of Makers
Must give us all Woad to put on.
O banks' moratoria
Isatis tinctoria,
Just nothing but Woad to put on!

I sent the poem off to Denys Val Baker, who accepted and promised payment in December. It was only November, and the Spring Number of the Cornish Review was not due until mid-March. When the proofs came, after Christmas, I was impressed by the fact that they needed no correction at all. The compositor had done a scrupulous job in setting-up my text.

The Worhipful Company of Mead Makers was, by this time, conducting a high class Sales Drive, with an impressive list of almost prehistoric tipples. They offered the following range to discriminating palates; MEAD, for use at table. SACK MEAD, a sweeter drink METHEGLIN, flavoured with mediaeval gruit, a herbal blending. SACK METHEGLIN, a spiced Mead. BOCHET, a burnt Sack Mead. PYMENT, a light table Mead. HIPPOCRAS, a spiced dessert Mead, and finally, MELSOMEL, as drunk in the time of Nero. There was no mention of Tiberius, nor of Caligula.

The ancient borough of Penzance was having greatness thrust upon it, willy-nilly. The Mayor, Aldermen, and Burgesses, under their

Common Seal, granted to the Worshipful Company of Mead Makers, at the request of the Worshipful Company of Mead Makers, a Charter granting to their Liverymen, their heirs, and assigns, in perpetuity, the right to parade through the streets of Penzance wearing yellow and green aprons, as in days of yore. It brought to my mind a celebrated phrase of Virgil: 'Rari nantes in gurgite vasto', which one might render as 'Strange beings swimming in an enormous whirlpool.'

Denys Val Baker let me know, early in March, that his Spring Number was due for publication on March 15th, and advance copies would be available on Saturday, March 12th. Very conveniently, this was a day I went to the Railway Hotel. After a pint or two with Bill Grafton, the Landlord, I allowed the conversation, somehow, to veer towards Mead, and after a modest interval, towards a poem about Woad, a copy of which I happened to have with me. Then I let Bill Grafton persuade me to read him *The Worshipful Makers of Woad*, and after that, I even gave him my spare copy, which he put in a glass case on the bar with a pile of meat pies and a round of chicken and ham. I said, "Goodbye", and left. Bill Grafton was a shareholder in the Mead Makers Company.

1> Denys Val Baker – see biographies

2 > Conversion from "old" to "new" money is approximate.
To get a very rough idea of today's values times x 15.

3> See appendix VI

VIII
Opening without my Bishop

JUST AFTER TEA on Monday, 14th March, Denys Val Baker rang me up and told me a tale of unlimited woe. He had, that morning, received from the printers the first half of the total printing of the Spring Number, and was happily engaged in working on the schedule for their distribution, when his labours had been interrupted by a telegram. It was from the printers, and ran: "Stop publication number four. Threatened with writ. Position serious."

Denys had telephoned the printers at Plymouth, who told him Col. Gayre had been on the phone to them. Apparently, after listening to a few bursts of rapid fire, the manager of the firm had scuttled for cover like a hare, and promised the Colonel to be good. The printers had undertaken that they would not now, or hereafter, print any copy of the Cornish Review containing *The Worshipful Makers of Woad*, and had promised to destroy all copies so far printed in their possession containing it, and to call in and destroy all other copies.[1]

Denys was then informed that the printers would not deliver the second half of the printing, unless my poem was completely cut out of the first half. He promised them to cut out, with scissors, pages 19 and 20, which contained my heretical text, and when he rang me up that evening he and his innumerable children had just spent hours doing so.

When Denys rang off I meditated for some time on the Law of Tort, then I went to bed.

On Tuesday I made two calls in Penzance. The first was at the Star Inn, an ancient tavern, from the vanished balcony of which the Riot Act used to be read in times of tumult. It was then kept by a friend of mine, Spencer Waters, a journalist. I outlined what had happened to my poem, and then I read to him, and everybody in the bar, not the Riot Act, but the forbidden text. I did this, at half-past one in the afternoon, as an oral publication, to assert my right as a free

Englishman not to be silenced by arbitrary authority, my poem having been banned from the public press by a private censorship, exercised by threats from a rich man to a poor Editor.

Immediately after Closing Time, I made my second call. This was at the Penzance Court, where I took out a Summons against Col. Gayre endorsed as follows:

> 'Plaintiff claims damages in tort not exceeding £10 on the grounds that the Defendant intentionally and without legal justification on March 14th 1950 induced Mr. Denys Val Baker Editor of the *Cornish Review* of 16 Morrab Place Penzance to break a contract with the Plaintiff to publish in the said Cornish Review in an issue at the date aforesaid in the printers' hands in course of preparation a poem entitled *The Worshipful Makers of Woad.* Plaintiff claims these damages for loss to his professional reputation as a poet.
>
> Plaintiff attaches copy of *The Worshipful Makers of Woad* to this statement.'

For this, the Clerk demanded the fantastic fee of fifteen shillings [75 pence], which I was able to pay, as I had worked out the mathematics of litigation beforehand, and had been obliged to limit my claim to my pocket. The end of the month was a fortnight away.

On Thursday of that week, a close friend of mine, Joe Martin, then on the staff of *The Cornishman*, risked his neck by contributing the following, in his column on the middle page:

> **OBJECTION TO LIGHT VERSE**
>
> **Cornish Review Withdraw Publication**
>
> *The Cornishman* understands that, following a strong protest by Col. G. R. Gayre, of Mead Makers Ltd., Gulval, *The Cornish Review* is withdrawing from its Spring issue a piece of light verse by Mr. Arthur Caddick, of Nancledra.
>
> Mr. Caddick's contribution was entitled *The Worshipful Makers of Woad.* It introduced at the end of each stanza a rhyming phrase in Latin.

Mr. Denys Val Baker, editor of the Review, considered it a brilliant exercise in light prosody, which readers would find highly entertaining. He told *The Cornishman* yesterday: "I thought that Col. Gayre had sufficient sense of humour to accept it in the spirit in which it was intended. Instead, he has threatened legal action, and so, I suppose, the poem must be withdrawn."

Mr. Caddick was equally surprised. He said: "Everyone who has read the poem has been amused – except Col. Gayre. It was passed on to him though Mr. Grafton of the Railway Hotel, who thought it very funny."

On Friday of that week, I received a Registered Letter from the London Solicitors to Messrs. Mead Makers Ltd. It ran:

'Sir,

Our clients, Mead Makers Limited, The Worshipful Company of Mead Makers, their Directors and Officers, take strong objection to the publication in the *Cornish Review* of a defamatory poem of which you are admittedly the author.

Our clients are contemplating legal proceedings against the Editor, printers and publishers of this publication, they also have in our view a cause of action against you as the author.

We further understand that you recited these objectional (sic) verses in the Star Hotel on the evening of the 15th March, thus effecting a further publication of the defamatory matter.

We are accordingly instructed to issue a writ against you claiming damages for libel and slander and we should be glad if you will give us the name of your Solicitors who will accept service on your behalf.

Yours faithfully

T S B'

The same day, I posted my reply off to them, unregistered. It ran:

'Dear Sirs,

Without Prejudice

Re. Caddick v Gayre. Penzance County Court

Hearing-13.4.'50

I thank you for your letter of 17th March, the subject of which is, substantially, a poem written by me entitled: *The Worshipful Makers of Woad.*

This poem is now sub judice, being the subject of proceedings which I began on 16th March, 1950, in the Penzance County Court against Lt. Col. G. R. Gayre, Master Mead Maker, on the grounds that he intentionally and without legal justification induced the Editor of the Cornish Review, on 14th March 1950, to break contract with myself for the publication of the said poem. I framed my claim in tort, and claimed unliquidated damages not exceeding £10 for loss to my professional reputation as a Poet. A copy of my poem is attached to my Particulars of Claim. It may still be necessary for me to apply for leave to join Messrs. Mead Makers Ltd. As principals liable for the acts of their agent.

I shall be obliged if you will withdraw your assertion that I recited my poem in the Star Hotel on the evening of the 15th March. I recited it in that place, to a few friends there assembled, at or about half-past-one o'clock in the afternoon. My poem did not become sub judice until shortly after half-past-two o'clock, when I commenced my action. You are therefore accusing me of a contempt of Court, and I would like this matter cleared up.

By what strange misconception you assert that my poem appeared in the Cornish Review I cannot fathom. I attach a local press cutting to show you what did really happen.

My poem is not defamatory of any person or body or guild or anyone at all, even if the meaning of words is stretched to the utmost distance of casuistical elasticity. Your clients have set themselves up as public figures in this district. They are not a secret society. They revel in publicity, and invite local Mayors, complete with Chains of Office, to their pageantries and ceremonies. They are prone to mediaeval ecclesiastical rituals, fascinating and beautiful, but in the twentieth century, the legitimate object of fair and light-hearted comment.

I shall conduct all proceedings myself, and, at whatever the cost in fees and labour, I will fight this matter of the suppression of my poem in the honest belief that I am fighting for the ancient liberties of Englishmen and what is left of the modern freedom of the poet.

Yours faithfully,

Arthur Caddick.'

Their reply to this was an invitation to write an open letter which could, if necessary, be read in Court.

This was an invitation to put my neck in a noose, and I rushed to comply, and pulled no punches. I pointed out that other people in Cornwall made Mead, but they made it quietly; Defendant, metaphorically, made it to the fanfare of trumpets, with the panoplied participation of the Established Church. One might say that bottles of Mead went out to America wrapped up in the pages of Crockford's Clerical Directory. 'Nothing in my poem' I added, 'is really as funny as what actually does take place at these pseudo-mediaeval pantomimes.' I never at any stage of the proceedings, denied that my poem referred to the Mead Makers; on the contrary, I kept on claiming that it did refer to them, and that it was my right to satirize them.

The next stage was rather sordid. I had to go out with Guido Morris, a close friend of mine, and borrow the money to raise the ante. We raised enough for a good morning out on Bass, and then we went to the County Court, and paid out forty-five shillings in genuine currency to raise the claim to 'damages not exceeding the jurisdiction of the County Court;' in those days the limit was £400. I also added the words 'by means of threats' to my recital of the Defendant's tort, and inserted a second paragraph, explaining why I had increased my claim. 'Plaintiff claims these damages for loss to his professional reputation as a poet, the enormity and extent of such damage only having become apparent since the date of Plaintiff's first filing of claim.'

The same evening I wrote to Defendant's London Solicitors: 'The damages to my reputation by reason of your client's cruel and irresponsible act are daily becoming more apparent. *The Cornish Review* has gone out with a thick black line through my name.'

There now began a complicated legal paper-chase, which I engaged in single-handed, while their moves and counter-moves were all settled by Counsel.

Their counter-attack started with a Counterclaim for damages for Libel, so that, automatically, in the same case, I was Plaintiff on one count and Defendant on another, which I found very exhilarating. There was an attempt on their part to get the case moved to the High Court, which I defeated; there was an attempt by them to have the case adjourned beyond the second date fixed, May 2nd, which I successfully resisted before the Registrar on the grounds that 'when Reputation is at stake the Common Law brooks no delay.'

There was a pile of papers as high as Tren Crom by the time we actually got to Court; Further and Better Particulars; Notices to Produce and Admit; Affidavits of Discovery and Claiming of Privilege; a huge wad of Agreed Correspondence; Exhibits, and Inspection of them, which meant I went into Penzance and gazed earnestly at their Coat-of-Arms in their local Solicitors' Office.

And, of course, the massive and monumental setting-out of the Defendant Gayre's Counter-Claim, settled by Counsel. I was gratified beyond words to find out from this what my poem was said to have meant to the other side. 'By the said words the Plaintiff meant and was understood to mean that the Defendant was an impostor who had been responsible for the foundation of a sham Company; that he was not genuinely and honestly interested in the mead making industry but was concerned solely with the performance of useless and ridiculous ceremonies; that instead of making mead he spent most of his time drinking in the company of titled people in expensive hotels; that he had improperly used the church for the purpose of advancing and promoting his interests as a Mead Maker; that he was responsible for marketing a useless coloured liquid bottled in curiously shaped bottles for the purpose of deceiving the public and particularly the Americans.' Phew! At times, I felt the old roof of my cottage foundering upon me and my little ones beneath a burden of infamy and guilt . . . but I still managed to keep very cheerful. Perhaps I am a Justified Sinner. I do not really know what Justified Sinners are, theologically, but they sound good company, and I elect for them.

Then, of course, I had to decide how to conduct the case, and what witnesses to call. There was, of course, Denys Val Baker, who could prove all the facts as to my contract for the poem, and his ultimatum from the printers. The printers had made it quite clear, from the start, that they did not wish any truck with poets who wrote offensive verses; so I served a subpoena on their Managing Director. I subpoenaed Bill Grafton, the landlord of the Railway Hotel, and so did the other side.

I served a subpoena on the Mayors and Town Clerks of Penzance, St. Ives and Helston, a subpoena Duces Tecum. This is a way of getting a witness to bring with them any vital document you believe him to have. I asked all the Mayors to produce a copy of the Standing Orders of their Borough Council, and the Town Clerks to bring 'any card or letter of invitation in your custody received during 1948, 1949, 1950, and issued to the Mayor, Aldermen, and Councillors to attend any ceremony at Gulval held by a Trade Organization known as the Worshipful Company of Mead Makers of Gulval, Penzance. And to bring into court full particulars of amounts of bottles of mead received by them(? . . .)

I was haunted, you see, by the thought of all those policemen being corrupted by the glamorous seductions of licensed premises; and, in my pleadings, I had already embodied a paragraph about the ecclesiastical halo placed round strong drink in a predominantly Nonconformist district.

I also served a subpoena on Canon Buckley, and so did the other side. This remarkably philosophic Vicar took it all, with a bland bonhomie, and the conviction that everything might still prove to be for the best in this best of all possible worlds. I was very fond of him, but I had to call him, in view of the Counter-Claim. So I required him to bring with him 'any Letter, Deed, or other Article, appointing you as Chaplain to a Trade Organization known as the Worshipful Company of Mead Makers.' I was prepared for anything, from the Thirty-Nine Articles, downwards or upwards, as you prefer.

I have profound respect for the Established hierarchy. It crossed my mind, therefore, that the only person I might properly call upon to pronounce upon the behaviour of a Canon would be a Bishop.I therefore served a subpoena Duces Tecum on the Bishop of Truro.

With all these subpoenas, I had to serve sums of ready cash, known as Conduct Money, and train fares for those outside Penzance. Once again, a wind-raising operation was imperative, and Guido and I conjured up the necessary velocity in the public bar of the Castle Inn, at St. Ives, with Michael, the beloved landlord, blessing our purpose, but shaking his head at our audacity. Then we took the bus to Penzance, and made a grand entrance into the County Court Office, which by now seemed like a second home. The Clerk seemed to sag a little at the knees when he read our list of compulsory witnesses, but he took our seven quid or so like a man, and assured me that the Bailiff would be prompt about my business.

Alas for my desire to do Canon Buckley proud! The Bishop of Truro failed to arrive at the hearing. Instead, there is now the following letter in the Agreed Correspondence in this melancholy case.

"The Registrar — LIS ESCOP
Penzance County Court — Truro
23/24 Market Jew Street
Penzance — 28th April 1950

Dear Sir.

F.62

Caddick v Gayre

As deputy Registrar and Legal Secretary to the Lord Bishop of Truro and on his behalf I am writing with reference to the Witness Summons which the Plaintiff in the above action has caused to be served on His Lordship.

I am instructed by His Lordship to request you to inform His Honour Judge Rawlins that the Bishop is unable to attend the hearing. His Lordship has to travel to London on Tuesday in connection with his Ecclesiastical duties including attendance at the House of Lords. I am further instructed to say that His Lordship has not been approached by the Plaintiff in this matter, has no recollection of ever having met the Plaintiff, has none of the documents specified in the Subpoena and is unaware that he can assist the Plaintiff in any way.

His Lordship has asked me to request you to assure His Honour that no discourtesy is intended by His Lordship's inability to comply with the Subpoena.

Yours faithfully,

Deputy Registrar and

Bishop's Legal Secretary"

Here was a new claim to Parliamentary privilege, with a vengeance. At the start of the case, the Judge passed me the above letter, accompanied by a note in his own hand assuring me that it if was necessary in the interests of justice he would have the Bishop sent for. I scented the necessity of being sweetly reasonable, handed the Judge's note back, as was requested by the Registrar, and decided not to mention the Bishop by name until it was necessary to do so. I merely complained formally that one of my material witnesses had failed to attend, and left it at that.

It was never necessary. The Bishop never had to come; but he kept his train fare and his Conduct Money. I think of the cash involved as my Pious-and-final-Endowment to the Diocese.

THE CORNISH REVIEW

EDITED BY DENYS VAL BAKER

SPRING 1950

[1]> The poem was published in full in Western Morning News, West Briton, The Cornishman, and in part (inter alia) Daily Telegraph, Daily Mail, The News Chronicle and The News Review. *See also Chapter X*

IX

A Happy Issue out of all our Afflictions

THE MIDDLE OF May-month in Cornwall often brings a blackthorn winter, when a cold spell matches the snow-white blossom which break on blackthorns before the leaves, and turn the branches into Chinese prints, so frail appears their framework in the air.

On Tuesday May 2nd, 1950, however, the morning was warm, and bright, and dry, as Peggy and myself sat in the front seat of the double-decker bus, which seemed far too big for the lanes in front of it, the deep bronze bank of blackthorns, bearing sprays which tossed ephemerally in the soft west wind, stood out in the sunlight with the vivid emphasis of Spring. The first sniff of the air you take when you go out of your home in the morning, is most important; it helps to determine the day before you. When you have wintered in a small cottage, the world starts to get bigger as the daylight lengthens. That morning, in spite of the battle before me, I started thinking of the splendid challenge of Pervigilium Veneris.

Cras amet qui non amavit, quique amavit cas amet. A neighbour was tending our five children, and here I was, off on a jaunt with Peggy, who had never questioned any single one of my acts in the case, and was bringing with her, and with me, her unshakeable faith that I would not go down. Well, we would shortly put it to the test.

I met Denys outside the Court, and carefully repeated to him that he must come straight out with the truth – that he knew all along the poem was about the Mead Makers. This he fervently agreed to do. Then my friend Guido Morris arrived. He was going to sit with me and Peggy to do a sort of secretarial watch and ward. When we went inside, we found the tiny Penzance County Court was full. My friends were in heavy support right at the back, where the Judge wouldn't catch the smell of hops. Michael was there, from the Castle Inn, and Alastair Harrissen, who kept the Gay Viking at St. Ives, with Elsa, his wife, until he died too young, not so long ago, and many of the artists had arrived with them, and they looked like lost souls, as they stared at the Royal Coat of Arms, over the Judge's Bench. This symbol of dominion is a very potent thing when you face it; it has all the majesty of the imponderable; but, unlike Abstract Art, it has a meaning, and an emphasis enough to make a tachiste take up knitting. The main body of the Court was very full, and there were several distinguished faces visible in the privileged seats in the front. The Press Bench had had to be doubled for the occasion.

I went up to the front of the Court with Peggy and Guido, and a lawyer from the other side said we had better sit in the dock. We all did so, in two adjoining docks, and I did not like it at all. When the Judge came in and took his seat, he handsomely invited me to take my seat with Counsel in the well of the Court. I moved my bundles of papers and files, and did so, leaving Peggy and Guido high and dry in a sort of felon's boxroom, which made both of them look smaller than ever.

I opened my case by formally reading the pleadings, which included the full text of *The Worshipful Makers of Woad*. During this His Honour had to silence some laughter in Court. The pleadings, Claim, Amended Claim, Defence, then the Counter-Claim, and my Defence to that, were exceedingly complicated, and took over twenty minutes to read. I then waded in.

"May it please Your Honour," I said, "the pleadings will have already revealed to this Court that I am a minor poet in major difficulties. For the sake of clarity, I will start by setting before Your Honour a synopsis of what I hope to prove a sort of skeleton from which you will observe, I trust, the anatomical structure of my case. I will then proceed to clothe these bones with the living flesh of evidence. There are some brief opening remarks I feel compelled to make. Had I been represented, no doubt Learned Counsel would have made them for me.

Firstly, then, I wish to make clear that other than the matters disclosed in the pleadings, there are no what might be termed petty or private quarrels between myself and the Defendant. We do not know each other. We have never met. What does separate us is something far more profound and irreconcilable. It is the difference between two totally opposed concepts of what in law is permissible to a writer in a free society.

There is my own view, which I have come here today to assert, that, by the nature of things, where there is a free press, public figures are always batting on a sticky wicket. It is open to any writer at any time to spreadeagle their stumps with a good hard ball provided he does not overstep the crease laid down by law." (I had discovered, outside the Court that morning that the Judge, whose first case this was at Penzance, was a distinguished cricketer.) "In other words, Your Honour, when public figures stick their necks out in public, we are entitled to chop off their heads.

Against this there is the Defendant's view, in so far as I understand it; a view, as benefits a Master Mead Maker, more archaic, more feudal, more mediaeval, that local big-wigs must only be referred to as most potent, grave, and reverend signories, in no terms other than stricken and almost anguished adulation.

Your Honour, you are today the arbiter in a contest between the twentieth century and the Middle Ages. I speak for the twentieth century.

Now, as to my brief synopsis of fact. I shall prove that I am a writer and a poet and that I have a professional reputation to damage. I will prove my side of the contract with the Editor of the *Cornish Review*, namely the offer. It was finally accepted for the Spring Number of January 19th, 1950. There was some delay between offer and acceptance, due to the financial teething troubles of the *Cornish Review*. These troubles are relevant because they prove how ill-equipped the Editor was to face the threats made by the Defendant.

I now move to March 12th, 1950, and at this point I must mention the innocent and very good-natured man who really caused this action to start at all, Mr. Grafton, of the Railway Hotel. He is subpoenaed by the other side but I shall call him myself, because his evidence will blow to the winds any question of malice in any sense of the word. Your Honour, by an irony which makes one despair of understanding the human heart, the two reasons this poem was placed in the Defendant's hands, through the agency of Mr. Grafton, on the eve of publication, were these – the hope that he might like to order advance copies, and the hope that he might commission me to write an official Mead Drinking Song.

I state now that when I wrote the poem it was inconceivable to me, and today, now, in Court, it is still inconceivable, that any man of standing, any man of culture, any man in the tolerant drinking trade, could take real offence at my verses.

This is not inconsistent with what I have already said about writers bowling public people out. All along, I have thought that the only dovecotes that might be fluttered a little by my verses were ecclesiastical. But, by another irony, of which this case is full, what happened was this; the parsons laughed at my verses, but the Defendant proved to be more papal than the Pope. What the Church laughed at the Defendant could not tolerate.

On March 14th, 1950, the Defendant read my poem, and proceeded to indulge in a little neolithic literary criticism. I shall call the printer to prove that he was telephoned by the Defendant, and that in a few, short, staccato barks, the Defendant terrified the printer out of his life. He told the printer he was going to put him in the High Court for defamation. To the printer, he uttered threats against the Editor to put him out of business. This was monstrous; it is further proved by the fact that Defendant's London Solicitors demanded, in two days, the destruction of the whole Spring Number of the *Cornish Review*.

Next, I will call the Editor. His evidence will fall into two distinct parts. He will take up the thread of offer and acceptance, and the making of the contract. He will then confirm the printer's evidence as to the threats, and the breaking of the contract. Your Honour, the Editor telephoned me at my home on the late afternoon of the 14th of March. From him, I learnt of his decision not to publish my poem. I never for a moment acquiesced in that decision. In the words of the Duke of Wellington, I told the Editor he must publish and be damned, for my verses were harmless. The Editor, however, was in a financial strait-jacket at the time, and he could not risk financial ruin.

When I finished talking to the Editor on the phone that afternoon, I realized that I was confronted with one of those things which a man who believes in freedom must fight to the bitter end. I suddenly recalled, Your Honour, that to my hand was the weapon of this ancient Common Law Action, dating back to the Writs of Trespass on the Case, in 1285, seventy years after Magna Carta.

In that faith, the very next day, I started these proceedings. I was then only concerned with fighting for a principle, and I limited my claim to £10. But, Your Honour, as the long days of winter dragged their weary length away, I began to realize the damage done to my personal reputation. The *Cornish Review* went out all over the Westcountry with a black line through my name, and my poem cut out. I shall call two distinguished members of the St Ives colony of artists to testify as to the slur and stigma the Defendant, and the Defendant alone, has caused to be placed on my reputation.

I come to this Court today to assert the rights of a poet, who is not rich, against a big local businessman. I shall ask Your Honour, in giving judgement, to rub out the black line over my name, and to replace my innocent poem in the columns of the *Cornish Review*."

By now, I had been orating in full throttle for well over an hour. The writer of an article in the last issue of *News Review* swore, later that I could be heard booming at the Land's End. Certainly, my breathing was beginning to sound a little erratic to myself, if not to others, and I was only too glad to start calling witnesses, so that somebody else might hold the stage.

I actually called Bill Grafton first, as he was on tenter hooks to get back to his pub. The dear man fell over his portly self to be fair to both sides, and, in consequence his evidence was neither help nor hindrance to either party. Except that, by sheer bonhomie, and without saying it, he managed to give the Judge the impression that no man of the world would have been quite so fussy as the Defendant over a scrap of paper with words on it that rhymed.

The printer, who was hostile to me, was next. He confirmed the phone call from the Defendant, up to a point, and told the Judge, very righteously, that my poem was not a poem he would care to publish; he considered it offensive, and had promptly undertaken to have the pages containing it cut out, and the title and my name obliterated. I then put a vital question to him. I asked him if he had been threatened with legal action during his phone conversation with the Master Mead Maker. The printer said very emphatically that he had not been threatened. I put the question to him again. He repeated that there had been no threat. I then read out to him his telegram to Denys Val Baker: 'Stop publication number four. Threatened with Writ. Position serious.'

Witness: "I put in 'threatened with writ' to ensure that Mr. Baker telephoned me."
Mr. Caddick: "When you want anybody to answer a telegram do you always threaten them with a Writ?"
Witness: "No."
The Judge: "I have got his answer. I have got to judge what the value is."

When Denys Val Baker, my next witness, started to give evidence, it came over me, with a flood-tide of chagrin, what Shakespeare meant by 'the thousand natural shocks that flesh is heir to.' Denys was loyal, friendly, anxious to help me; but he had stage-fright. Outside the Court that morning, I had drilled into him, again and again, that he must come straight out with the statement that he knew all along the poem was meant to refer to Mead Makers. He did the exact opposite, and Counsel went for him tooth and nail, and asked him, in one probe after another, on various details, whether he was really saying, as Editor of the *Cornish Review*, that he knew nothing about the Mead Hall, and its' ceremonies. Denys went on blandly professing ignorance of all sorts of things he knew about. Then, bless his heart, he got his second wind, and started fighting back.

Counsel: "Did you think it would be offensive to say of a businessman that he used the Church for the purposes of advancing his trade?"
Witness: 'I would consider it offensive if it was not true, but if it was true, I don't see how it could be offensive."

Counsel cross-examined Denys on a viperish letter from Sydney Horler he had printed in the Review, 2 and was questioning him about his declared editorial policy of 'living dangerously' when the Judge adjourned the Court for lunch.[2]

We went to lunch at an uproarious tavern called the Globe Inn, kept by three successive members of the agreeable Wilkes family. There was a crowd of us there, but I rationed myself to two pints of bitter, and wished they had been firkins. I was pre-occupied with higher mathematics – wondering how much it would cost to keep my witnesses on tap, and bedded and boarded, if the case went on for more than two days. Two days had been set aside for it, and this seemed to be a hallucinatory minimum. I foresaw endless legal argument about the precise meaning of 'without legal justification', as I had described the breaking of the contract in my Statement of Claim. I was convinced I was right, but there were awkward case-law precedents to be rationalized out of existence in the Judge's eyes, and some of the older decisions, suggesting that it is legal justification to act in protection of one's interests, were buried away in tomes to which I had little access. Once I succeeded in this, I had then to prove to the Judge that my poem was not defamatory. On this, too, I was convinced I was right. The Judge knew that all the pressmen in the Court already had complete texts of it, and he had given no sign whatever of giving any directions about these copies, though Counsel had pressed Denys Val Baker hard to admit that he had supplied them, and, indeed, had hinted at a contempt of Court. This hint, too, the Judge ignored. But I foresaw hours, then days, of argument, with the costs for my witnesses snowballing down a legal hill to an abyss of insolvency, with the final nightmare of paying for a Tipstaff to go to the House of Lords to dislodge the Bishop of Truro, the recusant prelate who had so nimbly slipped through my fingers.

When, therefore, Counsel for the Defendant approached me in the Court-room, after lunch, before resumption, and asked: "Need this go on?" I was willing to listen. It soon became clear that the working basis should be that each side should withdraw his claim, and pay his own costs. Mine, already paid up to date, were somewhere around ten pounds, and as far as I was concerned I was willing to write this sum off as money well-spent. The other side's costs were twelve times mine before the Hearing started at all.

But Col. Gayre would consider no settlement that would sanction the publication of the poem; I, on the other hand, had brought the Action to bring the poem out. On the face of it, an irresistible force had met an immoveable object. Under the surface of things, however, this was not so at all. I had already won, in reality. All the pressmen in Court had copies of the poem, which had been read as part of the Pleadings, and Counsel knew he could do nothing at all about it. What I also knew, and he did not, was that several national newspapers in Fleet Street already had either the whole text or very lengthy extracts from it set up in type, and all these would be going to press as the various papers were put to bed that evening for next morning's edition.

Counsel left me to confer with his client, and returned with the news that his client was adamant that the poem must be suppressed. There could be no argument; *The Worshipful Makers of Woad* was on his Index Expurgatorius.

We looked at each other in silence for a moment. We were both thinking of the same thing – the Libel Law Amendment Act, which meant that nothing on earth could stop any newspaper printing all or any part of the poem as fair contemporary and accurate reporting of judicial proceedings.

"Look," I said. "I am prepared to give a personal undertaking, only, not to publish. If I do that, your client must commission me, in Open Court, to write an official Mead Drinking Song for a fee of ten guineas. We each pay our own costs." Their Counsel, a wise man, now a High Court Judge, said no more, and actually smiled at me as we shook hands.

And that was that. When he took his seat, the Judge approved our happy ending, and said he only regretted he had not a case of Mead to celebrate with.

For that night only, the Mead Makers were convinced they had suppressed my nasty verses – and over four million copies went out, all over the kingdom, in the Dominions, and the United States, in the next few days. The BBC gave the settlement in its' six o'clock News.

The press coverage was staggering. *The Daily Telegraph* had three-quarters of a column, with the first three stanzas of the poem. *The News Chronicle* was lyrical. It had an enormous spread, heavily headlined: 'Mead, Woad, a Poet, and a Colonel who was not amused. Much ado about a poem – but it ended happily.' Its write-up ended happily too. 'Canon Buckley took Arthur Caddick's arm as he left. 'May I write the music, my boy' he asked.' *The Daily Graphic's* headline was: 'Woad banned, so Mr. Caddick will write on mead.' This was accompanied by a photograph which made me look like Dr. Crippen. 'That ode on woad was really a screed about mead, said the colonel,' was the *Daily Mirror's* headline. I have already mentioned the write-up in the last issue of *News Review* – it was bubbling over with friendliness and inaccuracy. Even the *Literary Guide of the Nationalist Press* wrote it up, with a grim judgement that they thought I had become too suddenly mellow. The *Daily Herald's* headline was 'Colonel and the Poet make it up.' The *Cornish Evening Herald* ran three stop-press columns on the case. The *Western Morning News*, the *West Briton*, and *The Cornishman*, printed the poem in full, and reported much of the evidence verbatim. Finally, the *Times* gave me an august nod with a headline: 'Mead Maker Sued by Poet,' and a concise summary of the legal issues involved.

But the fan-mail from the lunatic fringes was the most hilarious of all. Much of it was incoherent, most of it was ejaculatory, some of it was creepy. One man asked if he could send me a poem 'that has aroused most extraordinary interest in literary circles: the perusal of which cast one reader into a sort of trance, and from other readers has evoked comparisons with 'The Hound of Heaven' – in red ink – and caused a renowned Hermit to weep!"

A scorned woman wrote: 'You sound just the type of person I should like to contact, and I should be glad if you could make up a little poem about a particularly mean trick a certain well-known St Ives artist played on me. Having a brother a qualified Osteopath, she allowed me to go to an unqualified man to have the bones of my feet set. I am plump, fair and 29-ish. Take this, and use it as you wish.'

Another man admonished me: 'Probably you did not realize fully the import of the verses you composed, but, believe me, you stirred up a nest of snakes! Read *The Rosicrucians* by Jenning, also *The Two Babylons* by Hyslop, and you will see how mead-making, flora dancing, maypoles and countless other survivals are all Satan Worship. God Bless you – and glorify you to His Service!'

There were dozens of interesting and rational letters too, and a deluge of mail from old friends who had lost touch with me for years.

It is pleasant to record that I made peace with Col. Gayre, later on, and Canon Buckley did set my *Song of Mead and Merriment* to delightful music. The *Daily Telegraph* published the whole of this song.

I end this tale on a note of stark tragedy. When, not long after all this brouhaha, the Mead Makers went out of business, the last act of the Liquidators was to empty their vats into the millstream, and all the trout died of alcoholic poisoning. I wonder if it was MELOMEL he emptied, 'as drunk in the time of Nero'?[1]

[1]> See Appendix VII Madrigal of Mead

[2]> Val Baker published a letter by a Sydney Horler of Penrock, Bude in the Reader's Forum, Cornish Review No. 2, Summer 1949. I reproduce here the first and last paragraphs of one of the most unpleasant, pieces of writing it has ever been my misfortune to have read. All credit to Val Baker for publishing it.

"Pick up any book about Cornwall, and you'll find the writer expatiating about the lovely coast scenery, the different points of interest, etc., whilst remaining very reticent about the natives. I lived among the Bude Cornish — the variety in particular — for some years now, on and off, and I have been appalled by what I discovered in the local character. I have found a certain class to be treacherous, two-faced, sly, deceitful, flagrant humbugs (more especially when they profess themselves deeply religious, as many of them do) and although undesirable, in fact, in sheer self-defence, I now refuse to have anything to do with the "locals," and if newcomers to the country take my advice they will adopt the same precaution. If they don't, they will inevitably learn the same bitter lesson as myself.

Perhaps this sexual lust can be partially explained by the strange mixture of blood in the Cornish; the frenzied chapel-goer will deny it at the top of his voice, but in spite of the strenuous attempts to hush it up, there is undoubtedly a lot of foreign blood among the natives; you can see men in Newlyn and other places standing at street corners, unshaved and wearing filthy trousers, who are pure Iberian, and who might have stepped out of a picture by Goya. This may account also for the Cornishman's indolence, carelessness, and general shiftiness is some measure, at least; although the worst kind of Cornishman would be a natural rascal, I am afraid, in any case."

X
The Patter of Tiny Feet

HOME LIFE AT Windswept maintained its even swing of the pendulum from pandemonium to chaos, and back again.

Our three eldest children used up a great deal of their energy walking in all weathers the two miles each way to and from the village school, and Peggy spent more of hers taking them and collecting them, as she feared for them on the narrow, winding roads. Watching the summer fools in sports cars blinding down Nancledra Hill, I shared her fear, and took my turn as often as I could.

By 1950, our two youngest had reached the age when they fell from everything they could climb, and turned our cottage and its croft into a terrain of unsuspected dangers. Caroline was a year older than Duncan, and several years more wary of the unknown. When Caroline was born, at Windswept in 1947, my mother was visiting us, for, at that time, she was still not too old to travel down to Cornwall from the North alone. The day of Caroline's birth was a scorcher, and very oppressive for Peggy. So my mother held a tea-party for the three eldest, underneath a tree in the back garden, and kept them all entertained until I ran out to tell them they had a new sister. Caroline arrived at tea-time, and has been nuts on cups of tea ever since.

It always amused me to watch my mother's reaction to some of the more hit-and-miss aspects of Cornish rural life. Mother is a pure Scot, and her favourite city is Edinburgh. As all canny Scots know, if you don't run down Princes Street when the wind is coming hard from the East, you are liable to get nipped-off in your prime. So, unlike many Cornish streets, Princes Street in winter is not a place for the saunter. People who move briskly tend to make neater jobs of things than those who doze about the place. The gentle soft, often enervating, mists that haunt Cornwall have, it seems to me, drifted through long centuries, into the minds of many Cornishmen, so that they look upon precision as anti-social. In Penzance, the Market clock is invariably at odds with the Post Office clock a few yards below it, and nobody cares a hoot; in fact, I doubt if many of the natives of the town notice the discrepancy at all. For years now there has been a large clock-face, in a busy street at St. Ives, with no hands on it at all. The time it tells is always no-minutes to nothing, and it seems to suit the natives. All the same, I believe Cornishmen are the salt of the earth – kept in a very damp container.

Duncan, a year younger than Caroline, was born here at the aggressive hour of just-before-breakfast, and he has followed this pattern ever since. In 1950, Duncan was just starting on his amazing career as the Boy who had Unusual Accidents. They befell him thick and fast, and unpredictable in shape. How many boys just happen to be standing with their mouths open on Christmas Day at the precise moment when a tin-whistle, thrown into the air by a sister, just happens to be falling? Duncan just happened to be doing this one Christmas, and there was a hammering at the door of the room Peggy and I had slunk into after the washing up, and when we opened it we learnt that they might shortly have to open Duncan. The whistle was in his tummy. We gave him strong salt-and-water (a thing we later learnt was wrong) and he knocked tumblers of it back, and then demanded more Christmas Cake. A kind neighbour rushed us to Penzance Hospital, and Duncan was X-rayed. On how many boys would the verdict have been: "Just eat and eat and eat, and it'll help Nature to help it out!" A verdict followed by the reward of a kiss from an Irish nurse with eyes like Lake Killarney by moonlight.

How many boys would disappear at a School Sports, in a heat-wave, and be saved at the last moment from death by suffocation by the sharp eyes of a neighbour who saw a pair of small feet just-to-say sticking out of a large haystack? "Honestly, Mummy, it was nothing . . . the big boys just pushed me in for fun, and forgot to pull me out . . . Can I have an ice-cream, Mummy?" If the boy has accidents like this on our humdrum earth, what would happen to him if he were to land on Mars with the rest of Nancledra Youth Club, about 2000 A.D.? Nothing, I imagine, to Duncan. I do not guess what havoc he would wreak on Mars.

I remember an autumn day when David, our elder boy very kindly helped in the effort to keep Duncan out of the past tense. We had not, then, laid our pipe-line down the lane to the public water supply, and were dependent on a thousand-gallon tank, which collected rain-water from the roof of the Sub-Station. The Cornwall Electric Power Company had piped this down to the inside tap for us. We still kept, however, a five-hundred gallon tank, outside the door of our back porch, as an emergency supply, and this was always full. The ancient cast-iron tank was eight feet high.

Peggy and myself went out of the back door to stroll round the garden after tea, and discovered Duncan, way up in the air, wobbling on the rim of the tank. He had piled a broken chair on a heap of granite chunks to make his ladder up to the borders of the hereafter. I did not shout; the noise might have sent him toppling down into the tank. I jerked him backwards, and brought him down to earth without spreadeagling us both.

He could have drowned in minutes, had he fallen unobserved, so there and then, we opened the tap, and let five hundred gallons flood away to waste. David had been watching all this with the sober gaze of an elder brother, and, when we took Duncan inside to tell him off, and give him some cake as a reward for not being a fatality, David stayed outside. After a time, Peggy and I went out again, Duncan running in front, as usual, to see what David was doing. There was no sign of him. The water had stopped running from the tank, which was now empty. We looked at it for a moment, and as we did so, a jagged lump of granite flew upwards out of the tank, and missed Duncan's head by inches. Alas, it brained a point-of-lay pullet, which was clucking round the garden with us, in the hope that we would dig it a worm or two. It fell and died in a bleeding mess.

"What on earth . . ." I began. Then I stopped. There were muffled and hollow noises coming up from the inside of the tank. I heaved myself up the side and looked down.

"Just cleaning it out, Daddy!" cried David, nobly conscious of doing a job without being asked to. He was covered with red rust, and ooze, and slime, and deliriously happy. I sighed.

"Don't you dare to throw any more rocks out!" I bellowed. "You've killed a pullet and nearly killed Duncan!"

David's reply was mysterious. "Duncan's always in the way!" he muttered, broodingly.

"Wanna go in the tank with Day-day!" screamed Caroline.

"I can't get out, Daddy!" shouted David.

Clearly, he couldn't. He wasn't tall enough to reach the rim, and there was nothing in the tank big enough for him to stand on. Daddy had to go down into the slime and the ooze and the rust, and hoist the little helper up. Daddy's trousers were corroded with the bitterness of the years, and their seat stayed Burnt Sienna until they became the family's new floor-cloth. Nothing is wasted; all experience is an arch. And so on.

It is not surprising that when, in 1949, the BBC booked me up for my first broadcast, my talk was entitled: 'The Patter of Tiny Feet,' and it opened with Bacon's remark: 'He that hath wife and children hath given hostages to fortune.'

How true that remark was, the evening of the broadcast underlined. I had recorded the talk at Plymouth, and we were all excited by the prospect of sitting with me, listening to me. The children found the concept almost metaphysical, and David kept explaining that, if I was sitting with them listening, someone else must be making the voice in the box.

However, the day of the broadcast arrived, and Diana, in particular, was agog. She was five, then, and I used to think of her as Middle Miss, between two sets of two children, forming quite different groupings in the family. In the middle of the morning, Diana was very sick, and she had acute pains in her side. By the middle of the afternoon, she was in an ambulance on her way to West Cornwall Hospital. Right through my talk, she was still unconscious after an emergency operation for appendicitis. Peggy and myself heard my talk in the lounge of the Union Hotel, where we were standing by the telephone for the word to go up to the hospital, for the third time, after she had come safely round. We both listened to me, and thought of Diana. When I got my cheque for the talk, I bought her a huge and hideous Teddy-Bear which she loved. Diana was more disturbed at missing my talk than all the pain and fuss of her illness.

For years and years, until they were well into their teens, I always used to write my children Birthday Poems, which I read to them at the table after the candles on the cake had been blown out. My twenty years in Cornwall are symbolized for me by the blowing-out of birthday candles, more and more each year, as my family grew nearer to the world, and further away from me. I will give you two of my children's birthday poems now, as records of our golden years.

Lines written for Caroline's Ninth Birthday

I ask a miracle today,
I ask it for my Caroline –
Sit still! Don't talk! And I will tell
A magic thing concerning Nine!

In Greece, upon a sacred Mount,
Where runs an ever-holy spring,
There dwell disdaining time and death,
Nine Muses whom the poets sing.

Nine Goddesses the Muses are,
As beautiful as they are wise
(Don't pout, my pretty Caroline!
They all would envy someone's eyes).

Now let me give the Muses' names,
The graceful names of Greece, that leave
An echo from far golden bells
By moonlight on Midsummer's Eve.

EUTERPE, Muse of lyric verse;
POLYMNIA, Goddess of rich song;
TERPSICHORE, the dancing Muse;
URANIA, to whom stars belong;

MELPOMENE, the tragic Muse;
ERATO, Muse of lovers' wiles;
Grave CLIO, history's patroness,
And Wit's own THALIA, Muse of smiles.

Then – Callie – there is just one more,
CALLIOPE, that Muse sublime
For whom the epic poets make
The monuments that outlast time.

These are the Muses! Learn their names!
But get them right, sweet Caroline!
Don't copy me, who, watching you,
Have sometimes made them Ten not Nine! [1]

A Letter for my Dearest Anne
(on her seventeenth Birthday, 25th January, 1957)

How long ago it seems,
How lost in dreams,
Since last, so late at night,
I sat to write
A letter to a girl of seventeen!

I wrote one, yes, I know,
So Long ago,
To ... well, the name
Of that spent flame
Eludes me, but the girl was seventeen.

I think her eyes were blue –
If memory's true.
Her hair was dark and long –
Unless I'm wrong! –
And I was young and gay and seventeen.

And this is really all
I can recall.
It's nothing very much

To give the touch
For writing to a daughter, seventeen.

I somehow do not feel
Tonight is real.
You don't seem old enough
For all that stuff
That palpitates the heart of seventeen.

Older than Juliet?
Quite so! ... and yet
What Romeo, dear Anne,
What star-like man,
Stands sighing for the glance of seventeen?

What Romeo? ...A fool
Begins to drool!
Not young enough am I,
Nor keen in eye,
To track the tangled loves of seventeen!

Not young! ... Well, not so old!
My tale's not told.
I conjure something now!
It is just how
I felt so long ago at seventeen.

Quick happiness, black fears,
Rich laughter, tears,
Bright dawns of surge and glow,
Nights sad and slow –
The whirligig of life's at seventeen.

Jump on the whirligig!
The world is big!
So – feet off the ground,
And round and round –
Then happy landing, sweetest seventeen!

For most of their lives in Cornwall, my five children have been partnered by a sixth member of the family, Simba Caddick, a nondescript native of Windswept, born in a disused lavatory and a howling gale, on a spring night in 1950.

The pre-natal history of this remarkable dog is haunted by infamy. I will tell you the shame that hounds him down the years.

I was walking up the croft one morning when I met Jimmie Nicholls, a farmer with a twinkling eye, who farms Higher Trenowin. In our first year in Cornwall, in the other cottage, which he owned, he and his wife had proved friends in need to Peggy and myself. We had walked home from St. Ives one day, without being in good enough training for the long climb uphill, and Peggy had got very tired, and overheated, and developed pneumonia. I was trying to nurse her, cook for the children, and run the cottage, while I was in the middle of an attack of asthma so violent that old Dr. Matthew twice had to give me hypodermics before I could start on the chores. Jimmie and his wife, and their five-year old boy, Billie, rallied round, and whisked the children off to play, and did us innumerable kindnesses. We were strangers, among strangers, stranded in the high hills, and their goodness of heart pulled us through.

"I'm thinking of getting a dog for my children," I said to Jimmie. "I'd like a good watch-dog."

"Capun," said Jimmie, "I've got the very thing for you. A terrier, gentle with children, and as good a watch-dog as you'll find anywhere."

"You have? And you want to part with it?"

"I've got my old dog," said Jimmie. "And a new red-setter, that's bred to gun. Three's too many to feed. I'd like a good home for the terrier. You come up-along and take a look!"

I went up to the farm with him.

"Bundle's in the shed," said Jimmie. "Bundle's the name my lad liked."

"Locked up in a shed?" I asked, in some surprise.

"Just shut in, Capun, just shut in!"

Jimmie's old dog, Warrior, a fierce half sheep-dog, half Alsatian, growled and barked as we approached. He was on a stout chain, and I was delighted to see it.

We reached a shed, and heard a high, excited yapping.

"That's Bundle!" said Jimmie, proudly.

He opened the door, and a largish brown and white shape leapt out and started licking his gaiters.

"Hup!" cried Jimmie, holding his arms out.

The shape jumped into them and started licking his neck.

"There my handsome! Do anything with her!"

"Her!" I exclaimed. "A bitch! I really wanted a dog."

"Bitches are best with children," replied Jimmie. "Bundle loves children!"

Bundle was now licking my hand, and seemed quite prepared to love me.

"A year old. Got a bit of greyhound in her, and her head's very terrier. Fine cross! Of course, she's not had any puppies yet."

"That's the trouble," I answered. "It's so hard to find homes for puppies that aren't pedigree."

"The children'll love them, when they come," said Jimmie very benevolently. "Children and puppies go natural together. You'd get a lot of fun if Bundle had a family."

I looked down at Bundle. She looked up at me, head on one side, and put her front paws on my shoes.

"She likes you," said Jimmie.

I am a fool. "How much do you want for her?" I asked.

"Capun, I don't want a penny for Bundle. She's yours for a good home"

"Alright, then! And it's very handsome of you!"

"She'll soon settle down with you. I've not had her too long, she's so young. Feed her and pet her and let the children fuss her a bit, and she'll never notice the change. But you might keep her tied up for a week, to get used to her new home"

"Tie her up for a week," I repeated obediently.

"Or perhaps a fortnight might be wiser, Capun. Yes, I should tie her up for a fortnight." And without another word, Jimmie vanished into a stable.

I walked off proudly with my new property, tethered by a scarf. I took Bundle across the croft, crunching brown and brittle brackle fronds under my feet, and turned up the lane to Windswept. Coming down it was John Tregoning, a farm-worker from the village.

"Hello! I cried. "Seen my new greyhound-terrier?"

Tregoning stopped.

"Is that the one Jimmie Nicholls had, Capun?"

"Yes. He's just given me her. Wouldn't take a penny!"

John Tregoning's large, frank, weatherbeaten face seemed to change, for a fraction of a second. He looked at me, then at Bundle, and grinned and walked off.

I stared at Bundle. What had amused him? I decided it must be her tail, which was waving in the wind like a banner. Her tail was docked, and long, and curly, and its hair had as many waves in it as a Pop-singer's.

As I neared home, five children rushed out of the gate, shouting excitedly: "Daddy's got a dog! Daddy's got a dog!"

"A bitch," I said.

"A bitch is a lady-dog," announced Anne.

"A lady-dog bitch" I agreed. "Bundle, let me introduce you to Anne, David, Diana, Caroline and Duncan!"

It was a triumphant homecoming, and Bundle settled in at once, behaved beautifully, and stood like a pointer and gave warning if a stranger came near the cottage. But things are not always what they seem.

A few weeks later, we were all round the fire one night, talking about Christmas.

"I want to make the cake," said Peggy. "But, do you know, we're not getting any eggs!"

"What!" I cried. "Those pullets drive me scatty every day with egg-laying noises. They're pedigree stock. They must be in full lay."

"Well, then" said Peggy, "they are laying invisible eggs. That's all there is to it."

So we made a plan.

The next morning, we listened for the cackling chorus that should have meant eggs. Then we went, all seven of us, out of the front gate, and round a lane skirting the side of my land. It was mild and sunny, and one of those Cornish days in November, between the gales, that are as soft as the days of Spring. We went in Indian file, crouching quite unnecessarily, and very melodramatic. Even Caroline stopped talking. Up to the old wall we crept, a sheriff's posse of seven, and, where it was low and crumbling, I peeped over.

"Two pullets coming out!" I hissed.

"Can't see!" groaned Duncan, in an agony of tension.

Peggy lifted him so that his head just topped the wall. I lifted Caroline.

Then we saw it. Furtively, guiltily, with the slink of a practised sneak-thief, Bundle was sidling towards the henshed door. She melted through the doorway, the moving image of a culprit. For a moment, we saw no movement. Then Bundle slithered out. The driblets of one egg were dripping from her jaws, and another egg was between her teeth, and her fangs seemed to curl in a sinister grin. I shouted. Bundle jumped, saw me, dropped the egg, and streaked in streamlined fear for the safety of the croft.

She stayed away for hours. We called, and searched for her, and told neighbours what we were looking for. We got not sympathy at all from anybody. Instead, the macabre and sordid truth came out. Bundle was notorious for miles as an incurable and expert egg-thief. Farmers all round Nancledra were waiting for her with shotguns. Jimmie Nicholls had been keeping her in his shed for weeks, and he must have worried about being unkind. I have already told you what a kind man Jimmie is. Well, his chance had come to let Bundle out of jail and do me a wonderful kindness at the same time. I quite see how his mind had worked; the Cornish are gentle people, and do not like dealing out hurt or harm. So that is how we got Bundle.

As soon as we had untied her, after the fortnight wisely suggested by Jimmie – how tempted he must have been to make it four years, she had got up to her tricks again, and half the eggs in Nancledra and district vanished. We found out that Bundle even arranged the order of her maraudings to fit the times the farmers wives let their hens out in the mornings. We even discovered that a sort of visitation of neighbourly anger, in the shape of a deputation of one, was being planned against us at Windswept.

Many a dog in the country may steal an occasional egg, but Bundle was different. She had an incurable mania for eggs, an obsession for eating them that nothing could cure. No sort of punishment was any good at all. She was even too cunning to fall for the old dodge of filling an eggshell with mustard. The pattern of her life was fixed forever – every dawn, when sheds were opened, she would be slinking on her round of theft, every twilight, just before the sheds were shut, she would be there again for her furtive twilight call.

Peggy found the only solution that would save the neighbours' eggs without breaking the children's hearts. We let Bundle have her first litter, chose Simba, as the pick of the bunch, found homes for the other three puppies, and then, one day when Simba was out with our tribe for an uproarious walk up Tren Crom, we passed Bundle painlessly into the hands of an R.S.P.C.A. Inspector, and the hereafter. She would have been found dead in a ditch, shot up with pellets, had we kept her any longer.

If you were to keep Simba without food for two days and then roll a dozen eggs in front of him, he would never touch a single one. Ever since he was a puppy, Peggy has conditioned him to the knowledge that Eating Eggs is Bad for Good Dogs.

To the terrier and the greyhound said to be parts of Simba's ancestry, I should be inclined to add a few dollops of retriever and Alsatian. He is gentle, and fearless, intelligent, and something of a buffoon, and devoted with all his heart to Peggy and the children. Devotion, however, has not made Simba lead a careful life. I once had to lance his jaw with a razor blade, after he had been worsted in an encounter with an adder; one Sunday morning, we found him lying gasping in the front garden, peppered with gun-shot; when they were digging the septic tank for the village sewage scheme, Simba managed to get buried for three days under an enormous mound of clay and soil which had collapsed on top of him, and arrived home at last with a belly and a mouth and a nose and both ears plugged with earth. Once, when he was in his prime, and the moon was full, he ran off for a week with something that must have smelt like a vixen, for he came back reeking of fox. He has never acquired any traffic sense whatever; periodically, he gets sent flying for six by a car or a motor-bike, and limps home for another convalescence.

It was only yesterday that I wrote this brief account of Simba, our family dog, fathered by Warrior of Higher Trenowin on the felonious Bundle. Continuous snow fell on West Cornwall yesterday, and by dusk, ice glazed our upstairs windows.

This morning, March 2nd, 1965, Simba was eager to be out and away, and he left the cottage at breakfast time.

I was called from my desk in the middle of this morning, and went out into the snow, and found a neighbour waiting in the field that lines our eastern hedge. Through bleak and leafless branches, in subdued tones, he told me of a phone call he had just taken from a nearby farmer. The message was that Simba had gone down in a fight to the death with a younger dog, over a bitch that had lured them both out early on the same errand.

Duncan went for him, and he and a friend brought Simba home on a tractor. They have buried him in his box, wrapped in a blanket, deep in the black Cornish soil of our cottage. All our land is white today, except for one black patch.

1> Caddick seems to have liked the Muses — see A Is For Arts Club *Alphabet of West Cornwall. 1963.*

XI
Druids' Whoopee

THE MEAD CASE helped me considerably in the placing of my writing. I found several fresh markets for occasional journalism, and, even, several new periodicals that were willing to accept poetry, which is a perishable commodity in a buyers' market at the best of times. I think it also helped me with the BBC, although I had broadcast well before all the publicity that erupted like Vesuvius from that little County Court. I now started broadcasting fairly often, until I could chalk up the tally of a dozen talks.

The publicity also affected what genteel persons might describe as my 'standing' in West Cornwall. What other people think about myself has not worried me overmuch, though it has amused me a lot at times when I have accidentally discovered it. Before the brouhaha about Woad, I suppose such local opinion as might have been identifiably formed about me could be summed up as: 'A bit of a nut-case, but very well-spoken.' After the uproar, it began to be whispered about that I was very clever, although I did write poetry.

I recall a most gratifying moment when I was given the authentic chance of seeing myself as others saw me. One year, round about Michaelmas Day, Peggy and myself had walked several miles, with all five of our children, to a Harvest Festival Service in a neighbouring Parish. The Service had been pleasant, but very sparsely attended.

On Christmas Eve of the same year, I went for a drink into the Gentlemen Only Bar at the Western Hotel, Penzance. This is a spot where, by long tradition, many of the older farmers from all over West Penwith meet for a drink at Christmas. Farmers never seem to worry about modulating their voices, or toning down the volume to fit the nearness of the crony they are chatting with. They shout at full blast indoors, just as they do when they are calling Friesians in for milking across a ten-acre field.

When I went into the Western, I noticed two very elderly countrymen sitting together in a corner. As I ordered my pint, there fell, by chance, one of those intermittent and disconcerting sudden silences you always get in taverns. In the silence, one of the old farmers bellowed to another:

"There's that there mad poet from 'cledry!"

"Dang me!" the other replied, in a still louder voice. "He ain't daft. He come to my Harvest Festival with his missus and hundreds of children, and he puts them in rows, and dishes out hymn-books, and the whole bloody lot of them stood there singing like hell!"

My reputation has been saved by a Churchwarden.

One of the things that makes life in Cornwall so congenial to me is the lack of servility of class towards class. There is none of the sickening cap-touching that pollutes village life up country. You have only to look at the Cornish landscape to realize that it is populated by very independent people. They build their homesteads exactly where they choose, and as far away from the next man as they can manage it. It is a system that makes distribution a trader's purgatory, but it breeds men who do not lick boots. The Anglo-Saxons grouped their dwellings round the Manor; and its Lord, transformed to Squire, turned centuries of rustics into toadies. There are very few Squires in Cornwall.

Cornwall, besides never having invented the Squire, has also managed not to perpetuate the Parson. Wesley dealt a death-blow to Anglicanism down here, and harassed Vicars have to tend two rambling Parishes by preaching on alternate Sundays. Truro Cathedral was supposed to symbolize the resurgence of Anglicanism in the West. It is, in reality, a memorial to it, and, like the Church it commemorates, Truro Cathedral is a patched-up architectural compromise. The most interesting thing I found, the only time I visited it, was an inscription by a wife saying that she had dedicated a small organ to the memory of her husband.

At Windswept, high on the hills of West Penwith, which form barricades round scattered homesteads, we are surrounded by smallholdings. When we first came to Cornwall, market-gardening predominated; then the sheep appeared, as farmers learnt that all that their pasture lacked for the grazing of healthy flocks was regular dressing with cobalt. Far more of them, however, used subsidies for breaking up croft, which was first cleaned by early potato crops, then used for broccoli, and finally tried out as grazing for dairy-cows as the farming fashion veered towards milk production. Now that milk has, apparently, been too successfully produced, so that there is a planned glut of it, the crofts are being used for steers, and these frugal pastures are producing beef. They are also being used for the rearing of pigs, and, as you walk down the Cucurrian valley from Nancledra to Cockwells, you can see herds of porkers finishing off the job done by the bulldozers, churning up the topsoil, and ripping up the tenacious roots of gorse.

This countryside, punctuated by the stacks of derelict mines, scarred by the gashes hacked by disused quarries, occasionally whitened by dumps of China Clay at discontinued workings, farmed by marginal smallholders earning less than the labourers they used to employ, is now becoming a Geriatric Unit. Young people are leaving, and retired folk from up country are buying old cottages and converting them into quasi-suburban Shangri-Las. These are the new passive settlers; the active settlers, who, alas, do not often settle for long, are the dreamers and the drifters, the romantic fringe who arrive here because Penzance is the last railway stations in England, the visionary terminus of this century.

Behind this Cornish background, or superimposed on it, if you prefer it that way, is the Old Cornish Movement. This has several layers, of differing depth. The most profound is Mebyon Kernow, the Cornish Underground Resistance Movement in everything except that it publicises its rebellion. Then there is the Federation of Old Cornwall Societies which homogenises the activities, mainly historical, of parochial groupings of enthusiasts. Finally – yes, the absolute end! – is the Gorsedd[1]. This august and almost metaphysical band of scholars and patriots has King Arthur as its lodestar, but its' true Patron Saint was Morton, the late Morton Nance, Grand Bard of Cornwall, an eagle of a man with the flaming eyes of a fanatic.[2]

Morton Nance's English-Cornish and Cornish-English Dictionaries are works as much of impassioned imagination as of scholarship. At some time or other, across the subconscious mind of this remarkable man, must have flashed a thought similar to that once memorably expressed by Voltaire – if Cornish did not exist, it would be necessary to invent it. To a great extent, this is what Morton Nance really did.

I quote from the 1955 Preface to his Cornish-English Dictionary. 'It includes all recognised words, Celtic or otherwise in origin, that have formed an integral part of the Cornish Language, and, since its aim is to promote use of this language, where known words fail to supply an obvious lack, others which being both Breton and Welsh are assumable as Cornish also, or which seem likely Cornish loanwords, from Middle English, are given a spelling conformable with the Unified Middle Cornish adopted for the rest. Such adventitious words are used sparingly and given an asterisk.' As to 'sparingly', there are nineteen asterisks on page 94 alone. As to whether they are invariably used, I looked up 'aeroplane', and found it given as 'plen an ayr' – without an asterisk. This is, apparently, not a loanword, but a prophecy.

I was very friendly with Morton Nance, after I had published *Druids' Whoopee*, which I published as a Broadside in 1951. Here it is:

DRUIDS' WHOOPEE

OR

A BALLAD OF BARDS AND BONFIRES

I sing the Bards – long may they thrive!-
Who keep the name of things alive
When all the meanings gone,
Who sanctify Midsummer rites
(And what the heathen did at nights)
By calling on Saint John.

They light the flames of old desire
By setting heaps of straw on fire,
And baying to the stars
Strange relics of pre-Saxon runes
To ancient, atavistic tunes
In fragmentary bars.

Having no useful thing to do,
One year I kept the Solstice too
And joined the hill-bound crowd,
The climbing band of devotees,
The crackling of whose Celtic knees
Seemed singularly loud.

The air was damp – it always is
For firework activities –
It made the night seem stark.
They did not flag, their hearts were stout,
For once, their wives had let them out
To wander after dark.

They scaled Tren Crom and piled the straw,
And kept the necromantic law
By adding the herbal sprays.
They lit the pile (it took three tries,
An omen of great enterprise)
And then began the blaze.

It flamed beneath a waning moon,
They chanted Cornish rhymes and soon
A magic thing occurred;
Descending on the hill-top's crest,
A woman white, and quite undressed,
Moved lightly as a bird

'Twas Aphrodite, come to claim
A man, in sweet Midsummer's name,
To lie within her arms.
The Bards beheld, they gave one bleat,
Then on rejuvenated feet
They rushed to taste her charms.

She fled, and cast a smile behind.
The learned scholars were not blind,
They chased, they leapt like hares.
They shed their vests, they shed their age,
They shed their woollies stage by stage,
They cast all clothes and cares.

Over the hills the Bards pursued,
And one the goddess caught, and wooed,
And left the earth at dawn,
Dead from a night in love's own bowers!
The other Bards conferred for hours,
And secrecy was sworn.

The Times had several stately lines
Upon the unsealed shafts of mines,
And still the Druids grieve
Their brother Bard – O happy soul!–
Lost in a prehistoric role
Upon Midsummer's Eve.

[also published in *Quiet Lutes and Laughter* 1955. see also *'A Rocket for the Gorsedd' and 'Cradle Song for Mebyon Kernow;' Broadsides from Bohemia, also 'Lesvebyon Kernow;' Cornish Review No. 10 Winter '68*]

The reaction of Morton, Grand Bard of Cornwall, to this jeu d'esprit was magnanimous in the extreme; he came to two of my poetry readings not long after, sat in the front row, asked me to read *Druids' Whoopee*, and knocked his knees together with delight. This gesture distracted attention from the smallness of the attendance; had I not prudently brought my wife and five children with me, I should have been reading poetry in the wilderness. Poetry readings are precarious events; people promise nobly to come, and call for a pint on the way, to steel their hearts against the pending agony, and immediately forget all about poetry for the rest of the evening. The only full house I ever had for one of my readings was at Newlyn Art Gallery, and I suspect Peter Lanyon drummed up a lot of the victims.

The Broadside was splendidly printed by Michael Johnson, of Padstow, on hand-made paper, with one of his own drawings at the top, showing Aphrodite, naked, haring across the landscape. My poem originally referred to a waxing moon, but Michael had the block made for a waning moon, and I was quite agreeable to change the text. Michael Johnson was a dark, romantic, corsair-type, whose disappearance from our midst I regret. There was a rumour that he had set up a Press on a yacht, stationed just outside Portuguese territorial waters, to print either propaganda, or pornography, I forget which. But I do vividly remember helping him to escape from the amours of a beautiful woman; we crammed his suitcase with socks, and gulped red wine, then shoved in shirts, and drained the dregs, and fell through the doorway to liberty hiccupping ungallantly.

Though Morton took my satire in good part, he was always obdurate when I tried to raise with him the question of the Roman influence on Cornwall. He maintained it had never been occupied by the Romans; not long ago, they discovered a very considerable Roman encampment at Camborne. He even refused to admit that the Cornish for a church, 'eglos', was obviously a corruption of the Latin 'ecclesia'.[3]

I do not think enough attention has been paid to the theory that Cornish may, for the most part, be corrupted Dog-Latin. Here is a table of words that may set a few philologists to work:

English	**Latin**	**Cornish**
Book	liber	lyver
Dogs	canes	cun
Danger	periculum	peryl
Fish	pisces (pl)	pysk
Fisherman	piscator	pyscador
To follow	sequi	sewya

Foreigner	extranus	estren
God	Deus (or Dominus)	Dew
Land	terra	tyr
Law	lex	lagha
Letter	littera	lyther
To learn	discere	dysky
Moon	luna	lor
Nations	nationes	gwlasow
Night	nox	nos
Sea	mare	mor
Thief	ladro	lader
Thin	tenuis	tanow
Window	fenestra	fenester
Word	verbum	ger
Work	opus	ober
To write	scribere	scryfa

To this scant collation from hundreds of obvious derivations as many again may be added when philological changes are allowed for. Thus, after adjusting the opening letters 'gw' to 'v", we find:

English	Latin	Cornish
True	verum	gwyr
Virgin	virgo	gwerghes
Widowed	viduus	gwedhow

One of the most indefatigable of the present Bards is Gwas Galva, the mysterious name which hides, unsuccessfully, the form of Peter Pool, a Penzance solicitor. From Peter Pool, the lawyer, I have had innumerable kindnesses; of Gwas Galva, the Bard, I am terrified. The moment I mention Julius Caesar to him, he reaches for a massive two-handed sword, and whirls it round my head. This sword is carried before the Grand Bard when the Gorsedd is in session, and was made in Birmingham. One day I shall risk decapitation and ask Gwas Galva if the farm to our north, Borea, one of the oldest in Cornwall, could possibly be named after Boreas, the rude North Wind that blows through the pages of the Golden Age of Latin.

The most formidable rebellion of the Cornish people was against the Tudors, when Ultra-Tamar rose as one to save the use of Latin in their Churches. 'Give us back our Latin tongue!' they cried, until the grim arm of the central government stretched out and throttled them. Among those hanged was John Payne, that Mayor of St. Ives who was wined and dined as he watched the erection of his own gibbet.

In the Dark Ages, Saints from monasteries in Ireland descended like locusts upon Cornwall, some of them crossing the Irish Sea, or St. George' Channel, as you wish it, on miraculously unsinkable objects such as slabs of granite. At least, when they landed on these savage shores, in lonely coves or on the softer dunes near Hayle, these Saintly Eccentrics, preaching in mediaeval Latin, would find a race of potential converts whose Roman-Celtic patois enabled them to understand. Long after Rome had fallen and her legions departed, the isolation of this ancient kingdom preserved this fragmentary Latin dialect intact.

[1>] *In 1904, Cornwall was accepted as a member of the Celtic Congress. In 1920 all Cornwall societies started to encourage the learning of the Cornish language and the revival of old customs.*
In 1928, Morton Nance along with Henry Jenner formed the first Gorsedd of Bards of Cornwall, based on the ceremonies of Wales and Brittany. The first Grand Bard was Jenner, who was succeeded by Nance.
At the annual Gorsedd, titles are conferred on Cornish men and women who have made an outstanding contribution to Cornish life. Peter Lanyon (qv) was one so honoured.

In private correspondence with Diana Caddick May 2003 she wrote:
'I went to a very good talk about his life at the Morrab library in Penzance last Spring, given by a Dr Brace from Exeter University. It stirred up some of the Mebyon Kernow in the audience!'

See Cornish Studies 7
Chapter 8. Cornish Identity and Landscape in the Work of Arthur Caddick — *Catherine Brace.*

2> *Morton Nance – see biographies*

3> *I agree with Caddick here, I don't think the Romans stopped at the Tamar. Cornwall was simply too rich mineral wise for it to have been left.*

XII
My Career as a Café-keeper

FOR TWO DIZZY DAYS, Peggy and myself and our family of five once joined the fabulous and gilded company of Romano, Frascati and Ritz. We kept a wayside café[1].

How trite, you may feel, that a poet should herald the garlanded entry of June into Cornwall is these so sordid words! In a kindly season, after the Blackthorn Winter, which dies in early May, when the Chinese sprays of white blossom which break before the leaves have fallen from ethereal grace, the whole of Cornwall quickens and awaits the year's high-noon. June in Cornwall is a brilliance and a radiance and an oriflamme of molten sun, intense crystal light brings far horizons near, and telescopes the distance between the top of Tren Crom to Lizard with such intensity that you may stand on Celtic earthworks five hundred feet high and watch the waves, a score of miles away cascading their spray against granite and serpentine cliffs. In June, I once heard a nightingale at Marazion. It is also the crescendo of a Cornish Klondyke, when new potatoes are excavated as frenziedly as edible diamonds as the price sags daily at Covent Garden.

All this is very true. Yet, indigence detracts both from its beauties and its excitements. Hence our concept of a wayside café.

The inspiration for our wild leap into catering came to Peggy one morning in June about twenty-five years ago. We were starting on another lean day without cheques, and were finishing a bare-cupboard sort of breakfast. Even the cereal packet looked as if damp-rot had set in. Is there anything more sordid than a cereal that sags instead of crackling? We were traversing a seam of sorrow, through a time-tunnel of financial grief. Morbidity was beginning to seep-in, also. if a hundred Death-Watch Beetles, in our ancient walls and rafters, had started to tap out in unison their count-down to doom, I would probably have answered, resignedly: 'Dear Coleoptera, how kind of you to co-operate'.

The parlour-window in our cottage was wide open, and, in the rare and fleeting seconds when all the children were not all gabbling at once, we could hear the noise of tourist traffic, going up and down Nancledra Hill.

"Nothing but cars, cars, cars," said Peggy, severely. "Everybody in Cornwall is coining money from tourists except us!"

The morning post had dumped a thud of rejection-slips on my doorstep. When I opened them, I heard the far-off cry of wolves howling, as they edged closer and closer. Do wolves eat Death-Watch beetles? I know not. The last wolf in England is reputed to have been killed at near-by Ludgvan. But I knew better, it was not the last. It left behind a ravenous posterity. So I held my peace, when Peggy made her diatribe against cars, cars, cars.

She stood up suddenly, knocking her chair over backwards. "I shall go and count the knives," she announced, dramatically, and disappeared into the kitchen.

"I bet we've had burglars, "hissed Duncan, our youngest. "Burglars at dead of night!".

"What by dead of night?" demanded his mother, coming back into the parlour. Then without waiting for a reply, she went on: "Twelve! Twelve knives are quite enough!"

"What are twelve knives quite enough for? Twelve Lady Macbeths?" I asked, placatingly, fearing that her nerves had snapped under the sheer strain of living, and dwelling, and having one's being.

"To open a wayside café."

"A what?"

"A wayside gold-mine," she answered, very firmly.

Six pairs of blue eyes – ten bright, two faded – stared at her in stupefied silence. Diana was the first to come round. "I'll be the waitress, and keep all the tips!" she cried, boisterously.

A quartet of indignant snorts was silenced by Peggy, who gave her ruling: "All five of you can be helpers, and I'll look after the tips."

"I think we ought to have a trunk," said Anne.

"What'll we need a trunk for?" asked David, suspiciously.

"A trunk for pooling tips, like they have in hotels."

"You mean a tronc," I put in.

Anne looked at me calmly. "That's what I said, Daddy. A tronc."

"I bet those burglars will find the old tronc," grunted Duncan.

"Don't talk bonk?" said Diana.

"What's bonk?" cried Caroline, very wistfully.

"A bonk is what this family is going to get if you don't stop talking bunk," I replied.

"Daddy," said Peggy, pitilessly, "can stand by and do relays of stream-lined washing-up."

"Its kind of Daddy to do all the nasty washing-up," said Caroline, patting my arm as a reward.

"You'll be helping him, Callie, dear," her mother said. "We won't need four of you serving all the time. Not quite all the time. Besides, we'll need to save our strength for rush-hours".

I gave Peggy my version of a long hard look.

"You needn't wince, dear," she sighed.

"I want to know if this café idea is really serious."

"A wayside gold-mine," murmured Caroline.

"Another castle in Spain," said Anne, ending her words with a sniff.

Where's this gold-mine going to operate?" I wanted to know.

Peggy gazed proudly round our living-room. I gazed after her, and managed to conceal my pride. It has always seemed to me a very small space for seven people.

"This is a large room, really." She said. "Really a large room, when it's not cluttered".

"It is always cluttered".

"Well, then, we're going to de-clutter it. We'll move all the furniture out into the garden. The sunshine will freshen it up. Then we'll put four tables in. We can easily manage four tables, seating four people each."

"Sixteen people and twelve knives," brooded Duncan. "I can't make it come out right." He went on counting and recounting his grubby fingers in a mathematical frenzy.

"Little children shouldn't use sharp knives," said Diana. "There's bound to be hundreds of little children coming. Each table shall have three knives."

"Anyhow, our knives are all blunt," said Duncan. "Thank goodness a boy at the village swapped me a conundrum stone for my old bicycle bell. Now I can sharpen all our knives. Just you wait!" And off he marched; a man with a mission.

"That boy's very practical," said his mother, "I know which side he gets that from. But he's not touching my knives".

"How will people know we're a wayside café?" piped Caroline. "We're not a wayside. We're the top of a poky old lane."

"We're not a pokey old lane," I said testily. "One of the oldest bridle-paths in Cornwall runs up our lane and round our cottage. It's the ancient track for pack-mules, carrying Tin from Zennor to St. Michael's Mount."

"I don't see ghosts of long-dead mules selling Cornish Teas," brooded Anne.

"Do stop bickering," her mother ordered. "Daddy knows a lot of artists. Daddy will get one of them to paint us a lovely notice, saying 'Cornish Teas', and we'll stick it in the hedge at the corner of the main road. Daddy won't take long to get us a notice done."

"I do wish Mummy wouldn't talk about Daddy as if Daddy wasn't here", I grunted. "It sounds like a séance."

"Daddy," said Anne, very solemnly, "don't go asking any of those abstract artists for our notice. We want a notice people can read."

"What are we going to give these poor old customers to eat?" demanded Diana.

"Splits and cream and jam, and lots and lots of little iced cakes. I shall use the lovely icing-machine my Aunt sent me. It wriggles out fantastic squiggles."

"Lots and lots of little iced cakes at threepence each," chanted Duncan, almost like a new curate chanting the Burial Service.

"Little cakes included in a half-crown tea," explained Peggy.

"Some people –" Caroline's voice had become uncharacteristically bitter – "some people charge fourpence for mingey-stingey teeney-weeney cakes-and sixpence for big ones."

"All cakes in Cornwall go up in summer," said Anne. "It's a sort of Law the Council's passed. Like fruit and tomatoes just after Helston Flora Day. All the same, I don't see why our cakes are going to be free, Mummy."

"They're not going to be free, darling. They're just included in our half-crown Cornish Cottage Tea."

"People will be proper potty to come here and get charged half-a-crown just for a tea," pronounced Diana, like Portia going on about a pound of flesh.

"Most people are potty on holidays," her mother answered. "That's why most of them leave home-comforts, especially in hot weather. Anyhow, I'm not arguing any more. Splits and cream and jam and as many little cakes as they can stuff down – sweet little cakes with piskeyfield squiggles from poor old Auntie's elegant Victorian icing machine. Highly-praised by Mrs. Beeton. Let's hope it only works."

"Could someone eat twelve?" demanded Duncan.

"Certainly. But no one would dream of it."

Duncan scowled, and brooded for a moment. "I bet our customers do", he gave his verdict, slowly hissing out each word like a Judge with a Black Cap on.

"Cheer up everybody, we'll just have to see. Now, everything is settled. We shall open our Wayside Café the day after tomorrow. It's Thursday today, so we can open on a Saturday. Couldn't be better – a perfect day to start. We'll have our bright new Notice stuck up in the hedge by a quarter to three, and take it down at half-past six. That should be long enough – unless there are queues of cars lined up."

"Quite long enough". I said, emerging from my long silence in a sort of mental mortuary. I had just concluded that be it ne'er so humble there's no place like home, was going to take on another meaning from another planet. I shuddered and I sensed that somewhere in our ingle-nook our pet cricket lay petrified by a new and alien and baleful brooding presence. Thank God I am not a morbid man.

So that is how our Wayside Gold-Mine blazed the trail for Poseidon in its Blue-Chip operation.

By Saturday lunch-time, we were all ready for the gold-rush. (Lunch had been seven independent al fresco grabs at sandwiches in a cupboard labelled by Peggy "Family Food – eat this only or go to Bed!") Our bits of furniture had been bundled into an ex-hen shed with a mainly – ex roof. Luckily, I'd heard the Rector of Ludgvan was already praying, in vain for rain. Our cramped living-room had blossomed into a spacious restaurant, with four little table with four assorted chairs each, and three kitchen-knives each to give a touch of Cornish regional eccentricity. Our smoke belching grate (now, thanks to Summer disuse, damped of its vestal fires) was overflowing with pink Cornish heath. I had scorned the blasphemous temptation to tie it up in little bundles, beneath a label declaring, 'The Sacred Flowers of Saint Piran, Patron of all Cornish Miners – guaranteed fresh and very lucky – 6d per bunch, discount per dozens'.

I had rearranged our microscopic kitchen on the microscopic notions I had, of time-and-motion-study lines – that is to say, I shoved packets of detergents in a wobbly row at the back of the sink, and Peggy whisked them off again, as water was seeping upwards into their caustic and unspeakable contents. I put a pile of tea-towels on the top of an unstable stool, and on the stool's front leg I tacked an elegant placard saying: 'Clean'. But they were dirty all the time, as Caroline would insist on splashing every single pot we had with soapy water, so that she could make practice-runs at drying them, which Duncan tried to time on an alarm clock. He made it whirr every three minutes or so, and I got a horrible neurotic feeling that all my bright mornings forever and anon would be swept endlessly away.

At five minutes to three, I reviewed the Wayside Restaurant Chef, Waiters and Washers-up, and gave them all their last command before Zero Hour, and their going over the top.

"Nobody", I boomed, "is allowed to stand in the Dining-Hall and stare at eating Guests, or Guests eating."

Then I marched down our lane with the notice board, which David had nailed to a broom-handle. My long-suffering friend, William Redgrave, whom I had gone-off by bus to St. Ives to find, reassuring Anne that I was seeking out a Famous Painter, who was neither a Tachiste, nor a Cubist, nor a Surrealist, but an artist whose work I admired, had uncomplainingly left a canvas he was hard at work on in his studio in Island Road, and set out with a will to do me and my notice-board really proud. Hazlitt said he loved artists who did things with gusto. So do I. Gusto propelled Bill Redgrave's brush, and on my perpendicular length of jarra wood, painted yellow on black – the colours of the comity of Cornwall – he had inscribed, in elegant and elongated lettering, the talismanic words: 'Cornish Teas.' Bill had, at first, pretended to haggle for a Free Tea as a Fee, and when I enthusiastically agreed he straightaway stood me three pints of bitter in the Castle Inn, to prove that all great commercial matters are transacted over drinks. O, rare William Redgrave, long ago gone away to make his name in what I deem the exile of Chelsea, but still moving and talking through my memory down the Digey, along the Wharf, and in the bar where the fishermen gather in the Sloop.

I ceremoniously anchored the masterpiece, nailed to the broom-handle, in the thick blackthorn hedge at the bottom of our lane, where it joins the road from Penzance to St. Ives. I left it there proudly flaunting to the highway and high heaven its promise and its message, and trotted, rather breathless, up the lane, back to the headquarters of our catering-combine. It seemed to me that my cottage was already holding its sagging old roof high, pretending to be a Trust House.

By now, it was three o'clock, and Duncan and the whirr of the alarm-clock both said it was at once. The other five of my family sang out, in a sort of discordant harmony that the kettle was boiling. We stood round it fondly, watching each puff of steam. It was the donkey-boiler at our Klondyke.

At the end of about five minutes of our silent reverence round it, Anne shrieked: "it's boiling dry!"

But Peggy was already at the peak of her form – "Alright, then, refill it, and let it simmer on the side."

So now we switched duties; we stood and watched it simmering. It was a change from crescendo to rallentando. Each of the children went in turn on tip-toe to the café, to see if any customers had come; equally on tip-toe, I suppose. Each found it silent and empty, except David who found one wasp. All of them stamped back, very loudly, into our kitchen. Then they all began to chunter ominously to one another.

At four o'clock, Peggy doled out little iced cakes all round, to sustain morale. At a quarter past four, I repeated the bounty, and I tried to be hearty and sounded plain daft. Outside, on the croft, there was the scent of furze and heath and wild thyme; in the kitchen, it was sweatily cramped and warm, and the kettle's simmer had become a sneer. And instead of skylarks singing in the blue Cornish sky, I was listening to murmurs of mutiny, perhaps omens of mayhem. I sweated with Angst, which brooded over Windswept Cottage. I began to wonder if the four tables in our silent restaurant would break into a pavane, or behave like the furniture in 'L'Enfant et les Sortilèges.'

By half-past four, we were standing at our front gate in a sombre septet of deaf-mutes. Then, all of us at once, we spotted a figure trudging up our lane.

"Trade's starting!" screamed Peggy.

"I've got wind with waiting!" wailed Caroline.

We started down the lane through the curving hedgerows, with eagle eyes, stout Cortez multiplied by seven, silent by a battered gate-post in West Penwith. Then I recognized the pilgrim. It was Bill

Redgrave, ostensibly coming for his tea on the house; really, to back us up out of sheer goodness of heart.

“Why haven’t you got my notice-board up, Arthur?” he bellowed, as he came nearer.

“What?” I yelled back. “What??” shrilled six voices, eerie as air-raid sirens.

Then we all sprinted down the lane, like a lop-sided, mixed-age group, Seven-a-Side Rugby Team from Bedlam. Bill, left quite alone, was probably wondering if he looked like a Leper.

Our beautiful Trade Sign, tastefully embellished with the colours of a Royal Duchy, had toppled over backwards and now lay flat in a field full of Friesian cows. One of them stared at me, not in disdain, cows being incapable of unkindness, but in a restrained sympathy with my grief, which it punctuated by morose moos, its eyes were liquid with tears. Our Notice had lain for hours, unseen by any creature save crows and magpies and green men in Flying Saucers. Perhaps its underside had brightened the dark abysm of a mole or two, coming up to inspect a new roofing-system. In short, our Wayside-Wonder-Bar, like that feckless flower in somebody’s poem had been born to blush unseen, and waste its sweetness on a fertilized pasture.

I felt such a dam’ fool that I took the only way to stop myself being called one. I flared up like Herod and verbally massacred my innocent brood, with a torrent of snide innuendos against my harmless wife.

“I told everybody, every one of you, scores of times, not to fiddle and fool about with my Notice, for which I paid a lot of money, which I shall stop from your pocket money. Don’t start on crocodile tears! Do you understand what has hit us? We have lost several hundred pounds of goodwill before serving a Tea.”

“But we saved the little iced cakes,” said Duncan, loyally trying to comfort me.

I stared right through him, and he turned round to see what was behind him.

I went on, still dramatic: “Now, when I make out my Trading Income Tax Returns, I shall have to write-off loss of goodwill”.

I though you tore up anything about Income Tax," my wife remarked.

I scowled like a villain, and waved them all away. Bill had a half of John Bell concealed about his person, as policemen say in court. So, by half-past five, Bill and myself, and the Scotsman in the bottle, had stuck a Dutch-hoe in the field beside the blackthorn hedge. The shaft of the hoe had rope lashed to it, and the rope ran through the hedge, and was looped to the broom-stick at the other side. A chunk of granite, tightly swathed like a mummy in old sacking, bound round by three new handkerchiefs, and one of Peggy's chiffon scarves, was lashed to the base of the stick, and kept it pointing upward to the Milky Way, and thus the notice flaunted its dazzling black and yellow in the clean and clear Cornish air. Not a Witch in all recorded time could have done any better. You could see it from both sides of the road; indeed, you could not miss it. Horses might shy at it, but motorists would pause.

Then, without any warning, it started to bucket with rain. In no time at all, the notice began to change appearance.

"Poster-paints, you know," said Bill, regretfully, "I should have used Oils."

"I don't blame you at all, Bill. This is a staunch Nonconformist stronghold. An Anglican Incumbent had not right to pray for rain when some of the hillside hay's not even in. I suspect that the Tories have a pull Up There."

Back in our cottage that night, universal peevishness prevailed, tempered only by the children's appetite, as they munched their unprofitable way through Saturday's non-takings from splits and cream and jam and as many little iced cakes as you wanted for half-a-dollar, no Extras. I even ate too much sweet-stuff myself, and got wind for my greed. But Caroline's wind was cured; she got hiccups instead.

"That's my third half-crown's worth," she squeaked, swollen with the triumphs of Auntie's squiggle machine.

"Thanks for a jolly good blow-out," said Bill. "Best tea I've had for ages. Don't get depressed, Peggy!. . . I tell you what. . . "

"What is there to be depressed about?"

"I feel in my bones that this idea of yours will turn out to be – you'll never guess! – a little gold-mine. If it's stopped raining tomorrow, I'll try to get over to lend a hand, Arthur".

"That's handsome of you, Bill. It's big of you – er – could you do me a very small favour? You wouldn't like to help me out with bringing some bits and pieces of very, very, light furniture back from the hen-shed? It wouldn't take long."

"Arthur, I've eaten too much for removal-work".

Then, as he saw my disappointment, inspiration seized him. "As a matter of fact, I've got to dash away at once. I've a sitting fixed-up in less than an hour, and I must get to my studio as soon as possible. David, come with me, and I'll give you some Oils and you can make that blasted notice weatherproof. You can get the bus straight back."

And off William Redgrave fled, as a free man should, and I did not blame him one iota. David cantered after him, whooping with joy.

"The furniture can't get any wetter, so it can stay where it is till morning," said Peggy.

On Sunday, it rained perseveringly till four o'clock. Then, patches of blue appeared overhead. I rushed down the lane, and swarmed over the watery blackthorn hedge, prickly with piercing points of thorn. I fixed-up all the complex trappings of our hoarding-even by now admitting to myself that they were, in some ways, perhaps a trifle bizarre – and soon the sun had the pleasure of reading 'CORNISH TEAS' once more – this time in Oils. Then I rushed back to our place of business.

By five o'clock, the family was once more teetering on the verge of morbid hysteria. Nobody, as yet, was actually foaming at the mouth; but not a soul had come, not a drum been heard, not a funeral note, o'er the grave where our hopes lay buried. I was mephitically sick of it all. Law and Order were in tatters, and my staff was whirligigging round four flimsy tables in our spacious morgue of a café, throwing little iced cakes at each other in a demented frenzy. I got a direct hit on my nose, which left a sugared-violet almost up my nostril. Mack Sennett would have signed us up for life on the spot.

"Nobody will ever come to this dump," said Diana, who was prone to the grumps.

As her grumps slumped into total gloom, a car tooted raucously. Its sweet music ravished our senses. Then a second car tootled with more melodious two-toned horn.

We charged like the Light Brigade into our front-garden. Two cars were bumping up our lane. Two cars stopped at the top of our lane. Then people actually got out of the cars – real live people got out and started walking past our side-garden right up to our front gate. They passed through it and drew near to our Wayside Café. I counted an ensemble of eleven persons, marching towards our destiny, and two of them were carrying babies. Both babies were screaming. My insolvent ears misheard the squalls of brats as lullabies, trailing clouds of glorious lolly as they came.

My staff ran to their action-stations. Not me. I broke my own rule, and waited to welcome this happy throng of holiday makers to the joys of Cornwall, and the Cornish Riviera (invented long ago by a Board of Railway Directors when their line reached Penzance and threatened to make the last stop Penury).

A smiling, jolly, swollen woman led them to my door. She wore a gigantic necklace of Whitby Jet, and a bangle of innumerable lucky-charms, and they all wobbled with her.

"We'd like cottage teas for eleven grown-ups, and two babies-in-arms, please, Mister."

"At once, madam, please come in. You are all very welcome. Family-parties make up most our regular customers."

A short, tetchy, fidgety man came next. He peered into our parlour very cautiously.

"I don't think the gentleman has much room," came his reconnaissance report.

"There's plenty of room," answered Anne, in her best prefect's voice. "We just happen to have four tables vacant. You're very lucky, very lucky, indeed. We've been run off our feet for hours and hours."

A fat, Falstaffian figure ambled up. "Champion! Just the job! Stop picking holes, Alfie and park your you-know-what on a seat." He pushed the fidget aside, and stood inside the café, beaming at the world. He was sweating, wearing a thick blue serge suit, and a straw-hat with a black band which was lettered in gold 'Kiss Me Quick'.

"We'd all like to sit together," said purple jumper. "Alfie, tell the nice young lady we'd all like to sit together."

"We'd all like to sit together," explained Alfie, who was, I now discovered, the public mouthpiece of the party.

"Please, Miss, where's the Toilet?" gasped a pale young girl, who had thick pigtails, tied with out-size crimson bows.

"The Toilet!" gasped Peggy, going white with shock.

I nearly passed-out myself. A ghastly knife plunged into my innards. Our sanitation, in those days, was precisely the same as in the reign of good King Arthur, an earth-closet as used by the Lady of Shalott. In our rush of rapturous joy over our idyll of a gold-mine, we had utterly overlooked this sordid inconvenience. Now, eleven grown-ups, and two babies-in-arms wanted to enter its primitive portals. How could I tell them? What could I say? What would they say?

Inspiration chased desperation out of what was left of my mind.

"It is out of order," I declared, tragically. "I phoned the plumber at first dawn, and gave him the symptoms. He said something about a clump of bubbles in the sump. I think that was what he said, but the line is bad, in the village phone-box. Although it's Sunday, he promised to come after morning Service. Our plumber is a Sidesman at our Parish Church. A most respected figure for miles around. What he promises, he performs. Most unfortunately for us all, to-day, by ancient Cornish custom, is Common Christening Feast Day. There has been a remarkable rise in our birth-rate this year. It is possible that our plumber has been delayed because he had to lay on extra water."

They stared at me in awe.

"A plumber promising to come on a Sunday! Fancy that, Alfie," said purple jumper, believing every word I had said.

"They wouldn't do that in Macclesfield," said Alfie, most respectfully. "Nor in Huddersfield, neither. Nor Crewe, nor Goole, nor Pontefract. I travelled the lot in Fancy Goods and Junior Sundries."

Miraculously, the audience seemed to be on my side. The fat old buffer hadn't spoken a word – he sat stuffing himself with splits and cream. He had jumped the gun, and found food. A clinching column of support closed-in, in the shape of an etiolated old lady, in an ankle-length black dress, who wore rows and rows of huge white plastic beads. She tweaked poor, pale Pansy's pigtails with her withered talons, and spoke for the first time.

"Pansy will just have to wait. Auntie told Pansy to wash her hands on the sands. Auntie told Pansy this twice. Pansy has made her bed, and now she must lie on it. It just goes to show that children should be seen and not heard. I say, fiddle-sticks to Pansy".

"She was born self-willed, " said purple-jumpered Effie. "Dearie me, my poor old legs are playing up something awful."

"Come and sit down and rest them, Tea's all ready," cooed Peggy.

"Uncle George is already guzzling," observed Alfie.

"I wanna go to . . . " shrieked Pansy.

"That's quite enough from you! Disturbing people on a Sunday," hissed Auntie.

"Tea! Tea!" chanted Peggy, repeating it like a magic spell.

The incantation worked. It diverted the whole gaggle of them right away from Sir Galahad's unspeakable earth-closet. They took possession of our cottage, and we pushed cakes and splits and tea-pots at them like mad. They fell silent, save for the noise of munching and the smacking of lips, and the noisy squelch of sucked-in tea. Even Pansy seemed content to contain her unbiddable bladder. I noticed that six members of the party seemed to have walking-on parts only; they just sat and ate, and never spoke.

Then one of the babies pulled one of the crimson bows off Pansy's pigtails, and pushed it gleefully into a bowl of clotted cream. Pansy screamed to high heaven. At this, the other baby whooped with joy and threw a cup to the floor. Nobody seemed to dote very much on Pansy's charms. The cup smashed into fragments against her left sandal. She let out a sound like an air-raid warning. This sent both babies into gurgles of delight, and they knocked down two more cups and three saucers. But, this time, the clatter of their breaking brought on paroxysms of panic, and they began to wail and wail.

Effie mopped her brow with a large off-white handkerchief, stamped with a picture of the Queen in her Coronation robes. As she opened it, it spilt humbugs over lots and lots of little iced cakes.

"Alfie," she panted, "tell the lady we're really truly sorry."

"We're really truly sorry," said Alfie, after sucking some tea through a gap in his top teeth.

One of the babies pushed a jug of milk off the table.

"Wanna use the toilet!" screamed Pansy, by now as tragic as Ophelia about to jump off the deep end.

"There's another little difficulty about our lavatory," I put in, casually, "snakes, adders, vipers, you know."

"Snakes?" croaked Pansy.

I heard someone whisper that it was rude to call a Toilet a lavatory, but I plunged on.

"It's very hot, and it's June. And snakes have taken to sliding in under the lavatory door. I've put gravel and cinders outside, but you never can tell. Serpents are cunning. I slammed two with a spade, and they looked quite dead. But you never know. Adders live till sundown and die at close of day. . . still, they've got serum at Truro, I believe."

"I wanna wait for the Toilet," wailed Pansy.

"We want our bill, lady," chanted Effie and Alfie, in close harmony. Then they both turned round and dug Uncle George savagely in the ribs, and said it was rude to go to sleep at somebody else's tea-table.

"I wanna, I wanna. . . " Pansy's voice died away into silent anguish.

"The bill's eleven half-crowns and no charge for the babies or breakages," gabbled Peggy, desperate to be rid of her dread source of income. [Eleven half-crowns = £1.37 ½p]

Purple jumper beamed dotingly on her. "You hear that, Alfie? No charge for babies or breakages, the kind lady said. It just, goes to show-nicely-spoken, nicely-doing. . . Ask the kind lady if we could pour some of this lovely tea in our vacuums".

"Take anything you like," yelped Peggy, looking as though she was going round some private bend.

They produced three vacuums, and we started filling them up like mad. Uncle George got a plastic cup full of clotted cream. I prayed that it would raise his cholesterol to the point of no return. A baby tried to grab a plate of iced delights.

"Take some cakes", Peggy moaned in a broken voice.

They took some cakes.

"Twelve," came Duncan's sepulchral tones, as his outraged eyes counted-their disappearance into a paper bag.

"Take some splits," said Peggy.

"Fifteen", said our scorer, numbering them one by one like the sparrows in the Scriptures.

"Baby Willie's being sick, and please I wanna. . ." began Pansy – with the one-track mind.

The black-robed Aunt pushed Pansy out of our front door with one iron hand, and gave Baby Willie a backhand swipe with the other. "Children should only speak when spoken to," she pronounced. "Hurry up, the lot of you, or we'll be late for High Tea at that boarding-house we got landed in, and there's little enough to eat when we sit down first."

Suddenly, miraculously, we saw eleven adults and two babes-in-arms melting away from our little browned-off home in the West. The outraged walls of Windswept Cottage glared at us in proud disdain.

“Thirteen sat down!” chanted Caroline, like a witch-doctor.

“Thank God thirteen got up and went!” replied her mother. Then she raised her voice, and said adamantly: “Duncan, dear, run as fast as you can and take that beastly notice down at once. As fast as you can, Duncan, go like the wind!”

“It isn't six o'clock yet,” said Duncan, precisely. “And how can five of us share this mouldy old. threepenny bit they’ve left for the trunk?"

“Tronc,” corrected Anne, crossly.

“Do as you're told, Duncan,” ordered Peggy. “Don't argue-just get that beastly notice taken down”.

Duncan went off slowly, brooding over the commercial folly of his mother’s order.

“As from now,”announced Peggy “we have retired. This Wayside Gold-Mine-Loony-Bin-Café is closed for ever and ever and ever.”

“Amen to that,” I said.

“I don't think we should give in quite so easily,” began Anne. Then she stopped, and rubbed her freckled nose. “All the same, I’m glad we have.”

By Monday morning all traces of our catering-establishment had vanished into the limbo of things gone wrong, and we had quite forgotten that we had just organised another fiasco.

Monday afternoon was an exuberance of sunshine, and we lazed in our garden, and enjoyed the scents of heath and furze and wild thyme rising from the croft around us. Home had become home again, and the peace of it all covered up our penury.

Then I saw two people coming up our lane. They walked past our side garden in Indian file, and the leader leant over our front gate, waving a large-scale Ordnance Map.

He was very tall, and very thin and his bald pate gleamed in the Cornish sun like a Worcester Pippin. His shorts were ludicrously too long, and he wore a faded blue blazer, with an indecipherable badge, a very white open shirt, and enormous brogues. I wouldn’t have given generous odds that he was a master at one of those genteel places that take boarders, and try so hard to look like minor Public Schools.

As I went towards him, he asked, very politely; "Will you be kind enough to direct me to the Cornish Tea Café?"

"There isn't a café," I snapped back, trying to put on a really-ham act of a man whose privacy was being violated by a tripper.

"I have been definitely informed there is!" he bellowed back, giving me back twice as much as I'd given.

"You have been misinformed!"

A woman with a straggling bun, also wearing shorts, much shorter than his, unfortunately, for they showed her lean and stringy thighs – stalked up to his side, ready for battle.

"April, my dear! This is very odd, it is very odd indeed. Our friend here" – he winced at me – "who knows, one presumes, since, on the face of it, he lives here, informs me, quite categorically, that there is no café here. You will bear witness that two most respectable persons in the village at the bottom of that dreadful hill clearly said there was a café here, here at the top of this lane. This lane is marked on this map. I have my finger on this very lane. Yet there is no café, not here, nor anywhere further down it. The lane is a cul-de-sac. How very, very, disconcerting to have toiled up such a hill upon such a void assurance!"

"Typically vague, typically Celtic," boomed April. "I did tell you, Bartholomew, that I wanted to go walking in the French Alps, this year."

"They assured me there was a Cornish Tea Café," said Bartholomew, drawing closer, and glaring at me as if he were about to give me a thousand lines.

"Nowhere near here, never has been," I answered. "I am absolutely certain of that. As you say, I live here, and I should know. I do know. There is no café here at all."

He still looked very doubtful, and very superior, so I knocked him for six.

"As a matter of fact, sir, there is a Covenant running with my land against all Trade whatever."

"A Covenant running with the land," he repeated, most respectfully, and I could see his miserable insides twisting themselves in knots to kowtow to the rights of Property." I apologise, my dear sir. Clearly, in such a case there can be no café "

"We just closed it," mumbled Duncan, before I could pole-axe him.

"What did that little boy say? You, boy, come here. What did you say?"

I swept Duncan aside with a graceful back-stroke, and pushed my face nearer to Torquemada's. I moved nearer and nearer to him, trying to look pregnant with meaning, I mean. Then I stared at his horrible pink dome. Then I slowly lowered my eyes, and stared directly into his. He stared back, and blinked. I tapped my temples meaningfully with one fore-finger, and laid another silencing fore-finger across my lips, before pointing it furtively at Duncan.

The fuss-pot followed all this-finger-work of mine as if he were mesmerised. Then he repeated my movements, temples, lips, Duncan, with his own fingers, and gave a long sigh.

"Ah! I follow you, my dear sir. I quite follow you. What a tragedy!"

"Inbreeding," I murmured brokenly, "on the other side of the family, let me add."

"What an affliction! And how careless on somebody's part, too," was April's definitive summing-up. "Dear little soul! I sensed at once he was highly-strung. Here are three digestive biscuits for you, little man – be brave, keep a stiff upper-lip, you will come through." And she pushed a crumpled paper-bag into Duncan's hands.

The two of them stalked out past our gate, and went down the lane, stopping on their way to warn two young hikers who were wandering up. The whole quartet stared up the lane at Duncan. The bald fuss-pot tapped his temples, and so did April. The two hikers opened their mouths wide in amazement and embarrassment – and tapped their own heads, and followed April and her consort down the lane and out of our lives.

"Why's everybody tapping their heads?" demanded Duncan tapping his own, and going on tapping.

"Old Baldy's a special kind of hiker-scout, and that enchanted April with him is a special kind of hiker-guide. They tap their heads in hiker-scout -guide-sign language, in the tapping code. It means: 'No Cornish Tea Café here' "

"They all look plumb crazy to me" replied Duncan.

"As crazy as giving away millions of little iced cakes, and not charging smelly-yelly babies for breaking pots all over, and tipping five whole children one stingy-mingy, threepenny-bit, and. . ." he dried up, spent with anger.

"Duncan, my boy, you've been badly done to," I said. "Look, all of you. Next week it's the Midsummer Eve Bonfires. You can all go up to Castle-an-Dinas, and stay till the end. And I'll give you five shillings between you to spend on Pasties and Pop. And I hope that'll stop you falling into mischief if you get bored with Bards making speeches in Old Cornish fiddle-me-ree."

Duncan shivered with ecstasy, and rolled his eyes to heaven, and passed into a complete peace with his entire little world.

"What shall I tell the boys in the village about our café?" asked David. "I've just finished telling hundreds of them that it's open, and now I've got to go round telling hundreds of them that it's gone and closed. They'll all laugh at me like mad."

"Just tell them the café has fallen by the wayside," I answered.

"Down a mine-shaft, if you like," added Peggy.

The shades of Roman, Frascati, and Ritz, tapping their temples with contemptuous fingers, stalked mockingly away into a Black Hole in Outer Space, created specially for them by the explosive death of an erratic little star in the Constellation of Casse-Croûte à toute heure.

[1] *Although marked as 'Complete First Draft' pages 122-138 were missing from the manuscript. This was Chapter XII, 'My Career as a Café Keeper' – which appears on the original contents page. This chapter was found separately from the main manuscript in the boxes of Caddick's papers at Exeter University.*
The front sheet contains the title of the piece,
Handwritten: [The Month of June]
Typed: My Career as a Café-keeper
by
Arthur Caddick

With the number of words: 5,500 words, approx. The actual word count is slightly over 7,000 words.

It appears to have been re-typed and revised for submission to a magazine, possibly the Cornish Review *– but the date would suggest otherwise, the Review ceasing publication in 1974. Or, for possible inclusion in an anthology such as* My Cornwall *(1973) or* Both Sides of the Tamar *(1975) both of which included prose by Caddick. It was, I think, revised to stand-alone. As far as I know, it has not been previously published. The chapter is: 'Signed: Arthur Caddick – dated 8/X/75' – ED.*

XIII
On Art & Automation

LOOKING BACK OVER MY two decades in Cornwall, I am surprised to find how very few writers I have really got to know at all well, and how very many painters I begin to think I know a great deal about. It may be that writers are less gregarious than painters; certainly, compared with Cubists, Impressionists, Tachistes, Surrealists, and sheer bad makers of outrageous fancy doodles that end up in frames, writers appear to have a scarcity value round here. I must admit that part of the answer lies in my own dislike of Conferences, Councils, Committees and Co-Operatives for writers; they end up either as a back-scratching session, or a free-for-all, with the faint smell of sewage, like the uproars at the Edinburgh Festival. Then, too, there is the fact that the cleverest writers have the dullest conversational habits; they hoard their epigrams for their books, and add to them the epigrams that others let fall absentmindedly. Writers who live with gusto do not leave rows and rows of hard-cover hardware; they exercise their sense of style in the repartee of taverns, and their best paragraphs are drowned in rounds of drink.

However, I have made some friends among writers down here. About one of the closest of them all, Denys Val Baker, I have already told you something. In the days when the Cornish Review was foundering, friends of Denys tried to save it by contributing books, paintings, manuscripts, pottery, and some sculpture, and all these tokens of goodwill were put up for auction in aid of the Review. That was how I met Winston Graham,[1] that determined man from Manchester, whose brilliantly constructed novels are so underrated by the highbrows, because they are so successful. Winston Graham once told me something I have always remembered, and never benefited by, that his first success as a writer began to come when he rented a dilapidated bungalow well away from his home, and went out to it daily, as to an office, with a suit-case for his food and materials. It was not only the regularity but the physical separation that helped him to work so hard and consistently. I have never been able to practise a regime of this nature, and the books I have not written pile up behind me on invisible shelves, as the fertile years grow less. To do myself a scrap of justice, I might add that though I often, quite groundlessly, complain about the difficulties of writing with a large family in a small cottage, the only time I really find it difficult is when I am not writing. When I am really working, on verse or prose, with white-hot conviction, I would not notice if Windswept blew up, provided that the explosion left me hurling through the air with the scrap of paper intact on which I was concentrating when the fuse ignited. Nevertheless, quite contrary to nature, I have begun to evolve some sort of system; as I type this, I have two extra chairs, one on each side of me. The left-hand chair is for carbon-copies, and the right-hand chair – hum! That seems to have carbon copies on it as well! Yes; my system has broken down once more; it is time for another pot of tea. Funds don't run to beer this week.

Winston Graham opened the Auction for the *Cornish Review*, and I did the auctioning, which left me as limp as one of those pieces of blotting paper avant-garde poets write their doomery-gloomery-back-to-the-wombery masterpieces on. The Auction did not save the *Cornish Review*, which so disappointed us all that Denys had to throw a gorgeous party to save us all from suicide.

I met Phyllis Bottome several times at St. Ives; she read a play of mine, and very sportingly sponsored me for an Arts Council Bursary to write another. The fatal flaw in this plan was that I wanted to write a comedy with a plot, and I ended up with an elegant printed intimation of non-success (failure being reserved for geniuses).

I have met several poets down in Cornwall. I recall vivid meetings with George Barker, and walking with David Wright. John Heath-Stubbs lived near here for a time, and came one day and gave me a holograph of his *Last Will and Testament of the Cornish Chough*, which I enjoyed. My respect for his classicism, however, was dealt almost a mortal blow when I came across these two lines in his translation of *The Pervigilium Veneris*:

"Look, how the bullocks rub their flanks among the broom-plants all around,
Each with his own proper mate in natural conjunction bound."

It must have been a dull party.

Although I have had many letters from him, and exchanged poems with him, I am desolate to record that I have only met Charles Causley[2] once. I greatly admired the vigour of his *Farewell, Aggie Weston.*

Peggy and I had one protracted and uproarious lunch with Ronald Bottrall, before he went off to Peru, but the only poet I have seen consistently and often through the years is W.S. Graham.[3]

Sydney Graham, Nessie, Peggy and myself once met on Saint Valentine's Day, at the Engine Inn, Cripple's Ease, in the days of its glory, when old John Humphreys was the landlord. I know that John Humphreys ended that lunch-time with a medley of six different drinks in the bottom of his pint-glass, and I expect Sydney and I did the same, or better, or worse. My firm and tangible memory of that day is a copy of Sydney's *The Night-Fishing*, in front of which he wrote the following poem:

"St. Caddick's Day
Nancledra
14.2.56

Arthur Caddick this clear cold day
Is St. Valentine's Day
And we have gone on the Engine
All on a Poet's pay.

And where it is that each of us
Has gone I do not know
But engines of a genius fly
The poet or the crow.

Arthur Caddick, Peggy Caddick,
And all the Caddick five

Stick up for Arthur Caddick while
You seven are alive

Arthur with what love I seem
To have I write your name.
"Arthur Caddick" it is and this
Is a poem by Sydney Graham."

Sydney's sporadic visits to Windswept have always been unexpected, and invariably entertaining. He once walked here, two miles through the snow and ice of a bitter February night, with no overcoat, and wearing what looked suspiciously like dancing shoes, to borrow some bicarbonate of soda. I keep a good brand of this, and it soon soothed Sydney, who stayed till five o'clock in the morning, talking about poetry. He had a friend with him, whose name I forget. When Sydney stepped out into the snow, just before dawn was breaking, he was still talking about poetry, as I sagged down into my armchair and felt rigor mortis set in.

Another night, there was a disturbance in a huge clump of artichokes in my back garden. Simba was baying furiously, and I went out expecting to find a man on a flying saucer, or something. Instead, lost in the artichokes, I found Sydney, with Ruth Hilton, and a bottle of Scotch. I asked all three in, and made all three welcome, and Sydney, in full voice, harangued me on prosody till half-past three. I don't know, now, why we broke up so early, unless it was the emptiness of the bottle.

This clump of artichokes was once the scene of another singular rendezvous. It was in the summer, this time, and I saw the artichokes shaking madly, and the tops waving across the sky. I quite expected to find Macbeth's enemies approaching, as the Witches prophesied so long ago. Instead, I found a movingly innocent ensemble. Plumb in the middle of the clump, his face red with the heat of the sun, stood the Curate from Ludgvan, accompanied by five tiny Wolf Cubs. They were lost; they said so; they said so again, and again. It turned out they were supposed to be on a track nearly two miles away, and had climbed over my wall in desperation. I gave them all a glass of still lemonade, showed them the path they ought to take, and off they trudged, still sweating apology and contrition. How clumsy of fate not to contrive the perfect rendezvous among this clump of unspeakable vegetables! The Curate and his Wolf Cubs – ill met by moonlight – should have collided with Sydney, and Ruth, and the bottle of Scotch.

Before I speak of some of my friends among the painters in Cornwall, I must, in all frankness, uncage from my treacherous bosom a viper I have nursed there for years.

Since St. Ives became what Paris might have been, if only French painters had not painted quite so well, there have been more artists in the town than pimples on a schoolboy's chin. But the worst is yet to come.

One of the grislier threats of Automation is that the number of bad painters will increase by arithmetical progression, for it will spell the dawn of the Age of Compulsory Leisure.

Now, Painting is the most primitive of all the Arts. Whilst it may liberate the emotions, it is quite ludicrous as the expression of any highly developed intellectual concept. The brain of man has been enabled to develop from the brain of monkey mainly, it seems to me, through the use of words. Without the intricate range of articulate speech he has evolved, man might not have evolved at all; the orang utang might now be his equal as an end-product of evolution, might, indeed, by superior strength, have wiped the species homo sapiens, deprived of sapience, entirely off the face of the earth. Painting as an Art is a survival from pre-history, from the era of cave paintings; and all its' images and symbols and pictorial constructions have been infinitely pathetic since the publication of the first dictionary. Not only is Painting a survival from neolithic ages; it is, in our modern world, a cult of pseudo-regression to primitiveness for the sake of being primitive, and infantilism as lip-service to Sigmund Freud. You have only to study the popularity of Alfred Wallis,[4] the St. Ives primitive painter, to realize that this cult of pseudo-regression is being deliberately encouraged as a social soporific.

Probably the greatest day in the life of Alfred Wallis was the day he was acquitted at Petty Sessions of a charge of receiving stolen scrap metal. This brass and copper had been flogged to this simple rag-and-bone man by two unscrupulous fishermen, who had stripped it from a wreck on Porthmeor Beach, and then told poor old Alfred they had bought it. The Bench believed Alfred, who was too stupid to invent anything. The shock started him off painting. The work of Alfred Wallis may profitably be studied, from the pathological or the geriatric viewpoint; as Art it is as tawdry as the grocer's boxes he painted on.

It is, however, as quite another phenomenon that Alfred Wallis may now be closely regarded. He is one of the success symbols of Proletarian Art, plugged as a magnet to a people bored by Bingo, disillusioned with Soccer, and conditioned by egalitarianism to the belief that all men are as good as all men, provided many men may be persuaded to forget that some men are better. You, too, can be Aristotle – if you listen to *Any Questions*. You, too, can be Leonardo da Vinci – if you copy Alfred Wallis. In the coming Age of Compulsory Leisure, Painting will become the craze of the Proletariat – a quasi-aesthetic activity demanding little skill, and gratifying multitudes of petty vanities. The State will inevitably foster it as the cheap uplifter of the Common Man. The politician will surmise that voters engaged in self-expression may forget to poll during a depression. After all, if Art Schools all over the kingdom are busily engaged in bringing out the baby behind all the adults who sign on for Further Education, the politician will be entitled to expect a lowering of popular intelligence. This is clearly what all these State subsidies for Art are about. Miss Jennie Lee gave the game away when she ranked Art and Fun together. Existence for hundreds of millions is not funny. It is grim, agonising, fortuitous, and those who survive will be those who take it unfunnily.

I have no doubt that when all the world's an Art Class, and all the paints are free – for Anglo-Saxons that is – the climate of our society will be less overtly neurotic. We all of us know a painter or two who has been saved from crime or the psychopathic ward by a nice little one-man show.

In this sense, St. Ives has long been a Therapy Centre. Psychiatrists send patients down to it as a last hope before they try leucotomy; sometimes the healers follow the sick down here, and they all go mad together.

I should hate it to be thought that I am criticising Abstract Art. I am one of those who believe that the price the nation paid for the Leonardo Cartoon cannot be measured in sterling; the real price we have all paid is the indefinite survival of the Royal Academy. In my palmy days, before I pawned my last top hat, I once went to a Royal Academy Private View. It was a translation into pigment of Ivor Novello's candy-floss fantasies about the structure of a real man's world.

I have tended this snake-pit in my perfidious heart for twenty years, and still made friends of many painters. I excuse myself this treason with the thought that some of my friends are good painters, and all these friends are good men. What is a little thing like a canvas to come between us?

I have not been to an official Penwith Society Opening since 1951. In that year, I recall, Barbara Hepworth won a Prize, in an Arts Council Festival of Britain Competition, for one of her highly polished, internationally publicised, essentially second-class carvings with a hole in it. For many year now, the Penwith has been a Venetian oligarchy with a female Doge, and it has now received the final cachet of a Grant from the Gulbenkian Foundation.

> "And one can tell to what red hell
> His sightless soul may sing."

Nor far from the storm-wracked harbour of Mousehole, lives Albert Reuss, a consummate professional if ever there was one. His works adorn galleries in Berlin, Vienna, Moscow, New York and London, but he was rejected for membership of the Penwith. He survived it, though the gesture was an insult, and has continued on his lonely way, a law unto himself, and one of the best painters I have ever known.

Karl Weschke,[5] lives out near Cape Cornwall, and paints tempestuous abstracts of the concrete Cornish scene. Karl is a smallish man, who walks like a cat, and has eyes like a bird, and vaguely reminds me of Erich Von Stroheim. He has a brittle gaiety, which I suspect is backed by sadness, and this makes him the best of company. This idealist, with all his wits about him, this tender hearted sophisticate who is attracted to women almost as intensely as they are attracted to him, spent time, and trouble, and money, to do me a fantastic kindness at a time when Peggy was gravely ill. He was waiting for me at the hospital when I went to visit her and told me he had arranged with his friend, Buck Taylor, whom I had never seen before in my life, to take my two youngest children to stay for a holiday in a guesthouse. They had a hectic time, bathing, climbing, and listening to jungle noises from records in a local Coffee Tavern. I owe both Karl and Buck the sort of debt that cannot be repaid but should be recorded.

As distinct from the floating population of Bohemia, who are too busy sinking pints to settle anywhere, several painters have made their homes near Nancledra. Patrick Dolan has a house out at Towednack, in which he has had a mezzanine floor built. Patrick's conversation is laconic, abrupt, aggressive, and very agreeable, and I value his company because he keeps attacking my most cherished ideas with a pick-axe. Most of them survive, and I value them more than ever. His conversational style is reflected in his paintings, which are vivid and violent.

Down in the Cucurrian valley, lives Roger Leigh, the sculptor, who has laid out an attractive garden by the river and set out many of his sculptures in it. All modern sculpture seems to look better in the open air, and Roger's new work is fascinating. He spent years on teaching himself the quality of materials the hard way, by trial and error, and now his name is coming more and more into prominence, as he moves away from formalism. Pat, his wife, was one of the first Leaders of the Nancledra Youth Club, of which Caroline and Duncan were first Chairman and Secretary. This Youth Club is our dynamo of the future, and I am very proud of the fact that my own children's energy was its' initial driving force.

At Halsetown, three miles away, and conveniently next-door-but-one to the Halsetown Inn, lives Alan Lowndes and his family. Alan is a Northcountryman, but the traditional bluntness that this is supposed to mean is tempered, in Alan's case, by a subtle wit, and a quick mind. He is a vivacious mercury-man, a small length of quicksilver, swift to anger, quick to forgive, and, on the whole, an artist whose head rules his heart. Lazy critics often talk about the work of Alan Lowndes as derived from that of T.S. Lowry. It is not. T.S. Lowry influenced his early work, clearly, but his painting is now quite individual, and I suspect he has much more intellectual curiosity than Lowry has. There is something Gallic about Alan; none of the Northern placidity, much, almost, of a Mediterranean spirit. His one enormous weakness is a profound reluctance to believe that anybody with PRIVATE MEANS (of which he always thinks in upper case type) can possible be a serious painter. I quite understand how Alan has placed this chip on his own shoulder; there are so many playboys in paint, so many well-connected nonentities who get one-man shows through double-barrelled names, so many sycophants to wine and dine the dispensers of official patronage. But there are also very good, talented painters, who paint because they must, and treat their wealth as an inherited accident, like a cleft chin. It is, of course, a thing that makes life much more pleasant than a cleft chin does, but private means does not conclusively prove the existence of a cloven hoof.

[1>] *Winston Graham – see biographies.*
[2>] *Charles Causley – see biographies.*
[3>] *WS Graham – see biographies.*
[4>] *Alfred Wallis – see biographies — For a more balanced view of Wallis try Marion Whybrow & Robert Jones — see suggested further reading.*
[5>] *Karl Weschke – see biographies.*

XIV
Two Can Sleep Cheaper

THE HEADING OF THIS chapter is also the title of a short humorous novel I wrote in 1952. It was a roman á cléf, set in Trebogus-on-Sea, and concerned the loves and feuds and follies of a colony of artists. I put myself in the novel, as a dilapidated poet called Richard Tudack, which is an exact anagram of my name, and my portrait of myself was so libellous that, had the book been published, I should undoubtedly have tried to sue me, and one's defence would have been uncontrollable dichotomy of the moral fibre. To be fair to myself, I also lampooned several of my friends, quite indiscriminately. Had they sued me, I should have pleaded justification. I put Guido Morris in the book, under the name Bembo Aldine, and he was so pleased at having been so delicately exposed that he sat down and wrote me a letter in his exquisite script, giving me permission to defame him ad infinitum.[1]

I record from this novel a verse Richard Tudack recited one wild night in the Rampart Inn, Trebogus, to whose landlord I accidentally gave the true name of Michael. Dear Michael Mitchell! He was a Cornish Saint, unrecognized, and unsung by all save myself.

Poem for a Public House without a Proper Privy

It is a solemn thought to think
That every single drop we drink,
That trickles through our middle,
Has yards of guts to travel round
Before it passes to the ground
Transformed to ...... Solve the riddle!

But when we come a-drinking here
No welcome privy standeth near,
Which makes existence sadder.
We have to wander half a mile
Holding water all the while
Which lacerates the bladder.

And now and then an urgent call
Makes topers use the outside wall,
Or even drives a fella
To dash out with a frenzied stride
And liberate the flowing tide
Down in a handy cellar.

It is not just, it is not fair
To drive our kidneys to despair,
It gives no chance to Charlie,
Who spends his mornings with a can
Removing from the sight of man
What once was hops and barley.

[Published in Cornish Review *summer 1963, also* Broadsides from Bohemia *1973 where it is dedicated to the beautiful thirst of Guido Morris, Esq. I was told by David Caddick that the pub was The Engine Inn, Cripplesease].*

Alack-a-day, as lovesick Mousehole maidens say, my novel *Two Can Sleep Cheaper* moved inexorably forward to a macabre destiny. The following letter, which, though it was written in 1958, concerns my industrious nights in 1952, will tell you a tale of grief and mincing mallicho and hell-hatched frustration:-[Pages 152 –154 of manuscript missing * to * taken from *More Laughter at Land's End – Cornish Review* No.6 Summer 1967 — Ed][2]

*Windswept Cottage
Nancledra
Penzance, UK

14th November 1958

To the Postmaster-General of the United States of America,
Federal Post Office,
Washington, D.C.

Sir,

I have the honour, and at the same time the infinite distress, to lodge with you a complaint that for upwards of five years I have been piratically deprived of my property by executive action of the Department which you are held out to the public as controlling.

On August 22nd, 1953, I sent by surface mail the typescript of a novel I had just completed, entitled *Two Can Sleep Cheaper,* to a firm of publishers in the United States, the Seven Sirens Press (Inc.), of New York. On the same day I sent to the same firm a covering letter by air-mail.

I had no news of the receipt of either. So on November 14th, 1953, I air-mailed a reminder to the firm.

Again, I had no reply. So, on December 12th, I air-mailed a second reminder.

This brought a brief reply from the publishers, by air-mail, on December 21st. Their reply was more alarming than their silence.

The publishers informed me they were in a state of chronic confusion, as you were interfering with them. They did not mention my novel at all. So I air-mailed a reminder on January 5th, 1954.

I heard nothing until March 29th, when I had the astounding news from the publishers that my novel had been intercepted and impounded by your Department, on unstated grounds, and that their Attorney had filed process in the Courts for its release. I may here remark that, neither then nor at any time since, have I had any notice whatsoever from your Department that my property had been seized.

On May 18th, 1954, after consulting the Foreign Office, I put the facts before the American Civil Liberties Union. They were eventually able to inform me that my novel had been impounded solely because it was addressed to the Seven Sirens Press. Under what has now become notorious as the McCarthy legislation, it appeared that you, Sir, as Federal Postmaster-General, had used your powers to make an Order for the impounding of all mail whatsoever addressed to this firm, on whatever subject, from whatever quarter, on the sole ground that you, in your sole discretion, had decided that, at some time or other, the firm had sent obscene matter through the United States Mail.

The Civil Liberties Union also informed me that I had no right to sue your Department without the permission of your Government. In passing, may I remark that we changed all this sort of thing in this country a century and a half ago?

I was further told that the McCarthy Legislation gave you power to cut off most of the Universities of America, and nearly all the publishers, from all communication with the outside world; and that the Supreme Court was being asked to declare the Statute under which you impounded my novel, *Two Can Sleep Cheaper*, ultra vires the American Constitution.

On December 3rd, 1954, I sent, by surface-mail, yet another enquiry about my novel to the publishers. This brought no reply.

I heard nothing from anybody in 1955. In 1956, nobody told me anything. In October 1957, I began to receive a melancholy series of postal packets, with terrifying messages stamped on them. Five of my letters to the publishers were returned by your Department, after upwards of three years' detention, marked successively:

UNLAWFUL-IMPOUND.

ILLEGAL-AWAIT FEDERAL ORDER.

FORBIDDEN MAIL-SEIZE.

CRIMINAL-AWAIT INSTRUCTIONS.

IMPOUND-NOTIFY WASHINGTON.

This, Sir, was a macabre postbag for a respectable British subject, the father of five innocent children, to receive and the effect on our village postman, an upright man, who once played cricket for an Australian touring eleven, was sinister. His eyes began to avoid mine. My eyes began to avoid his; I felt like Lady Chatterley's Lover on a dirty night.

It is now 1958, and I still have not had my novel back. I demand it back. *Two Can Sleep Cheaper* is an anti-communist satire, centred round the behaviour of Left-Wing Bohemians, in an imaginary Cornish town, which I have called Trebogus-on-Sea. It may not be good, but it is pure. As far as obscenity goes, there is nothing that could not be read aloud, in the evenings by the fireside, to Whistler's Mother, were that revered American figure still happily with you. It would not displease Grandma Moses herself. It is a jeu d'esprit, and you have charged down upon it like a bull-moose.

Not only is the typescript harmless; it is unique. It is the only copy I have not mislaid, and you have kept it locked up, presumably in Fort Knox with all that bullion, where no one but Federal Marshalls can read it. I have not even been able to rewrite the novel. Your depressing form of literary criticism has robbed me of the necessary high spirits, and is now turning me into a tragic writer, and a martyr to flatulence.

You have no right to my property; you have no right to detain it even temporarily; you have no legal justification for not having given me notice of your intention to detain it. You have denied me the elementary right of protest, and have behaved like Louis XIV, sending books to a literary Bastille under private letters de cachet. Stalin and yourself, Sir, have acted as judges, in your own cause, to Pasternak, and myself.

You are not dealing with a scribbler of pornography, nor am I seeking to subvert the Constitution of the United States. I am a Life Member of the Oxford Conservative Association. This cost me five shillings in 1929; say £200 sterling, at present rates. I am also a baptised Member of the Church of England. This cost my parents nil, and the value is still unchanged.

I am, Sir,
Your obedient servant,

ARTHUR CADDICK

How did it all end? In 1959, the Federal Court ordered the release of *Two Can Sleep Cheaper*. Six months after the Order, the typescript was returned to me, with no apology, and no covering letter whatsoever. What compensation did I receive? Nothing – except the deep satisfaction of having been the author of a book which helped to cause nine old men in the Supreme Court to declare ultra vires the American Constitution the Statute under which it was impounded.

I also had the masochistic joy of realising that I had master-minded another catastrophe for yet another of my projects. I celebrated this joy in a lyric of haunting beauty:*

Lines written to boost my morale

Here lies Arthur Caddick
Whose next-of-kin may
Have to make him a
Posthumous bankrupt today.

And were he to learn
He was bankrupt, deceased,
He would not be surprised
At the news in the least.

For here in this modest
And still-owed for earth
Lies one who was nature's
Insolvent by birth.

Since earth is the final
Container of all,
No other Official
Receiver need call.

What assets avail him?
Three drawers stuffed with verse,
And some prose they can't sell
For the price of the hearse.

Let him settle, unbalanced,
With no more ado,
And a stone, carved on credit,
"R.I.P. – I.O.U."

[One of my favourites – Don't ask! As far as I know unpublished in any collection. Although published as a Phoenix Broadsheet 331 by Toni Savage of Leicester. See Published works of Arthur Caddick. Ed.]

1> *Aldine Bembo — a clever choice of name by Caddick as Morris used the typeface Bembo for his work. The following is set in Aldine Bembo.*

Bembo was an Italian classical scholar, a friend of Lucrezia Borgia and many leading figures of his day. He regularised the Italian language itself by publishing grammars. He was made a cardinal in 1539.

The Monotype Corporation of London gave his name to their typeface Bembo in 1929. The design is based on the type cut by Francesco Griffo for the Aldine Press of Aldus Manutius, and first used Bembo's work De Aetna in 1495/96.

See Guido Morris: a brief biography, page 275

2> *Further extracts from the Cornish Review No.6 appear in Chapters, X, XV, XVI and XX*

XV
The Speech of Phantoms

IF SOMEBODY WAS kind enough to send me three hundred pounds, unexpectedly, in the post, I know that the money would bring me nothing but grief.

How do I come to name an exact sum? Why do I stand so confirmed and adamant in my melancholy bodings?

Well, I dreamed it all last night, and this morning there was a snail crawling up our bedroom window. As all Cornish miners will tell you, a snail is an unpropitious start to a day. If you meet one on your way to work and do not spare it a scrap of any food you are carrying, evil will befall you. I had heard about the malevolence of snails, but forgot about the propitiation as I do not eat solids for breakfast. My doom is therefore sealed inside my dream. This is how the fatal scenario ran.

Somebody did send me three hundred pounds, in fivers, in the post, and Peggy was holding her breath so they wouldn't blow away.

"I think fivers are beautiful!" she intoned at last, like a priestess in a trance. "Is it true that the old ones used to crackle like brittle leaves in autumn?"

"It is."

"Do you think this sort will crackle?" she asked wistfully.

I was quite sure they would not; they had all the grace and style of Share-Out Coupons in a Second-hand Underwear Club. But I could not ruin Peggy's rapture. "They might," I lied. "Given the right temperature."

Before she could ask for a demonstration, I made an important announcement.

"This morning, I'm going to open a bank account. I shall walk straight in, and wave three hundred pounds in fivers in front of the manager's nose, and he'll whisk me out a whopping great cheque book."

"You don't want me to mind the money, dear?"

"You are quite right, darling. That is what I do not want."

I went in by bus to a small Cornish town, and carefully studied the facades of banks. They all seemed the same, dignified but depressed, so I chose one opposite a Free House.

I marched in and hailed a man behind a counter. "I wish to open an account with three hundred pounds, sterling, in five pound notes."

"Position closed," said the man, without looking at me.

"I'm not applying for a position," I began, but he waved his right hand peremptorily at me, and pointed to another man a yard or so from him.

I repeated my terms of trade.

"Current notes, of course?" he queried, staring at my collar. I'd forgotten to put my tie on.

"Brand new notes!" I snapped back.

He sniffed at me and my wad as if we were both out of season. "You had better see the Manager," he said.

He went away, leaving me clutching my money. When I get apprehensive, I sometimes wobble my top palate. I wobbled it now.

The man came back, and said I could be seen, and I followed him into the Manager's office.

"A new account, eh? Sit down, Sir, and I'll take some details, then the Cashier will attend to you."

I told the Manager my name and address and my occupation. He noted them all down.

"You did say poet?" he asked, severely, looking at where my tie wasn't.

"I did."

"Now, Sir, you wish to open an account with three hundred pounds in cash?"

"Brand new five pound notes," I answered, earnestly.

"Well, I think that this will be all straightforward... Now, Sir, what about references?"

I was quite surprised.

"Oh, we needn't bother with those," I said, largely.

Now the Manager was quite surprised.

"Needn't bother with references? My dear young man, I've never heard of such a thing. It's a simple matter, really. Two tradesmen will do."

"It's very good of you," I replied. "I do appreciate it."

The Manager looked very puzzled. "It's routine practice in all banks you know. Now, what about the two tradesmen?"

"If you really insist," I said.

"I do insist. Give me two names, Sir."

"But it's no use my guessing," I said.

"Guessing?"

"Well, how do I know two tradesmen who bank with you?"

"They needn't bank here at all."

I was amazed. "What good are they as references if they don't bank with you?" I cried.

Now the Manager was amazed. "You flatter us, Sir. There <u>are</u> other banks, you know."

"Yes," I told him, feeling the time had come to be firm, "there are other banks. But I am not putting three hundred pounds sterling in brand new five pound notes into another bank. I must have references to support your bank. Now do you see my point?"

The Manager seemed to be trembling, and his voice was unsure, as he muttered "What – er, what did you say?"

"I only said what you said. I wasn't going to bother with references. I believe in trusting people. But you insisted. After all, three hundred pounds sterling is a very considerable sum, and on reflection I see you are right. But you surely understand that I must be given two references from customers who bank with you, if they're to be any good at all. I suggest people who know you. There may even be people who've known you for a long time. I shan't quibble with you – just give me two names I can check up with, and you can have my money."

The Manager breathed very heavily down his long nose, as if two adenoids were playing a scherzo out of time with each other.

"I have to give you two references as to the stability of my bank," he said slowly, biting the end of every word.

I looked at him sharply and began to wobble my top palate again. This man seemed odd – was his manner furtive? I began to get alarmed and bit my tongue. I ignored the taste of blood and looked long and hard at the Manager. Was I on the track of the swindle of the century? I glanced round the office. The polish on the furniture had a sinister gloss, and there were plastic roses on the desk. That was enough!

I broke the ominous silence, and replied to his last strangely uttered words. "You have to give me two references as to the stability of your bank."

He started to sweat, and his cheeks went puce. I have never before seen such a sudden flush of guilt to a face. Instinct told me what to do. I thrust my wad through my shirt-front, and tucked it next to my ribs, behind my woollen vest. I got quickly up from my chair, and it fell backwards and crashed against a safe. Keeping my face to the Manager, I backed to the door, twisted myself through it as I wrenched it open, and turned and ran like hell.

When, with part of my wad escaping down my trouser-legs, I knocked over a policeman standing outside the bank, I found myself being frog-marched to the station. It took several hours to explain everything, and longer to get my wad back. I had to get references as to my stability. Lots of references. And they still harbour doubts.

Such was my dream, and the omen of the snail reads that it must all come true. To have such a morbid dream about money you must be a poet. Money dogs the poet's days, haunts his fleeting hours of happiness, and drives him to sordid chicaneries, such as making two short lines out of long lines in a poem, because the BBC pays poets by length. All poets are always thinking about money, but few of them ever get any.

Nevertheless, they have a duty, to themselves at least, not to drop dead, too young, in respectable neighbourhoods. Poets are much more choosy about their milieus than painters; for one thing, poets are usually a little bit cleaner, because ink does not make quite such a mess as paint. Neighbourhoods, therefore, are not quite so finicky about them, in turn, and the two attitudes interact, and, on the whole, poets never sink so low as painters. All the same, they have to avoid dropping dead in elegant joints. To do this, they need to have, at the minimum, five shillings to spend on their stomachs on Mondays, Wednesdays and Fridays. Eating at weekends is not so costly; you can usually catch people at home if you call early enough, without warning. Drink is much more expensive than food, but poets, mercifully seem to come by it more easily. You will usually find that the amount poets drink is in direct proportion to the pressure of their anxiety state. The more Angst, the more hooch. Since all poets develop an anxiety-state about money, all poets drink deeper at times when they can least afford it. This increases the anxiety, which increases the drink . . . The whole subject is distasteful, and I never raise it.

Even if poets got paid much for poems, the papers that will print them are becoming rarer and rarer, except for the contemptible periodicals that announce: "No payment for verse, which is occasionally accepted." It is a buyers' market on Parnassus, and thank God my hideous example has trained my children not to try to write sonnets. I reckon my awful warning will be worth about five hundred a year to the lot of them, as it has made them prefer writing cheques to writing anything else. I hope I am right in my reckoning – I dread a frugal old age.

If there is even so much as a hint of an echo of a whisper that a new publisher is going to bring out a poetry series, there will be a scurry among poets all over the kingdom, and even, strangely enough, in India as well, to prepare and send manuscripts for consideration. So it was, when Guido Morris announced the proposed publication of the Crescendo Poetry Series, under the very distinguished imprint of his Latin Press, at St. Ives. The initial series was to contain six issues; all by different poets, and the financial arrangement was that subscriptions for the whole series of twelve, totalling thirty shillings, were invited from the public. The Crescendo Series was a laudable venture, and it was very well subscribed. The format was Crown Octavo, unbound, hand-sewn, in Aldine Bembo type on Abbey Mills heavy Art paper, with a very attractive grain in it. Each issue was a different colour. I had the great compliment paid to me by Guido of being selected to be the first poet in the list, and my "Speech of Phantoms" was published on September 1st, 1951, in an austere grey paper, which in the event proved to bear wear-and-tear much better than some of the more vivid colours. The price of a separate single issue worked out a half-a-crown, and Guido promised me, and paid me, the very generous royalty of sixpence a copy, or twenty per cent. Typographically, the Crescendo Poetry Series was superb, and I cannot understand why an Arts Council exists at all if it lets a venture like this flounder, as flounder it did, for want of a few pounds. As usual, Guido had grossly underestimated the production cost of each issue. He skimped nothing, used the best of everything, ink, type, paper, thread, and found he was running the Series at a fantastic loss. It failed, gloriously, and ridiculously, when you consider the official patronage doled out to painting and sculpture in golden bucketfuls. The five issues after my own were:

No.2 Aphrodite's Garland by John Heath-Stubbs
No.3 Songs at High Noon by Guido Morris
No. 4 Moral Stories by David Wright
No. 5 Ten Poems by Noel Welch
No. 6 Godolphin & Other Poems by Bernard Bergonzi.

This is one of my own poems, included in *The Speech of Phantoms*.

The Mare

With tops of old drumheads left out for her grazing,
The mare was let loose in a field of her own,
But, sun coming out, she was heated past feeding
And galloped and whinnied, insistent in tone.
The stallion, divided by lane from her pasture,
Alerted and answered as to a whip
She jerked and she jumped over hedge to his gateway
And trembled and nuzzled him, foam at the drip.
Then, baffled by gate, she raced off swiftly veering,
Confronting the spring with a tumult of lust,
Pounding the winter to death with her hoofbeats,
Pounding it pounding it down to the dust,
Thundering out on the black Cornish earth
The beat of the rhythm that triumphs in birth.

The companion piece to this, in the same publication, a poem called *North Wind* was splendidly read by Godfrey Kenton, in a BBC Poetry broadcast.

Prompting my memory, like a spectre from the wings of time, is the word "Speech", from *The Speech of Phantoms*. When, as a boy, I was very often forced to become what the Cornish call a bed-lier, I found solace in my father's books, as I told you in the early pages of this chronicle. Among these books, was a series of heavy, handsome, tomes, entitled *Crowned Masterpieces of Eloquence*. I gave the household no rest until all twelve of these had been carried up to my sick-bed, and my counterpane was covered by the collected words of an international array of honey-tongued high priests of speech. When poor little Arthur wanted to wee-wee, my ever patient mother had to shift hundredweights of eloquence before I could move out of the sheets.

What wealth I quarried from these pages! Here, I found enduring monuments built of words: the speeches of Pericles in the miraculous years of Hellenic flowering; Cicero's "How long, O Catiline, will you continue to abuse our patience?"; mediaeval orations from all the kingdoms of Christendom; the forensic to-and-fro at the Trial of King Charles the First; a formidable flow of speeches, impassioned, yet always elegant, from the great Eighteenth Century Parliamentarians, Chatham, Charles James Fox, Burke and Sheridan; and Gladstone's massive Old Testament denunciation of the Armenian Massacres, with that unforgettable phrase (if I remember it rightly) about the Bimbashis and their Bazookas being hurled bag-and-baggage from the Christian land the Infidels had pillaged.

The sheer vastness of this range of content gripped me for weeks on end, when I was ill; when I got better, they went on fascinating me over the years, until I left home; and now, forty-five years after I first began to read them, when I go up to Yorkshire to see my mother, I always find time to take down some of these volumes again.

It was reading these volumes that made me decide that, if ever I were called upon to make a speech in public, I would fashion it as near perfect as hard preparation could make it. There is nothing I find more repugnant than the sound of a person who, having intrigued twenty years for public position, has not even spared twenty days to study public speaking. They order this sort of thing better in France, where every small town Mayors have had some sense of forensic style drilled into them at school. In this country it is more than an even bet that His Worship will stand up and bray.

More, I suspect, for my own pleasure than for the interest of the reader, I have unearthed beneath the debris of the years the bare bones of a speech I made in 1954, when I opened the Spring Exhibition of the Newlyn Society of Artists at the Passmore Edwards Gallery. I must not cheat; I did no unearthing at all. I asked that obliging friend of mine, John Page, Editor of *The Cornishman,* if he could trace any records of it for me. John Page was kindness itself; he told Douglas Williams, one of his reporters, to get down to the donkey-work at once. I suspect that, as yet, there is nobody that Douglas Williams can order about, so, in his turn, this obliging man did all the drudgery. "It was a bit of a job sorting out this stuff," was his comment to me, when he passed on the skeleton's bones.

The Newlyn Society of Artists, galvanized by the energy of Michael Canney, with the wholehearted help of Peter Lanyon, over the last decade, has always appealed to me as being, on the whole, far more masculine, and much less precious, than the Penwith Society. One painter whose work I particularly enjoy seeing there, is Jack Pender of Mousehole. I once told him so, at a lush party given by Denys and Jess Val Baker, where the supply of cold roast turkey legs seemed so lavish that I began to class turkeys as feathered centipedes. The painting I complimented Jack on was of the harbour entrance at Mousehole. He had made the harbour hold the terrors of a trap, not the safety of a haven, and the painting made a powerful impression on me. Jack Pender thereupon said he was giving me the picture. I was delighted inside me, but managed to put on the front of grateful and embarrassed refusal. It was too much, I told him. So Jack repeated his gift to me, and, this time, I accepted, and poured him a double scotch. The gift cheered me through the mists of the morning after, and I kept remembering it, and taking another aspirin. But Jack Pender completely forgot about it, next day, and I have never dared to remind him since. I do hope someone lends him this book.

So Peggy and I went off in high spirits to Newlyn, on a sunny Saturday in May, which was the day of the new moon. Peggy presided carefully over the lubrication of my throat with two pints of Bass, at the Queen's Hotel, Penzance, where we called before walking along the beach together to the Gallery. There was a fair slice of local Upper Crust in the Cocktail Bar, when we went in, and I soon discovered that some of the wives were nagging on and on about Art Exhibition Openings, while their husbands kept muttering about Golf. I shall always be sorry that the wives spotted me before I could steal away, and sealed their husbands' doom by saying so loud and clear. Several sheepish golfers, their last getaway destroyed by their own innate good manners, left for the Gallery shortly after we did. They could afford to linger. Poets walk, tycoons go by car.

The speech I made was described by Judge Scobell Armstrong, in his Annual Review of the Year in *The Cornishman*, as "the speech of the year." Here is the skeleton of it, resurrected from *The*

Cornishman's archives, including Stiffs' Corner, where reporters hoard advance obituary material.

"Cornwall proliferates with carpet-baggers of culture, and with band-waggoners of the Arts. Encamped in every cove, alert on every carn, stand earnest cohorts of intelligentsia, waiting for the tocsin that will summon them to unveil a plaque, lecture about Braque, or dedicate the hillside traque where D.H. Lawrence discovered he was the Messiah. As they watch and wait for the Dawn their Cause is destined to inherit, all these regiments of cantankerous rivals while away the time by taking pot-shots at each other. It seems to me that there is a great deal too much cultural in-fighting in Cornwall nowadays, and that it is vastly over-publicized. I do not forget that a battle that does not rattle in the columns of the Press does not count, among the aesthetes, as a battle at all, but the public is wearying of artistic dog-fights, conducted in headlines. And, as for cats . . . well, you have only to start at the Malakoff and walk down-a-long.

In this period of brouhaha, and cut-and-thrust and cloak-and-dagger intrigue, it occurred to me that the Newlyn Society had decided that they wanted someone safe, someone circumspect, a prudent person who would refrain from putting any more kittens among the turtle-doves of Art.

So, today, I feel compelled to the duty of saying nothing gracefully. I come as a lay figure, stuck in your shop window, to stop someone else having designs on it.

Somebody might have come here today and started commenting on some of the artistic sinks down which buckets and buckets of public money are now being poured, at the seemingly arbitrary whim of a lunatic and private caprice. But that sort of thing would not be fitting here today, so I shall step over the sinks in silence, without a mention, and conduct you all amiably along the pavements of platitude.

Somebody might have arrived here today to tell you that there is an unseen political poison many artists are feeding to the present day public; to warn you that there are far more subtle ways of attacking a society in which the artist is still free than sticking a red label on a suitable part of your anatomy and grabbing a hammer and sickle, though these are the tools that many sculptors in this generation seem to prefer to the traditional hammer and chisel.

You can cheapen and destroy values by working as if there were no values. The few can make the pursuit of what is right seem ludicrous to the many, by repeatedly asserting that nothing, at any time, is ever absolutely wrong. Indeed, if you do this with just the correct amount of incoherence, you will swiftly climb the golden ladder of twentieth century patronage.

I sometimes shiver uncontrollably, as I reflect that if some of the exalted personages in this kingdom were to discover the real significance of some of the things they were graciously patronising, a lot of Advisory Bodies would lie stretched out stone-cold on Tower Green next morning. Truth is being shrouded by calculated indehiscence – a word used by Madam Chiang-Kai-Shek, a lady whose second nature is subtlety. Realities are being obscured by strategic smoke screens round high places. Single-minded fanatics use double meanings to wrap up infamies. If we really understood much that we now worship, and then continued to worship it, we would be like men proud of having cancer.

For three decades now, all the Arts have been dominated by "womb-doom-tomb" boys and girls on adult errands. I invite you to examine this business of despair, for business it is, on a cosmopolitan scale. One of our leading critics, Mr. Cyril Connolly, has stated that he measures an artist by the quality of his despair. An horizon bounded by despair! What a way to look at life! What a way to look at death! What a way, even, to look at the hydrogen bomb!

An artist may look at the hydrogen bomb with anger, loathing, contempt, seeing it as a perversion of man's unconquerable mind. If he looks at it with fear or despair, he allies himself with the destructive madmen now playing with it over the great waters of the Pacific. Man has learnt to make such things; man must learn not to make such things. That is all.

There will come a time when man will come to terms with his true self, and with his power over these inventions. Then the nightmare of nuclear fission will become the means of fulfilling a dream – a dream which our snivelling, half-epicene, intelligentsia despise – the noble nineteenth century, radical, dream of a fuller, freer, richer life for all mankind, on the basis of the bounty provided by the machine.

If this is not so, then all history, philosophy, science, all religions, and all the arts are meaningless. They are not meaningless. We, who have met here today in this little gallery in a remote corner of the West, are far truer tokens of the future of humanity than all the tight-lipped tycoons in the New World, busy now turning the very word "Pacific" into a meaningless mockery.

We are met here to show our faith in the painter's vision; in the light that never was on sea or land, the consecration, and the poet's dream.

That light, which we seek forever, is more brilliant and will be more abiding than a thermo-nuclear flash."

XVI
A Parson & Some Potters

1952 WAS, IN MANY respects, a most irksome year for me, personally, though it ended hilariously for all the family.

In the spring, I had an accident to my right hand, at the Sub-Station, while I was closing a Switch I had several times before logged as being faulty. The accident resulted in my right arm being in plaster from the elbow downwards, for almost two months.

During the period of time I passed with my arm plastered, I had to go into Redruth Hospital, nearly twenty miles from us, for an operation for the removal of a large cyst in my upper jaw. I blame this on opening my mouth too wide, too often.

Have you ever been admitted to one Hospital, for an operation quite unconnected with a very conspicuous mass of plaster put on you by another Hospital? It shakes the Health Service to its' foundations.

I was bustled into the Ward for dental cases at Redruth Hospital, got undressed, and sat up in bed to survey the battlefield around me.

A very young Irish student nurse bubbled up to my bedside.

"And phwat may I ask are yez doing in here? We aren't Orthopaedic!"

She certainly did not look it, and I found the task of explaining my double-meaning to her quite pleasant. To the Irish, any coincidence has something of a miracle about it. She seemed enthralled by my plight, and called over another student nurse, also Irish, and made me repeat my tale. Well now, I thought, I may be too limp to play the Lothario, but it is very soothing to act like a Leprechaun.

The two youngsters bustled off in a giggle of goodwill, and a Staff Nurse came up to the bottom of my bed. Her mental processes were much slower, but much surer, than those of her juniors. She stared hard at my plaster, then took up the card at the bed-end and stared at that harder still, and then looked at me and said "Hum! Upper Jaw!" and walked off, down the Ward.

As she did so, the Ward Sister came in at the other end. Ward Sisters know everything. That is why they are Ward Sisters. This Sister knew everything. She marched to my bed-side and gave a bleak, staccato cry.

"Staff!"

The Staff Nurse came quickly to her side.

"What is all this nonsense? See that this man is removed to Orthopaedic at once!"

The Staff Nurse, in a few lucid phrases, explained that the Sister was wrong.

Do you imagine that Sister apologized? Not on your life! Her voice rang out over the Ward like a bugle as battle begins.

"Nurse O'Hara! Nurse Moran!"

The two Irish girls sprinted to her side, like Olympic medallists.

"I want to make it quite clear to you both," announced Sister, "that this man is Dental. This man is not Orthopaedic. That's all! See you don't forget it!"

"Yes Sister" the students intoned, reverently, hypocritically, but, I think, prudently. Ward Sisters know everything.

By the time I was being wheeled off to the operating theatre the next morning, I was a little confused myself. The pre-operation hypodermic was taking effect, and I don't suppose I would have argued if they had suddenly decided I was a Maternity Case down for a Caesarean.

However, all went well, and after an extremely painful week, Denys Val Baker, with Peggy, arrived at the Hospital to take me home. I had a little plastic plug in my jaw, as a souvenir, and I had to go back to Redruth once a week for them to reduce the plug in size as the gap in my gizzard filled up.

What the Americans call the pay-off for my accident arrived on Christmas Eve, in the shape of an Insurance Company's cheque for £99.10.0 (£50 for pain and suffering, and the balance for special damage.) There was an element of comedy about this transaction. I had, of course, taken the elementary precaution of threatening my employers with a High Court Writ for Negligence. This had put my correspondence with their Insurers on an exalted plane from the start. After a month or so, they wrote me a letter saying that they admitted liability. The next sentence puzzled me: "We would like however, to study details of your loss." I duly sent these details, congratulating them affably on their good sense in the matter.

The reply I received told me that they had admitted liability through a typist's error. The relevant clause should have read "we do <u>not</u> admit liability." Nevertheless, they proposed, under the regrettable circumstances, to stand by their error, and make me an ex gratia payment of £99.10.0. My heart warmed to them, and burnt white-hot for their sweet little typist, and her inexcusable, dastardly, beautiful mistake.

We arrived in St. Ives that Christmas Eve, with two shopping hours left to use. I was a Rothschild, and Peggy was Mrs. Rothschild, with five excited Rothschildren to buy presents for. I hate spending money on Necessaries so I left all that to Peggy, and crammed all my pockets with Luxuries (anything over ten shillings in my family, from time immemorial.)

We bought picture books, and whisky, and Wellington Boots, and wine, and a fancy waistcoat, and a meat safe, four pairs of blankets, some rum, some feminine gew-gaws, a paint-box, a wrist-watch, a green coat for Peggy, and bi-carb for me. Old Mr. Ingram, then landlord of the Queens, a Free House, had coughed up fifty pounds spot cash in exchange for my cheque, and was giving me the balance when cleared.[1]

The thought of the balance unbalanced me further; I lashed out on fruit, apples, bananas, oranges, dates; nuts took my fancy, I bought them in bulk. Then I remembered Peggy had just told me she had got all these already, and bought some more rum. Our taxi home that night was the relief-train whose cargo made Windswept a transitory outpost of the Affluent Society.

The balance arrived before New Year; I was mighty glad. We were down to rock bottom, already. There stood on my desk an empty bottle, labelled "Lemon Hart Rum". Lemon Hart was a Penzance Jew, who had the contract to supply the whole Royal Navy with rum, in the days of Nelson. I wish this benefactor had opened a pawn shop in St. Ives. I could have pledged my fancy waistcoat.

1953 brought a great change in my way of life. The Sub-Station, whose welfare I had fussed over like an electrical mother, become non-operational, as the supply lines were re-routed, and I became a redundant Bus-Bar Isolator. I was well treated by the South-Western Electricity Board, on leaving, and had been given half a year's advance warning of the legal notice. The Board realised, as well as I did, that they would be terminating my service-tenancy of Windswept, when they ceased to require my services on the spot.

Windswept Cottage was leased by the Board, at an annual rent of £10, from Mr. Henry Sandow, then our farming neighbour at Borea, of which farm it was once a tied-cottage. The Board placed no difficulties in the way of my seeking a transfer of their head-lease to myself. Mr. Sandow, a good-natured, friendly Cornishman whose family have farmed here in direct line for over four centuries, was quite willing to have me as his tenant. I remember clearly what he said when I told him I was a little worried over the future.

"Don't 'ee fear, Capun! I'd never see you and missus and the little uns turned out of Windswept!"

Had I trusted to my own instinct, there and then, we would have been spared events which, in five years time, were to bring myself almost to the point of death, and my family to the brink of tragedy. I wanted to carry on at Windswept as a controlled tenant, and eventually buy it from Mr. Sandow through a mortgage from the West Penwith Council, which I could easily have been granted, as a sitting-tenant. For material things, from as far back as 1946, my dominant desire had been to keep Windswept as a home, and build it up over the years.

Timeo Danaos et dona ferentes. I now translate this as "I suspect priests, especially when they bring gifts." An outsider in Holy Orders stepped into my affairs.

In 1945, in the first month of our stay in Cornwall, we had met someone who became our friend until she died in 1954, Mrs. Dorothy Lewis, then staying in her own caravan, near our temporary chalet. I met her through her own good nature; I was crocked with asthma, and she very shyly came to our chalet to offer me a capsule, from a box she carried about for the heart complaint which finally killed her.

From that first meeting, until she died, Dorothy Lewis, Peggy and myself, although she was much the oldest of the three, became close friends. Between herself and myself, there were two natural bonds; she was born and bred in Oxford, and we could exchange all sorts of reminiscences about Town and Gown; and she loved books, which we both liked talking about. Between Peggy and her, there was the spontaneous affinity that springs from shared qualities, shyness, tenderheartedness, placidity, and an amusing distaste for life's little filthinesses. When we found the cottage at Trenowin Downs, she told us she had two cottages of her own in Nancledra, and a parrot boarded out in the village. One of her hobbies, which she very sensibly turned into profit, was discovering attractive old cottages, doing them up, and then either letting or selling them. Although she spent a great deal of her time visiting friends up country, Dorothy Lewis was almost a fanatical lover of Cornwall, its' landscape, its' history, and its' legends. Without any evident enthusiasm, she let slip one day the existence of a husband, the Rev. H.A. Lewis, a retired parson, living in the Scillies, where he was digging up prehistoric remains.

Mrs. Lewis turned up at our cottage, unexpectedly, less than three hours after Duncan was born, in my study, promoted for the event into a Maternity Ward. She was amazed to discover how small new-born babies were, because she had never seen one before in all her life. She was delighted when we asked her to be Duncan's godmother, for nobody had ever asked her to be such a thing before. She came to his christening, the triple event he shared with his two sisters, and, when she died suddenly, in her caravan, by now moved to Mousehole, we found she had left Duncan £25 in her will.

Before this, I had only met Mr. Lewis once. After this, he came to live in Penzance, and started to ask Anne and Peggy to tea-parties in the private hotel he lived in. He was one of those clergymen whose charm only unfolds to the full in the presence of buttered toast, with only women to share it. He and I, from the first, treated each other with that studied courtesy that masks heartfelt hostility.

Still, it seemed, then, that he meant well, and he was bereaved, and not robust, and elderly, and, clearly, rather at a loss how to pass his time now that he had stopped digging up the Celtic dead in the Scillies. He came to Windswept several times, and poked at the walls, and gazed at the roof, and inspected the garden. Then he suddenly told us he was going to buy the cottage, and put it in trust, eventually, for Anne. He went to see Mr. Sandow, and told him he wanted the place for Anne, and Mr. Sandow, after some hesitation, agreed to sell it to him for £350. Then Mr. Lewis took Anne round the village, and told his wife's old friends what he had done.

Well, that seemed that. I was wary of the whole business, the more so because of a letter from my mother. I write to her twice a week, and always have done, and she continually amazes me by the acuity of her perceptions as far as I am concerned. When I wrote to tell her what he had done, the reply I got contained this comment. "Watch your step! I do not like the sound of things at all."

When Mr. Lewis bought the cottage the lease to the Electricity Board had still some time to run, so became their Landlord, and received a certain amount of rent from them after my work for them was finished. The Sub-Station was closed down when there was an unexpired remainder of the Board's Lease. Mr. Lewis told me he would have a Repairing Lease to me drafted.

I heard no more until I learnt he was off on a cruise round the world, a luxury he had not been able to indulge in during his wife's lifetime. I wrote to him about the cottage, and, a week before he sailed, had a reply telling me not to be anxious. "The cottage is in trust for Anne," he went on. I relied on this implicitly, and ceased to worry about Windswept. Anne had already promised to sell it to me sometime in the hereafter.

If you can convince yourself that a vague benevolence is beckoning to you from the future, it is easy to drift towards it as though you were guided by a rational purpose. This I did with the cottage, continuing to treat it as I had always done, as my destined home. The living room had been dark when we first used it; I added two small windows to the west wall, and a larger one to the north, through which the setting sun shot oblique and glorious rays, at an hour when the room had formerly been shrouded by the first shadows of night. Peter Lanyon remarked that my windows looked like machinegun emplacements. He must have intuitively sensed future hostilities. He presented me with a pot he had thrown, and fired himself at the Leach Pottery, a rope-handled pint tankard, with a slight starboard list, and a yellow and black design that proclaims the unique hand that made it. I built two extra windows, one on top of the other, in my study, and Peter's tankard was always kept in the larger, lower, window, until I had them made into one just after his death. It is here I keep this fragile memory of him now; it opens on to a view of Tren Crom across the Valley, and the morning sun streams through it and lights up the black and yellow slipware, moving all too soon away from it, as it did from Peter when his glider crashed and he had to die so young.

We always enjoy using pots for our table that our friends have thrown; it adds a small embellishment to the dullest food, and it has made our children appreciate, without having been told, that Cornish Pottery does not mean mass-produced egg-cups, showing piskeys turning somersaults in pink pyjamas.

Over a period of about three years, we used to have a guest from the Leach Pottery for Sunday Dinner with the family, at quite frequent intervals. The first of these was our amiable friend, Peter Wood, who was studying with Bernard Leach, before setting up his own kiln in Leiston, Suffolk. Peter's step-father is A.S. Neill of Summerhill School.[2] Once, when Peter had been back there, I was very pleased to be told by him on his return to Cornwall that the pupils of that School had spontaneously chosen one of the poems from my book, *Quiet Lutes & Laughter*, for display in bold lettering on the blackboard. They had picked out this poem, entitled *Roads*:

Roads

The road is slimy with squashed dead frogs.
If it's been raining hard, they cross this road,
Drawn from the field by a spout of water.
Cars come along and hit and crush and kill them
Exactly as they do to children.
The roads are bloody with squashed dead children.
When the sun comes out, they cross the roads,
Eager to gather flowers and jump ditches.
Cars come along and hit and crush and kill them
Exactly as they do to frogs.

Peter Wood used to amble up our lane about noon, with a bottle of Chianti. After Sunday Dinner, at which my children behaved with an antique decorum which shattered his Summerhill habits, we used to ramble over the croft, if it was dry, to the pool at the old China Clay Works, surrounded by white, soft, mounds of kaolin, glistening with fragments of crystalline rock. If it was wet, we sat round our old, oval, oak table, and instructed the children, as a Sabbath duty, in the mysteries of Poker and Pontoon, played for matches.

When Peter left Cornwall, after a farewell party I am sure he does not remember attending, another student at the Leach Pottery, Len Castle, carried on his pleasant habit of visiting us on Sundays. Len went off to New Zealand, to start, I believe, his own pottery there, and we got as far as The Engine Inn to see him off.

The longest-lasting of all our pots in daily use have proved the Leach Pottery bowls, which are like Chinese rice bowls. They last partly because of the hardness of the interior glaze, and partly because of the inherent strength of their structure. We have also used two casseroles, made by David Leach, for the best part of ten years.

Many of our friends have Potteries round here. Jess Val Baker [wife of Denys] started hers at St. Hilary, and it is now the Mask Pottery, at St. Ives. Anthony Richards started his at Penzance, with Len Missen, who was tragically killed in a car crash, after a day at Helston Flora. I still have one of Len Missen's vases left. Anthony Richards now sweats his guts out at his Arch Pottery, St. Ives, where he sits at his wheel all day, throwing pots with bearded frenzy that seems to increase with the years. Alas, last year, I knocked over a dozen pots waiting on a rack for the kiln! I stood in chagrin, expecting a reproach. There was none. So I started to apologize; by the time I had stammered to an inconclusive end, Anthony had replaced the loss and thrown another twelve pots, and I left full of admiration, and wishing poets had the same output as potters. Still, versifiers are sky-bound; potters, by the nature of their trade, are earth-bound, and it takes longer to travel to the stars. All the same, I wish poets could sell off their failures as "seconds", as potters can; I have a laundry box full of "seconds" under my table.

It was through Anthony Richards that I first met Donald Swan, who is now our nearest neighbour of all the painters. He has a long pleasant house a quarter of a mile from us, made of two cottages converted into one, with a studio built on.

Donald is one of those agreeable Scots, who manage to veil a strict moral fibre behind the curtains of convivial gaiety. He buzzes round the district like a dynamo, on errands of good nature. He is the Chairman of the Plymouth Society of Artists, and has painted at least one portrait which the Westcountry will be looking at for many years to come, his rich, glowing portrait of the late Judge Scobell Armstrong. It is a striking study of a man not usually found on a judicial Bench; a man who allows his intellect to be dominated by his largeness of heart and depth of compassion, when Viscount Simon called him, at a late age, to the County Court Bench to meet a clamant war-time need. In this portrait, Donald has succeeded in depicting a Judge in full robes who looks like a gentle dreamer.

I will now steal from Donald what I hold to be the best of his large fund of true stories; since he is busy, in the intervals between being a dominie at Camborne and a Daddy at home, on the writing of a History of Western Art, and not on a frivolity like my book, I have hopes that he will not too much dislike my petty larceny.

In the first year of the last war, Donald was a Sub-Lieutenant in the Royal Navy, travelling from leave in Glasgow to London by overnight train. As he went down the subfusc corridor, something in front of him abruptly stuck itself out of the door of a first-class compartment. Donald bumped well and truly into it, and discovered that it was the largest bottom that had ever thrust itself upon his notice. It veered majestically to larboard, while, from a body still bent double, the largest head he had ever seen in his life wheeled slowly into vision on the starboard bow. There was a monumental grunt, and Donald found himself staring straight into the umbrageous eyes of the great Churchill himself. Donald scuttled down the corridor to safety, like the Graf Spee[1] seeking refuge in the River Plate. Luckily, unlike the Graf Spee, he survived this encounter with the First Lord; but, as the Grand Cham[2] might have observed, he had assuredly plumbed the fundament of Admiralty.

[1]> I'll Raise the Wind Tomorrow *gives the Castle as the pub.*

[2]> *A S Neill — see biographies*

[3]> *At the time of the scuttling of the Graf Spee, December 1939, Churchill was First Lord of the Admiralty, he became Prime Minister in May 1940.*

[4]> *Grand Cham — An obsolete form of the word Khan, a title applied to the rulers of the Tartars, Mongols and to the Emperor of China. Dr Johnson, of Dictionary fame, is also referred to as the Grand Cham of Literature.*

XVII
One Hundred Doors are Open

Eleven More Shopping Days To Your Beloved Father's Birthday

AS HIS BIRTHDAY APPROACHES, the prudent father does not passively rely on the affections of his family. He stimulates the rising of love in their bosoms by delicate and unobtrusive words, largely-lettered, however, and displayed on a notice on his study door well before the happy day.

I did this in 1955, and was delighted by the results. My children borrowed the money from me, to buy me their presents a week before my birthday. This is much less sordid and embarrassing for tender young hearts than borrowing it breathlessly on the very eve of Daddy's happy day. As the modern jargon goes, it enables them to adjust. Some of them adjust too far. By the end of the birthday party, feeling slightly sick with jellies and too much sugar in the diet, they become convinced they have saved up the money themselves and go to bed looking wistful. By the next morning, they are conscious martyrs, who have over-saved for the sake of others. By Saturday, they feel saintly enough to borrow double the first sum to go to the pictures. You stump up because your feelings are still stirred by the gifts of shaving soap, hair oil, and a red biro from the youngest.

So stirred, in 1955, were my feelings; not only by the presents, but by the pitiable sums I had been able to lend towards them, and by the wish that I could quadruple their microscopic pocket money. In other words, I had once again been making the discovery, which I had been making and conveniently forgetting for fifteen years, that there is an inherent unbalance in a family where the wife keeps on producing children and the husband keeps on producing poetry.

In this year, I published my third collection of poems, *Quiet Lutes & Laughter*, which had a delicate drawing on the cover, designed by William Redgrave, of a mediaeval troubadour. The volume was selling at ten shillings [50 pence], of which the bookseller got his immemorial three shillings and fourpence, [17 pence]and I was to get sixpence [2½ pence] when the publication started to make a profit. I will leave my hypothetical sixpences, for the moment, lying in the gutter from which I have never yet retrieved them, and say a word about the contents of *Quiet Lutes & Laughter*.

The title itself will convince anyone experienced in the ways of publishing in this country that the book had a fatal flaw; it contained poems, grave and gay, in alternating sections. This meant it had the worst of all possible contents. It is just as much a crime in England for a jester to weep as it is for Job to laugh. Both these forms of behaviour offend against the public's mania for pigeon-holing poets; and, of course, they rob the publisher's traveller of a simplified sales approach. He needs this, especially, when he is trying to sell books to Chemists.

Chemists? . . . . Yes, Chemists! Have you ever tried to explain to a Frenchman how Chemists used to prescribe the length of first novels in England? I once tried to convince a Professor in Brittany of this, and he left his aperitif and bowed himself off in a dignified hurry, as if I had gone round the bend. But I was quite sane, on this subject at least. In the case of an unknown author, it used to be most important that a publisher should be able to rely on the nation-wide chain of Libraries attached to a great pharmaceutical firm. Now, these Libraries got a great deal of their custom by providing old ladies in Bournemouth and Bath and Brighton with novels that will last the dear old things from Friday to Monday, right through, without fail, and practically without interruption, except for Saturday Night Theatre, and Sunday Morning Service. So the new young novelist was set a target of 100,000 words, or else. . . . What a lot of wadding, what a lot of padding, what a lot of puffing-out, this silly thing entails! It killed any attempt at emulating the brilliant French tradition of the short, astringent, nouvelle. The market terms were set at so much per pound of paragraphs.

My volume — ca va sans dire — was uncommercial. Even in its' uncommerciality, it was out of pattern, for it mixed the grave with the gay. In twentieth century Britain, versatility gets a worse reception than unnatural vice, which at least has the Third Programme carrying a torch for it.

I return to look at my sixpences in the gutter — too late! Somebody else has just picked them up and gone for a beer.

The arithmetic of my sixpence and the bookseller's three-and-fourpence has always revolted me. The nigger in the woodpile of all creators is the man-in-the-middle.

This applies to new potatoes equally as to new poetry. I remember a backbreaking experience in 1946, when I signed on with a local farmer to help him lift his earlies. In those days, the price the farmer got for his earlies dropped with the speed of a comet from sunset to sunset, so as soon as it was possible — and even sooner, I fear, in some cases, the lifting started. Every available man, woman and child in the village, who could walk and bend, and many who couldn't do either, turned up in the fields in the morning, and followed the tractor, down a furrow of black soil and then back up the next, picking up the scuffled-up earlies with one hand and carrying a basket for them in the other. The farmer got his subsidy according to seed sown, not harvest lifted, which meant that many barren acres of croft threw up unhappy potato plants where, a year before, gorse and heath and bracken had been struggling at will. So it was a matter of indifference to many farmers if, for the first few days, they lifted green marbles, to send to the early market, from haulms which would have quadrupled their yield in another month. They wasted food but beat the calendar; even so, I do not think any farmer ever got for his crop a tenth of the price it brought in the shops. I visualize the hard hands of the farmer and bulk-carriers at the one end, and the detergent-cracked hands of the housewife at the other end. Between these two termini, twitch pairs and pairs and pairs of podgy off-white hands, attached to bodies that toil not, neither do they spin. Yet Solomon in all his glory is not arrayed like Mr. Middleman.

With such morose thoughts about my five per cent royalty from my book of poems, I was delighted when, in the autumn of 1955, a well-known Cornish entrepreneur had suggested that he might commission me to write a Guide to Cornish taverns, and then publish it in a large edition, and pay me a twenty per cent royalty. I do not say I jumped at his offer; I fell off my bar stool in a surge of emotion, and signalled acceptance upwards by semaphore.

That was how I started on my new career as a Pub Pundit, which was merely a matter of giving up my amateur status and turning professional. The result was *One Hundred Doors Are Open*, a Guide to one hundred Inns, mainly in West Cornwall, which was first published, in a handy pocket-size edition, in March 1956, by Pendragon Publications, Penzance.

For this Guide, I was free, by contract, to make a collection of any inns I liked in Cornwall, and write what I liked about them, subject, of course, to the ordinary laws of defamation. It was agreed that no Landlord should be allowed to buy the right to be included in my Guide by payment of a fee of any sort; and no fee was ever asked of any of the hundred Landlords. The Guide was to pay for itself, firstly by what advertisements we could attract, at either end of the text, and secondly by sales, through the hundred new bookstalls, namely the bar-counters, we hoped to create by letting the Landlords have copies to retail at a handsome discount.[1] I think harmless vanity is one of the main motives that lead all sorts of men to become Publicans, that is to say, either Licensees of their own Free House, or Tenants. For the new race of Managers wished upon the public by the Brewers I can say nothing; indeed, I generally try to say nothing to them, by avoiding, except rare cases, Managed Houses altogether. This system is destroying the happiness of English tavern life. I believe it was Arthur Young who made a wise remark about the magic of property turning sand into gold. This is particularly true of taverns. The Landlord who puts his all, or most of it, at risk to become Mine Host, is on his toes all day, when he can still stand, to do the pleasure of his guests. The Manager with a salary is a Cost Accountant, selling liquor for cash to turn-over units. Best of all, are the Landlords of Free Houses, and there are still some Free Houses left in Cornwall, though they pass to the Brewers year by year, and their splendid eccentricities are stamped out by the hard trademarks of mammoth combines, and a pert, prim, fussy, prettified, prissiness, rears itself by the village green, by the lifeboat slipway in the ancient harbour on the savage coast, by the wayside where a crumbling Celtic Cross still stands, and the skyline is punctuated by the stacks of derelict mines.

Although one never reads an Appeal for Brewers in Distressed Circumstances, they are not really the villains of the piece in this matter of driving out Tenants and putting in Managers; the real Mephistopheles is the Exciseman, and his Taxes on drink. It is the Treasury Fiend that has driven the Brewers to their excesses. In the sale of a bottle of whisky, two-thirds of the price is Duty. What other tradesman has to deal in misbegotten arithmetic of this sort? The miracle is that there are not illicit stills in every village in England. We are a cowed and subject race, and Bacchus would disown us. Here is one of the verses I put in the first edition of my Guide.

The Virtues of Bacchus

Bees, so runs the ancient legend,
In the days when he was young,
Swarmed on Homer's lips, and sweetness
Gave the bard his golden tongue.

Chancellors, in honeyed phrases,
Speaking from their Budget notes,
Always bring in Beer, and Bitter
Gives us all our golden throats.

Revenue flows down our gullets,
Tonsils bathe in fiscal wealth,
We are patriotic martyrs
Doing public good by stealth.

All the pints we sink are allies
In the fight for sterling's rise;
Bankrupt Landlords act unpaid as
Tax Collectors in disguise.

When shall thirst for hops win laurels?
Hang-overs gain O.B.E.s?

Blossoms (Grog) get Birthday Honours,
And a Peerage crown D.T.s?

I passed the very agreeable winter of 1955-6, entering taverns for business reasons only. It is not always as easy as it sounds to persuade a Landlord to be written up free gratis and for nothing in a forthcoming Guide. Once he has got over the shock of finding out that there is nothing to pay, and nothing at all to sign, a Landlord is apt to dream up weird suspicions of your motives.

"Capun!" he grunts, suddenly turning round to you from tapping a barrel. "Capun! You do say this here Wascom" — Cornish for what-d'ye-call-it — "is to sell in a whole hundred houses? You did say a whole hundred, didn't you, Capun?"

"Yes!" you say, proud of your labours of Hercules.

"Well, that ain't no passel of good to me!"

"What do you mean? Think of the advert it will be to all the tourists and motorists!"

"No good to me, me lover!"

"Whyever not?"

"Capun! This is my house, now ain't it?"

"Why of course it is! I love this house – that's why I asked you to be in."

"I ain't a-going to tell my customers how to get to ninety-nine other houses! So there.... No, Capun, you can count me not in this Wascom."

Nothing will shake him. You leave him out, and go on to the next port of call. Then, when the Guide's published, and everyone in the trade is talking about it, you get an angry letter from his wife accusing you of promising her man to put him in, and then leaving him out.

One or two of the country Landlords in remote parts played a pretty game with me for a time. They would promise to produce old title-deeds, romantic evidence of ancient smuggling, all sorts of things: "But, Capun, I can't just lay my hands to it for now. You be off down-along, Capun, and come back tomorrow, and I'll have a rare old search. Wonderful old parchment, Capun, which I can't read. You'll be finding it quite easy, when I lend you it, to spell out the old black writing. But not me. Bye for now, Capun. Tomorrow, then!"

Well, I'd go back, and nothing would be shown to me. The Landlord would be all apologies for losing it, and promise another rare-and-tear of a search. Then I'd suddenly realize that, on most of these calls, I was the only man in the bar for most of the time, and the reason for all the delay would make me choke over my pint. I was a one-man godsend of winter trade in the dark days before Christmas; a sort of pre-Christmas goose, in fact, and the longer I went back on the forage, the more the Landlord could put on his weekly investment in the Pools.

Here is part of the foreword to *One Hundred Doors Are Open*, which I finally had to write overnight a few hours before my promised Press deadline.

"This guide does not claim to be one of those expert books that teach you What to Drink, How to Eat, Why to Breathe, or, When to Die. I do not hold out my name as an equal of the names that make waiters swoon, the unforgettable names, Escoffier, Bon Courtenay, Ashley Viveur.

My modest aim was to write a guide that could be flogged at half-a-crown, retail, without bloodshed. This book isn't labelled *The Hundred Best Cornish Inns*, or any such poppycock. I believe that I've gathered together a hundred very agreeable places for a drink. I know that several hundreds of equally good places have been left out. Except around ten o'clock, a hundred is a constant number. This was the most rigid of my bonds, the inescapable fact that anything more than five score must be more than a hundred. . .

At the start, I realized that a list of a hundred inns, selected on the grasshopper method, would not do at all. All liquor is liquid, but it is a solid subject. It commands profound respect. Drinking shows man at his most human; there is no evidence that a gorilla ever became a licensee. So I decided to give the guide a coherence, however rough, that might enable you to read it as a whole, if you wished, and consult it as an index, if you needed one.

Taverns lend hope to the horizons of travellers. The pattern I have followed is the simple fact that all travel is a moving forward to the next drink. This seems to me to have the sublime ring of truth. I shall leave you to trace the pattern, and to test the truth, for yourselves. If you are going to read the guide, it is pointless for me to set out the details. If you decide not to read it, the purchase price is definitely not returnable. . .

This is a guide to a hundred inns, mainly in West Cornwall. So it starts on Bodmin Moor. This is quite reasonable and need not vex you in any way. Even before arrival, say, at Mousehole, travellers have been known to get thirsts. . .

After that, we make various tours, circular, triangular, oblong, rhomboid, all sorts of shapely tours. There are little sub-guides to regional drinking, which is the opposite of regional teetotalism. Regional teetotallers are people who never drink on their own doorsteps. We drink on everybody's. . .

In many inns, after the Landlord has bustled up to meet us, you will find a Saint hard on his heels. Even the Free Houses have Saints tied to them in Cornwall. Similarly, I often discuss a village inn and a village church together. They are old partners, these two, and their dates often run close to each other. Humble curates got the gout, in former times, when drink was given the respect due to an essential, not the penalty dealt to a luxury.

Lastly, a word in your ear. All true hearts bleed a little at closing time. This is a guide to something near to the bosoms of all good men. But don't get carried away and try to take a glass at all these hundred inns on the same day. It can't be done, not even by helicopter. I know, I've tried. The lay-out of this guide is very good. The pages are numbered and all the words are the same way up. My printers fixed all that; they are right on top of their job, of course. But my own lay-out was better. It was perfect. I took it with me when I tried to make a century in one day, and me and my lay-out got laid out, and I lost it. You can't do the hundred in one day. Don't leap over the moon of Bacchus. Be calm and patient. Take time. Take two days."

I have just been reading through this Foreword again, and the mention I made in the first paragraph of Escoffier, the famous chef, brings back to me, vividly, and insistently, the characters of two widely dissimilar men, one in London, the other in St. Ives, to whom, after a short acquaintance, I gave the private nickname, in my own thoughts, of Escoffier. The first of these was on my staff when I was at the War Office, and his name was Christian Auguste Bang. This remarkable man had written a book on gastronomy, and had been, at one time, a Director of Heinemann's, and Licensee of His Majesty's Theatre, in the Haymarket. He was bon vivant, gourmet, and gourmand, all combined, and he used to invite me to his Club, the Junior Carlton, which was near my office, to sample his favourite sherry. I had an office in the building where Nell Gwyn gave birth to the son Charles II created Duke of Richmond and Gordon. Christian Auguste Bang had practised, until it was perfect, his own unique method of driving away the boring, the ponderous, the ultra top-heavy respectable.

He would suddenly announce "I am the only Eskimo in Who's Who!"

So he was, and this sounded very, very, posh, even to the ears of Top People.

"And, if you look me up, you will find" — a dramatic pause, "you will find that I was born at Middlefart!"

So he was. Pop went the Weasel, and off went the pukka sahibs. Foreigners are very odd, you know, even if there is a war on.

The other Escoffier in my life was not a famous but an infamous chef. He was a gaunt, stooping, not undistinguished man of sixty or more. He arrived one summer at St. Ives for an engagement as Chef-Maitre at a well-known Hotel, and quickly endeared himself to the variegated dreamers who haunted the Public Bar of the Castle Inn, in Michael's days, by arriving about nine o'clock with packages of breast-of-chicken sandwiches, which he handed round free as tokens of his love for all painters and poets. They were delicious. He would then give a little lecture on how to make chicken sandwiches for six out of one plump rabbit.

"I slice, so! . . . I chop, so! . . . Presto! Chicken for all – run, rabbit, run, rabbit, run, run, run!"

These lectures were very pleasant, and we all looked forward to a rich diet until the autumn.

But Escoffier started to look very haggard, and his hands to jerk uncontrollably. One morning, unexpectedly, he met us all and wept salt tears, and said he had come to make his farewells, and did so, and disappeared from St. Ives, that night, forever, incoherent with grief and hooch.

The next day I found out that Escoffier had been involved in an argument with the Hotel Manager over Lobsters. What the argument entailed, I never discovered. But Escoffier had shown his own claws. He had got up in the middle of the night, put dinner for fifty people to cook in the Hotel ovens, turned them full on, and decamped. What he did for the rest of that night I never knew. But he had sought us all out at eleven in the morning to make his tragic adieu.

The next week, a flood of light illuminated his strange conduct; two Special Branch Officers arrived in St. Ives, to seek him out. They were from the Narcotics Squad. Escoffier had run out of snow in Cornwall, and hurried back to London to get a fix. The only other fact I ever found out about him was that he was a devoted father, whose only daughter had just finished her education at one of the most expensive schools in Paris.

[1]> *The second revised edition of* One Hundred Doors *(1957) has a full page advertisement on its inside front cover for:* "The Home OF BABYMEDE at GULVAL, PENZANCE . . . The Ancient Drink of Cornishmen."

XVIII
Tycoon on a Tiny Scale

IN 1956, I DID what Dr. Johnson warned his readers not to do, in his opening paragraph of Rasselas, which that mighty man wrote in three nights for £40 to pay for his mother's funeral. I allowed myself to "listen with credulity to the whispers of fancy, and pursue with eagerness the phantoms of hope." To be precise, I went insane, and into business on my own account, and set up as a publisher.

I did it thoroughly and on a proper scale, on credit, and on the telephone again, which I insisted to Peggy I should need now that I was running my study as an office. When, inevitably, my telephone was cut off for an enormous unpaid account, which I settled, eventually, by installments by Order of the County Court, a most pleasing thing happened. A fortnight after the Post Office had signed Judgement against me for the bill, a beautiful man in a black suit tripped up my lane, and said he had come specially to see me from Plymouth. He was Telephone Public Relations Officer, on a mission to express the sorrow of the Postmaster General that I had decided to discontinue the use of my apparatus. He described to me, in glowing phrases, the special new Terms for Business Subscribers, and said that if I would just sign the Form he waved at me, I would be reconnected tomorrow. My telegraph pole was still in the lane; the wire would cost nothing to reconnect. As a previous subscriber, there need be no question of any deposit.

Oh, how tempted I was to sign, and let the beautiful man go away, his mission fulfilled, to face the music when the Postmaster General waved his left hand and demanded to know what in hell his right hand had been doing! But I have always abhorred cruelty to children. I thanked him warmly for his interest, told him I had had a nervous breakdown, and my doctor had warned me against sudden noises of any kind, particularly tintinnabulations. Yes, tintinnabulations, and things that went bump in the night. Then I gave him an earnest look, the sort of look John the Baptist might give if Billy Graham were trying to convert him, and he sprinted away from me down the lane like a stricken gazelle.

In March 1957, however, all these recondite types of contretemps were still in the future, and I became a publisher, in a gallop of eagerness and total ignorance of the trade.

There had been what Mr. MacMillan calls "a little local difficulty" over my royalties on the first edition of *One Hundred Doors Are Open*, and this had ended in my obtaining the cancellation of the Licence to publish it, granted by myself. I decided to re-write it, and publish it myself on June 1st of that year. This was March 20th, my birthday.

I found a splendid firm of printers who were willing to print 10,000 copies, on pre-payment by me of £140 cash. I borrowed this, paid it over, and started my race against the clock. The printing was going to cost 10d a copy, about £400, plus inevitable extras such as blocks. As I was going to sell each copy to the booksellers at 1/8, each copy sold to them paid for the printing of itself and another copy. I was going to sell the copies to inns at 2/-, so each copy in this market was going to pay for the printing of two and a third copies. I kept singing this magic formula to myself, and jotting it down on blotting paper. I wrote it up in charcoal on the white wall of my room, and it looked very impressive, and when friends stopped me to ask if I knew exactly what I was doing, I chanted the formula to them, and they looked suitably surprised at the commercial talents I had been modestly hiding all the long years.

Then, somewhere round April 1st, clearly, Peggy asked me what we were going to live on until June 1st, when the millennium was due.

I had my magnificent one-word answer pat: "Advertisements!" And we did. My Guide was obviously a valuable commodity; it was the Second Edition, in a Guaranteed Printing of 10,000 copies. That was another magic formula I evolved. I was introduced to Major Mike O'Neill, an exceedingly popular member of the St. Ives business community, who agreed to be my Advertising Manager, acting as Agent on a Commission basis. He worked miracles, producing somewhere round £300 worth of first-class names, which filled twenty-two pages, divided into two sections, one at each end of the text, which I kept completely free from advertising matter.

As I sent in the advertising Copy, the printers started mentioning it frequently on the phone. I was filled with emotion at their interest in my project; then I realized that, quite naturally, they were expecting some of this revenue to be used towards settling more of their account.

By this time, however, the advertising revenue had become the sole source of income for a family of seven, and the sole source of finance for my expenses for travelling round forty new inns, as replacements for forty in the first edition; and, moreover, I had to pay the fees out of it for a considerable number of new illustrations of inns, or their Signs.

Now, of course, I could not sink to sinking pints in Public Bars. As a potential Member of the Penzance Chamber of Commerce, I had to sip shorts in the Lounge. It all mounted up; it always does. The only certainty I have ever known is that all things are uncertain, but the bill always falls due.

It was a new pleasure to me to seek out artists and offer cash for small drawings. I could not pay lavishly; but I tried to pay fairly, and nobody was dissatisfied. Old John Barclay, who died at a ripe age in 1964, did me four whole-page drawings of inns, and several quarter-page drawings of Signs. Jeremy Le Grice, just down from the Slade, did me three delightful drawings in a more modern style, and should have done four; but two odd things stopped my printing his fourth drawing.

It was supposed to be of the Star Inn, Penzance, kept, as I have told you, by Spenser Waters. To my horror, on the morning before Press Day for all the Copy, Jeremy produced a drawing of the Star Inn, Newlyn, with the justification that he liked it much better. Well, no doubt he did, but it is a different inn, in a totally different style from the one I had commissioned him to draw All the same, he was very hurt, at first, when I went up into mild smoke at his switch-round, and it took me some time to persuade him to draw the Star Inn I wanted, at once, and to leave the finished drawing that night, with Spenser Waters.

I have often wondered, since, whether Jeremy Le Grice had second-sight, on this occasion at least.

I went into the Star Inn, that night, and collected the new drawing. Both Spenser and myself liked it, and I felt relieved that my Copy was now complete. Then an absurd situation began to develop. I was telling Spenser something of my hopes for the guide, when he started lecturing me, very solemnly, about Castles in Spain, and Counting Chickens, and ended up with a morbid crack about impoverished poets. He was, it seemed to me, letting loose a pent-up flood of unfriendliness towards me that I had never suspected, for I had always liked him. I now know that he had other, graver, matters on his mind than myself and my small beginnings in business, and that I was really a sort of stand-in fall-guy for something he was bottling up against someone else, not me at all. But I was very hurt, and also very tired, after nine weeks' full-pressure writing and organising. So I asked him, very sweetly, if I might use his phone, and went upstairs and phoned the compositor in charge of my guide, who was working late because the firm were newspaper printers. I told him to scramble the whole page write-up of the Star already in type, and promised to let him have Copy to replace it over the phone next morning, and also Copy to replace the planned whole page of the Star drawing. It cost me £4 in type-setting to scramble and replace Spenser. Then I went downstairs and thanked Spenser for letting me use the phone, and walked to the Farmer's Arms, a cheerful inn, scheduled as an historic building, and wrote a write-up for it on the spot. I phoned this to the printers the next day, together with the text to replace the Star drawing. For this, I used the text of a lousy poem I had recently written about the Mayflower, for which I had received the princely fee of twenty guineas. The poor impression the poem was to make was doubled by its' length, which meant that it had to stand, alone, in the book, in six-point type. It was a silly business, altogether, and I regret the malice of not telling Spenser straight out that he was not in the Guide. Instead, I let him wait till publication day, to find out for himself.

Peter Lanyon made me a generous present for the guide. He spent a day at Newlyn, and did a striking line-drawing of the harbour from the heights above the jetty, and presented it to me as a token of goodwill. On the way back from the printers, I left this drawing in someone else's studio in St. Ives, and I have been seeking it ever since. Alas, it has gone, and so has Peter[1].

In the interests of impartiality, I decided not to sell the back Cover of the guide as advertising space. Instead, I drew a sketch of a Temperance Workers' Protest Rally with these lines to contain it:

> What is the meaning of this dreadful Guide?
> Why all this flaunted temptation inside?
> Why such indulgence in Bitter and Stout?
>
> Ask your M.P. why this Guide is let out!
> Stamp on it, step on it, stop it, oh, stop
> This glory in Grape and this homage to Hop!
>
> Ale is the threshold to laughter, and Sin
> Always commences where mirth doth begin!
>
> Wine leads to wooing of Women, and Song —
> Both these pastimes are certainly wrong!
> Stamp on it, step on it, ban this Bad Guide!
> Satan is lurking and laughing inside!

I had, in fact, for a few brief months, been fairly friendly, round about 1950, with a St. Ives Salvation Army Captain. One night he had come into the Sloop, and asked me to buy a copy of The War Cry. When I replied that I would if he would let me go to his next meeting and try to sell a drinking-song, he saw the logic of my words, and we had a very friendly talk. To my surprise, a few days later, he arrived at my cottage on a motor-bike, for another friendly talk. I found out that he was popping into the most unlikely studios to do the same thing. He was clearly developing a morbid longing for Vice, so, one day, the long arm of his Headquarters whisked him peremptorily off to uncorrupted pastures.

Once I had got the Copy off for my 10,000 Guaranteed Printing, it would have been rational of me to relax a little until Publication Day.

I had finished my hectic round of new inns that I had chosen as replacements in the new edition; though there were one or two elderly Landlords I continued to call upon fairly regularly. They were surprised by my new enthusiasm for their company, and more surprised still when it waned, immediately after publication. In the actuarial tables, the trade of a Licensed Victualler stands permanently at the bottom of the Longevity League. I was, in reality, making a quasi-medical round, to make certain that some of my new entrants stayed the course till Publication Day. Fortunately, I had chosen wisely and well; none of them had the bad taste to perish before June 1st.

Instead of relaxing, I had a publishing brainstorm. I wrote *Curiosities of Cornwall*, which was subtitled *A Miscellany to divert the Tourist*, which I illustrated myself, with four line-drawings; I also designed the cover of this, which was in yellow type on black, with a drawing of the Cornish heraldic shield, in which I replaced the fifteen bezants with fifteen small sketches of ships, and basking sharks, and witches, and the like. The page-size was the same as that of the guide to the inns, which had a fine Front Cover, designed by Michael Buckland, in black type on yellow. The two made a striking show of contrast on the bookstalls. This second publication only had twenty pages, and, without batting an eyelid, the printers agreed to have 5,000 of this ready by June 1st, also, to retail at a shilling, the cost to me being fourpence. This cost for a copy fitted beautifully into my magic arithmetical formula, and I began to dream of publishing a Quarterly Review of the Arts in Cornwall.

I should have just kept on dreaming. Instead, I had another publishing brainstorm. As I kept jumping on and off buses in my wanderings round West Cornwall, a pattern of jingles kept beating at my brain. I sat down for two days, and wrote *Lowdown on Uplift!* This was a complete guide to Modern Culture in the form of an alphabet, written backwards, Z to A, of 26 verses, flimsy nonsensical, topical, and frothy. The novelty was that the booklet was printed on two sides of one long strip of fairly heavy paper. This was then folded so that the booklet became a concertina; when you reached the last verse on the front, you turned over, and began on the first verse on the back. I arrived at the printers with this brain-child about a fortnight before June 1st. Without any demur, they promised me 5,000 copies of this, to retail at a shilling, and costed on the same magic basis, which, I had now convinced myself, had been the basis of my fabulous fortunes since the turn of the century. Actually, this concertina was much in evidence in St. Ives all through the summer, and delighted many people. I have no copy of it myself, and the children have all lost theirs, but I recall the letter H.

> H is Henrico — you know him, of course?
> He writes all his sonnets entirely in Morse.
> An amateur station transmits them at noon,
> And skippers of trawlers translate them and swoon.[2]

For years after it appeared, burly Mousehole fishermen bawled Henrico's biography at me in the Ship on Tom Bowcock's Eve.[3] (I have a different ritual with the St. Ives fishermen, who ply between Seal Island and the harbour every summer. I have been friends with many of them for years and years. When I draw near, shout "A light on the starboard bow, Sir!" They reply: "And heading straight for us!" I close the dialogue by booming: "God help the ship!" This dialogue is a memory of my earliest childhood when my father used to take me to see Old Captain Gladstone, who was ninety-nine the month before he died in his sleep. He had been round the Horn in sail, and had a magnificent head, and a terrific, fleecy, beard of drifting snow, and he gave me sandalwood curios, and a Chinese Wind God, and an ebony walking stick with an elephant's head. With him, he was the one to begin the dialogue, and he ended it with "God help the ship!" in a voice you could imagine flowing from the mouth of Moses as he came down from the Mount.)

I now had twenty thousand copies of the three different publications due to appear on June 1st. Thank Heaven there was no time left for any more publishing brain-storms — though I did toy with the idea of running off the drawings as postcards, and also committed the folly of ordering one hundred very handsome display stands, in yellow and black cardboard, from Mike Buckland. I am glad I paid him for the Cover design, on the nail. I still owe him for some of the stands.

The printers, Messrs. Lake & Co., of Falmouth, were the peak of efficiency, and speed, and their head-compositor, Mr. Lander, was a delight to work with. They brought all three publications out dead on time, and the binding of the inn guide was strong, and all the reproductions were crisp and clean. Their Managing Director came to see me, and he put out the suggestion that he might form a limited company, into which I should bring my copyrights, and be would bring some funds. We did, in fact, call on my lawyer and discuss this, and it would have been a splendid thing for me and mine.

I decided, before publication, to appoint a sole distributor, and asked Mr. Bernie Durrant, a well-loved figure in Penzance, to act as this, at an agreed percentage per copy. He cordially agreed to do so, and I set out the terms of his appointment in a letter, which stated, among other things, that no Sale or Return transactions was to be entered into by him without my express sanction. I did this because all I had in the world was now tied up in these publications, and I had told the printer that this was a condition of the contract. I was far too inexperienced to realise that the big chain bookstalls would only handle the guide, and the other two guides, on a Sale or Return basis, probably with a half-yearly account. In other words, I would be expected to lend millionaires money in order to trade. Bernie Durrant soon put my visions of the bookselling trade into the terms of hard reality, and I was glad to follow his advice on this part of the transaction.

The Landlords, however, seemed to me quite a different matter, and I did not see that it would be just for me to let them have the books on a Sale or Return basis, when no other of their trade suppliers did so. I have had several slates, in several pubs, but I do not try to conduct my normal drinking on the never-never basis. Moreover, the Landlords were selling guides advertising their own houses, and many of the Landlords were most enthusiastic about my write-ups. I therefore expected that all sales to inns would be on a cash basis, and I was jumping for joy when the printers rang me up, at the end of a week after June 1st, to say that Bernie Durrant had sold the first five thousand copies, and wanted the second five thousand at once. I never had any doubt in my own mind that these must all be cash sales, as stated in my letter to Bernie Durrant.

Bernie, full of enthusiasm, and working like a Trojan, had done the one thing neither the printer nor myself ever contemplated. He knew that many of the Landlords had passed through bleak months in the winter, and relied mainly on the summer trade for their living. This was particularly true for many of the remote, unspoilt, country inns I had chosen for my book. So, never thinking for one moment that he was not doing exactly what I wanted, Bernie rushed round Cornwall in his car, and delivered five thousand copies, and collected no cash at all.

"Pay at the end of the season!" he said, as he dumped my books on all these counters. "Arthur's alright! Arthur won't mind!"

Well, Arthur did mind. I was flabbergasted, even though Bernie did give me a cheque, by way of advance, against sales of my twenty thousand printing. I was now doomed to be the creditor of one hundred Landlords till nearly Christmas, longer in some cases, and all my long training had been for the role of a debtor. There were no nice firm figures to take to the lawyer to discuss with the printer; there was a nasty cold blast, and the printer lost interest in the formation of a company, and concentrated on the financing of my astronomical debt to him. It was eventually paid off, by the re-delivery to them of enough copies to meet the liability, plus a small fee for their distributing them. It took months and months and months to get all the money out of all the Landlords. Three of them took until spring to pay. One of the best know Free Houses in Cornwall still owed me for a gross — fourteen odd pounds — over a year later and I had to use distasteful pressures to get settlement. I had to put the bailiff in; when he called, the Landlord blandly persuaded him to accept a cheque, and the Court had to get my express sanction to this transaction; otherwise the bailiff would have started distaining on the liquor. I would not have done this to a Landlord who was hard-pressed. This one was affluent, and uncivil.

[1] *The drawing appeared in the* 2nd *edition of* One Hundred Doors are Open *(1957). The original hangs in Diana and Ken's Devon home.*

[2] *See Appendix VIII*

[3] *Tom Bowcock's Eve — December* 23rd

Owing to bad weather, the fishing fleet could not leave Mousehole. People were starving and Christmas was coming!

Tom Bowcock, and possibly his cat, went out onto the stormy seas. He returned with seven different types of fish; more than enough to feed the villagers. Star Gazey pie was made, a fish pie with the heads and tails of the fish poking up out of the crust of the pastry; the pastry representing the sea, with fish swimming and diving, heads gazing at the sky.

XIX
The Roof Falls In

WHEN, IN TIME OF deep unhappiness, events crowd upon each other with disconcerting speed, it is easier to face it than it is to confront tragedy with a grim slow stride. In 1958, misfortune for Peggy, myself, and all our children moved upon our home like a hurricane, and stripped us of our roof. It was, perhaps, more bearable for me, in some ways, than it was for Peggy, for I was whirled into a hectic fight against the storm; on the other hand, I was, I believe, more deeply rooted in our cottage than any of the others, and it was upon me that the more lasting wounds were left.

The Rev. H.A. Lewis died in 1957, and we quickly found out that our cottage was not in trust for Anne. It had never been in trust for Anne; not a shadow of a shade of legal preparation had ever been undertaken for such a trust. It was all tea-time tattle, and Mr. Lewis left the cottage to someone whom he had once vaguely mentioned as one of Anne's possible future, or present, or hypothetical, pretended, or potential, whatever you will, trustees. His Executors now asked for vacant possession of Windswept.

I will not now revive in my memory all the personal, painful, details of this affair, but content myself with sketching for you some impression of how calamity first moved into our foreground to threaten us, and then fell on us all when we were in no position at all to cope with its' consequences.

I decided to try to establish the Trust, and fight the Application for the Possession Order on the Trust, firstly, and on an implied Repairing Lease from year to year, as a second defence. So, one radiant June morning, Peter Lanyon, grave-faced and most attentive to Peggy, called for us early in his estate-wagon, to take with the two of us four of the children and two of our witnesses, both elderly men, to Redruth County Court, where, through Legal Aid, Counsel was to appear in our Defence. The case was held at Redruth because the Registrar of the

Penzance County Court, Mr. Barrie Bennetts, was one of the co-Executors who were Plaintiffs.

Well, we lost the day, after a hearing of over nine hours, and His Honour made it quite clear that he disbelieved my evidence on the letter stating that the cottage was in Trust for Anne. The last time I ever saw that Letter was on a Saturday morning the year before, and it was on Mr. Barrie Bennetts' desk in his office in Penzance. His clerk gave evidence that Mr. Bennetts was ill, but that enquiries of him had elicited the fact that he knew nothing whatsoever about such a letter.

The Judge made an Order against us for Possession of Windswept, to take effect on August 12th, which was, that year, the week after August Bank Holiday Week. It was also Caroline's eleventh birthday. I was stricken into numbness, and Peggy and the children wept. The Bailiff of the County Court bundled us all into his own car and ran us the twenty miles home; a spontaneous kindness from a humane man.

The next day, a Penzance Solicitor gave me some astounding news. Not only was Mr. Barrie Bennetts ill; he was mortally ill, stricken by a stroke, and this unfortunate old man's memory was as if it had never been. Yet it had been my recollection of the vital letter that had been attacked in the Court, while no one had breathed a word about the fact that Mr. Bennetts knew not his own name.

I brooded over this fantastic news for some time. Then I decided to go to Mr. Bennetts; office, and tackle his clerk, once again, about the letter. The clerk was a pleasant young man, and he assured me that he had personally searched the office through every file, and the letter was not there. I believed every word he said, because he was the truthful sort. Then he calmly made a remark that almost made me faint.

"I had a word with the Judge before the case, Mr. Caddick, and he said he was quite satisfied with my enquiries."

I went to the Public Library and wrote out in long-hand an Affidavit, setting out my discovery about Mr. Bennetts' condition, and the silence about it before the Court, and then detailing my conversation with the clerk. I went to Mr. Barton, A Commissioner for Oaths in

Penzance, and swore my Affidavit before him. He declined to take any fee, and wished me luck.

The last day of the Trinity Law Term before the recess until October was very shortly due, and I had to act quickly. So, the night before, I went up to London overnight, without a sleeper, which I couldn't afford, and in which I could not have slept, in any case, for sleep had abandoned me, and on a chilly July morning went into the Law Courts in the Strand, and, after much trial-and-error, and one disconcerting trespass into the Judges' Rooms upstairs, I found the Court of Appeal. It was packed that day, because of a sensational application under the Fugitive Offenders Act, and Counsel were there in dozens, and the public there in scores. Because mine was a Personal Application, I took precedence over all other business that day, and made my plea to the Bench for leave to appeal out of time on the grounds of vital new evidence, reading out my long, long, affidavit in support. Even in the papers that reported it, it looked like a legal marathon race; reading it was like trying to get through "Gone with the Wind" on a three-minute trunk call. I kept remembering that a copy was up before Their Lordships, and that I could gabble if I wished, but something made me deliver it deliberately and resonantly.

Lord Justice Ormerod, who was presiding that day, whispered to his colleagues one either side for a minute or so when I had finished. Then, very precisely, but kindly, he told me that I had not presented new evidence on the merits of the cause at issue in the County Court, and that, since leave to appeal was not my proper remedy, it must be refused, and accordingly was. I bowed, and plunged through the legal throngs, and went out into the Strand. There I was nabbed by a reporter from the *Daily Herald*, who said he thought I had had a shabby deal. He took a photograph of me outside the Law Courts, which was published the next day. It made me look like grief on a monument scowling at patience.

I went back to Cornwall overnight. I was glad to see the Mount and the Bay, but loath to dispirit my family still more with the tidings I bore. It was too early for the first bus, so I did a sort of sleep-walk to the little bridge over the mill-stream at Ludgvan, and sat there for about an hour till my home-bound bus came. Poor Peggy! Poor children! How disconsolate they looked, how desperate. They, and all their friends, had been scouring West Penwith ever since the morrow of Redruth for somewhere for us to live, but there was nowhere, nowhere at all. There were thirteen days of home left to us.

Then it struck me that it was harsh and inequitable to make a Possession Order against a family with five children to take effect on the Cornish Riviera at the peak and pinnacle of the holiday season.

Five days later, with eight days to go to Zero Hour, I marched into the Law Courts again, to make a Personal Application to the Vacation Judge of the Queen's Bench Division, Mr. Justice Elwes. Again, they put back other business, because I came as one of the Queen's liegemen, exercising my right to seek justice before her. Her Majesty is technically in Court whenever a High Court sits.

"May it please Your Lordship, I have travelled from Cornwall overnight to ask you to stay the operation of a County Court Order made in Cornwall against me for possession of my family home, at a time when every farm in Cornwall has its' caravans full, every field its' tents full, and all Hotels are showing 'No Vacancy' notices. My Lord, it is impossible to rent even a kennel for a poodle under six guineas a week. Other proceedings I shall take in respect of my cottage can not be so commenced until October. I ask Your Lordship to use the residuary powers that must reside in Your Lordship, until my Application for a Prerogative Order quashing the County Court's decision shall have been heard and determined."

I then handed Mr. Justice Elwes the Affidavit I had made and read in the Court of Appeal last week. He went through it meticulously, and looked up and sighed, and then smiled at me most sympathetically.

"You overrate my powers, Mr. Caddick. There is no such thing as a Vacation County Court Judge, and I cannot turn myself into one. You have my deepest sympathy; you are in a dreadful predicament. But, I repeat, I have no power at all to help you. I must therefore dismiss your Application."

I bowed to him, and again went out into the Strand. Again, I was buttonholed by a reporter. I told him my story very wearily, and he was absolutely on my side. He said he would do what he could with a story, in the hope that publicity might help.

The story he produced, in the *News Chronicle*, was an addition to my nightmare. "Poet must quit Dream Cottage! 'No more poems', declares Bowed Bard in Strand."

> I'm a Cornish elfie-welfie
> Shut up by my selfie-welfie
> In a bubble in the mittel
> Of a blob of cuckoo-spittle.
> Cuckoo! Cuckoo!
> Who the hell are you?

To get home this time I had to put a call through to Peter Lanyon from the Paddington Booking Office; he had told me to phone him if I needed help, and written down his number for me on the back of a card I had in my wallet from a Penzance taximan, a palmy relic of my publishing past. Well, I had got through the day since leaving the Law Courts by raising the wind on my brief-case with a great friend of mine from time long past, old Mrs. Daley, Ma, as we called her, who kept the Lord Nelson in the King's Road, Chelsea. I do not recall how much I had to drink there; all I do know was that each drink made me feel more sober than ever, but also more exhausted. I was financially and physically spent up when I reached Paddington hours before the night train left, sagged down on a seat, and counted my resources. Fourteen shillings, [70 pence] six Woodbines, one asthma-inhaler, a dozen moth-eaten pencils, and a bag of battered soda mints. Hardly the trophies of a successful career.

I fished out the taximan's card, wilted over to the Booking Office, gave the clerk Peter's number in Cornwall plus the cash for a cheap Trunk Call, and asked him to go through the routine necessary for putting a passenger on a train without a ticket. Obviously, Peter quickly assured him that I was a householder and a person to be trusted with tick, and gave his own name as a guarantor for payment if I defaulted, for the clerk soon came back with my safe-conduct to Cornwall, which he exchanged for a Form I filled in.

Then, in the confused wrong order of calamity, I did next what I had bemusedly planned to do before contacting the clerk. I went to a call-box, put in the cash for my Trunk Call, and told Peter how the legal day had gone against us once again. The sympathy in his voice when he heard my tidings almost unnerved me. Clutching my ticket to Penzance in my fingers, I asked him if it would be alright with him if the Booking Office rang him, to verify me, so that I could get a ticket home. Then I broke off, and bellowed: "Christ, Peter, I'm awfully sorry! I've got a ticket already!"

The laughter this nonsense caused us both took away tension, and we felt better. But I was sorry to stop talking to Peter when the pips went. Weeks later, I found out that he had instructed British Railways to send the account for my ticket direct to him, and under no circumstances to claim the money from me.

I spent most of the change I had left on a sausage-roll, two bitters at the buffet, and one hot bath, and felt more cheerful for a while. I was so early at the station that I managed to get one of the unreserved seats on a train crowded with holidaymakers. Perhaps I pushed to get it; perhaps insomnia made me look sinister, or dangerous, or destined to a vile end; I had a poacher's pocket in my loose tweed coat, crammed with the overflow of legal papers from my brief-case, a sponge-bag, copies of the *Star, News and Standard*, and no supply whatever of Law Court Rock for my children. I suppose I really looked like an abortionist gone to seed. Anyhow, there had been a mis-carriage of justice.

The train rocked through the summer night to Cornwall and eyes all round me closed, but I could not sleep at all. I kept thinking that by the time I reached home there would be six days left before eviction, and Caroline's Birthday. She had just passed her Eleven Plus, the youngest in the school to sit it, and the only one to pass it. What a grisly celebration for her, and for us all!

I reached home about half-past nine the next morning, once more the croaking morning herald of failure in London. I was amazed and very reassured to find how calm the whole family was. They seemed to be taking things in their stride; I went to bed and slept till six.

We still had no home to go to. All our friends who had spare space in the winter were letting it for hard cash in the summer. For miles around, cottages denied to local workers from September to April, when the farmers kept them empty, were now crammed with quasi-rural couples pretending to find paraffin stoves and oil-lamps great fun. The West Penwith Council's most helpful suggestion was that we might all go to a County Council Hostel, forty miles away, where the hopelessly unhouseable, the feckless, and the reckless, and crippled tramps, and quite unfragrant vagrants, met together in the chance medley of adversity. We thanked them very nicely and fled back to our croft.

Then Donald Swan did the trick for us; a friend of his at Porthleven, Dennis Pattison, would lend us, very temporarily, and quite unofficially, a long large room he had in Penzance, big enough to curtain into two, and with its' own sink, and electric light. It was a room he kept for parties, and no one was supposed, under the Council regulations, to live there at all. I felt quite sure the Local Authority's officers would carefully not notice us at all, if we parked there for a day or so, and saved them the final show-down of arriving en masse to demand shelter in Penzance, where we had no claim to it, or in West Penwith which had the real duty of re-housing us. Cornwall is not a place where officialdom ever runs riot; it is kept in check by the Cornish Irregulars, the guerrilla freedom fighters who make it their business to see that little things like statutory regulations end up in their proper place in Cornish files — in the waste paper basket, torn up and ignored.

So we went to see Dennis Pattison's little pied-a-terre. Being congenital optimists, and also being about to be saved in the nick of time from sleeping on the beaches, or the hills, or in the streets etc., we naturally did not expect what Dennis Pattison had sensibly warned us, quite openly, to expect. The room was in a derelict house in a decayed off-shoot of Chapel Street, fittingly named Chancery Square, and littered with scraps of rubbish, and frequented by horrible cats.

We unlocked the door by pushing it open, and went in. At the foot of a flight of crumbling stairs, stood an apparition, a lay-figure, such as dressmakers use, wearing nothing but a crash-helmet. I was gazing, horror-struck, at the evidence that it was female, when it wobbled, and I swear it — or she — leered at me.

Then we all began to feel rather sick. The reason for this, and one of the warnings dutifully made to us by Dennis, was that a persevering young man on the ground floor kept an aviary there, which was crepitating with pedigree and oversexed budgerigars, from which a Stygian stench rose to our destined room above. The lavatory was opposite the largest cage of these birds, and the tap, dripped opposite to it, too. By a sink, Donald had not been supposed to mean a sink, when he told us of the amenities. He should have said an enamel bowl upstairs, for use with the piped, municipal, water supply downstairs — right in front of the stinking feathered love-birds. It was, of course, a very hot summer that year; since the birds were not supposed to be there the Local Authority treated them as if they were not there, and no man in his senses ever came near enough to the aviary, to measure its' odour with stinkometers, or stenchographs, or what your best friends use on you before they tell you.

Peggy wept, I cursed, the children fell into glum despair. Reality had sent make-believe reeling, and adventure was no longer the spice of life. We wanted the safety of a home, and we wanted that to be Windswept. Up to the Sunday night before the Monday we were due to leave, we made increasingly desperate attempts to find somewhere else, and our friends ungrudgingly took us in cars on more and more goose-like wildgoose chases.

On Monday, we discovered we were legally in order if we remained up to midnight, so we decided to move on Tuesday morning, at as near to eight o'clock as we could manage. Monday was made tolerable for Caroline and Duncan by an invitation to a tea-party at Tredorwin. For us, it was made quite macabre by the appearance of D. Gilbert, of *The Cornishman*, representing that day, the *Daily Express*, and David Hughes the now well-known free-lance TV photographer. They arrived at noon, and asked Peggy and myself if they could photograph Caroline, and do a story about her birthday. They were both kind men, and both extremely sorry for us. It was the honest opinion of both that such a story might prompt, out of the blue, an offer of a house or some sort of housing from a well-wisher. So we agreed, half-heartedly. But we grew keener and keener as the task of finding Caroline grew more difficult with every hour that passed. We all went up the rough road to Tredorwin in a car. Miss Baker said that Caroline was out with friends in their car, and she half-thought they were making for a beach, which she was inclined to think might be Porthtowan.

Off we bowled along the A30 in chase of Caroline and her little hour of glory. We couldn't find her at Porthtowan, but a man said a car with children in it had just left for Hayle Towans. We drove to Hayle Towans, and scanned the beaches desperately, like Irishmen looking for a pub in Wales on the Sabbath. Then we drove slowly along the side of the sand dunes, inspecting as we went. But Caroline withheld her diminutive presence.

We sped back to Windswept; there was nobody there. By tomorrow, there would be nobody there, permanently. We drove over the ridges again to Tredorwin; Caroline had been and gone, and nobody had remembered to give her any message. So we drove down to the telephone box in the village, and Gilbert called his news-editor, and learned that the time limit for flying films up country for the morrow's use had just expired.

I was glad, at the end that we did not find my youngest daughter. Children should not be involved too prominently in these matters in the national Press, for all sorts of reasons. The reporter and the photographer dropped us at the end of our lane, and when we reached the top, Caroline ran down to meet us, gay and fresh as ever, and ready for anything as long as we were all together. She was delighted to hear we had been playing hide-and-seek all day in a posh car. And very glad not to be in the silly old papers — so there. But she was very cross that nobody had photographed Simba. She said he would have looked lovely in a nice big photo for a change, instead of a teeny little snap.

A staunch friend to us all, Tony Barritt, called late on Monday night, to report no luck in the search for cottages. Throughout all our trials, he stood by us, and would go the most tedious journeys for us, with infinite patience, if he thought it would help. He promised to call at Chancery Square the next night, ready to do anything we wanted. He looked very, very, worried, and he had seen our destination. What was worrying him was a sense of guilt at not inviting us to his own house. But he could not. It was a new Council House, just big enough for their family of four, and he was in a responsible official position in the County, working closely with the officials whose concern was overcrowding. How could he invite seven people to his house? Seven people already the subject of local talk through the Press reports of my successive appearances before wise old men in horsehair wigs. Seven extra would blow the regulations affecting his own house wide open, and sky-high, and local gossips would tell their tales.

I could not afford a proper removal van for all our stuff; I was spent up with extra expenses for London, and all sorts of emergencies, but the ghastly exodus of Tuesday was made bearable for us by the way three friends came to our aid, and toiled like slaves for ten hours, and moved all we had in the way of worldly goods to our new town address.

The first, of course, was Donald Swan, always in the lead when it was a question of helping his friends. He was driving an old Singer, and minded not at all what we wished to cram into it.

Not long after him, the next day, arrived Bryan Wynter, who used his Land Rover from dawn to dusk, and manhandled beds, and wardrobes, down the yawning gap in the ceiling we had made by taking out the ancient coffin-boards. With him, in his own Land Rover, came Patrick Heron [1], that kindly artist who lives at Eagle's Nest, the granite house that towers over Zennor, where Arnold Forster stocked the gardens with shrubs from the Antipodes. Patrick has a quiet, amused, rather withdrawn manner, and an elegance similar to Bryan

Wynter's, but less baroque. I have often puzzled over the problem of reconciling Patrick's reserve with the startling flamboyance of some of his paintings. I suppose that Abstract artists have intellectual emotions — or do they have emotional intellects? I must ask Patrick this question one day.

With Patrick, there came another addition to our logistic assets — a young and witty French woman, from Paris, where she had a TV programme of her own. When we had temporary breaks from our hideous labours, in the Globe Inn at Penzance, luckily near our budgie dump, she solaced my stricken soul by letting me use my rusty but once fluent French — with a Swiss sort of accent — to tell her of two great days in my past — the day I went to St. Stephen's, Westminster, to make General De Gaulle the unofficial offer of spare time help from fifty accomplished linguists, and got brushed off by him like a fly the moment he understood I was not officially calling on behalf of any Department of the Government that still refused to give him full recognition (how much goodwill has that great and good man squandered by his strange line in Olympian hoity-toityness?); and the day I met both Dr. Axel Munthe, almost blind, and M. le Comte de Paris, Pretender to the Throne of France.

I recall these contrasts with the sombre sable that clothed our agonies, for they reassure me that gaiety is, in itself, one of the great virtues, and should be accorded equal respect, from the wise, with the honour paid to the gravitas of Cato the Elder. I am full of awe for the stiff upper lip of Republican Rome and Warwick Deeping, but I infinitely prefer the twinkle in the unscrupulous eyes of Figaro.

How would Voltaire have viewed the budgerigars? He would probably not have noticed them, for in those fusty days, a man who could not bear a bad smell would have had to live like a recluse to avoid them all — but where would he have lived like a recluse? Monasteries conceal bad smells with the odour of sanctity; St. Simon Stylites must have had the pong of a pole-cat; and Montparnasse may have obscure hide-aways, but I am sure they reek of unwashed bodies.

I went in with the last of our loads and started to sneeze at the first waft of our new feathered friends. I found Peggy holding a sort of macabre At Home. Bill Rieou, a cheerful ex R.A.F. man, had chosen that night to make a courtesy call with his parents. His father is an Hotelier in the West End, and he displayed the manners of Cesar Ritz that night, and his wife emulated him. They sat on a mattress that was leaking horsehair, and exuded sympathy for an hour, and then went. Not a nostril twitched as they said their farewells.

From that moment onwards, my life in the condemned budgerigar flatlet grows hazier and hazier to me. I know we curtained off the room. I think we tried to sleep. I know that Tony Barritt called next day, and whisked the rest of my family off to his home, and let all Council regulations go to hell. I remember that I said I would stay to look after all our things, but would go get some air first, and then have an early night. Peggy kissed me goodbye, and promised to call early next day. I watched her go, and felt the walls were closing in on me, and I rushed out and walked the length of Penzance Promenade. I remember no more at all.

Peggy told me later that, in the middle of the evening, something urged her to go to Chancery Square, though she was comfortable and safe with Tony; and Christine, his wife, who had laid on baths, and food, and all sorts of things to clear away the depression that wrapped them all in a pall, had been trying to get her to bed, with some aspirin and hot milk to make her sleep. But Peggy would not be gainsaid. She came all alone to Chancery Square, as Childe Roland to Dark Tower came, and there, in the dusk, she found me lying on the mattress, raving in a delirium, shivering all the time with a skin like the sands of the Sahara at noon. Then Tony arrived. Between them, they managed to locate an available doctor; we were far away from the kindness and care of our own Dr. Slack in St. Ives. At last a doctor arrived, diagnosed pneumonia with a fever of 105 degrees, and set about getting an ambulance to rush me to hospital. I knew nothing about all this at the time. I know now that if Peggy, tired and unwell as she was, had not determined to come all the way back from Madron to Penzance, so late that night, I would have become the late A.B. Caddick, B.A. (pre-war Oxon) by midnight. Well, she did, and I didn't.

I felt too shattered the next day even to wonder for several hours about my family. I suppose that, in addition to the infection on my lungs, some mental spur that had kept me fighting so long had finally snapped under the stress of an unequal combat. I started worrying at once when Peggy told me, brightly and cheerfully, that she was taking Caroline and Duncan and Diana and Simba on a lovely camping holiday, at the Eastern Green caravan and camping site on the road from Penzance to Marazion. Poor girl, she was going there because it was impossible to impose on the Barritts any longer, and, after the aviary, the idea of open air life in August really attracted them all. They pitched a large tent, which Tony had found for them, and then the most violent thunderstorm for ten years burst over them, and they just-to-say saved their belongings and their tent from being washed away. However, they stuck it out, and the weather got dry and warm again.

When the children had all been in to see me, and then Peter, and Tony, and Bryan, and Donald, I felt much less stranded. My mother's letters, too, began to hold mysterious hints. Then, one afternoon a young Irish doctor came up to my bed, with a telegram he would not let them bring me to open until he could be present. He was a bit fussed over my nervous state, and the rapidity it gave to my pulse.

He need not have worried. The telegram was from mother. "Stop worrying. Lawyers negotiating for Windswept. All love. Mother." I began to hope again. Then my hopes faded, as I realized that Windswept was being put up for Public Auction. Obviously, there would be a limit beyond which mother, whose income was mainly derived from my father's estate, could not possibly go. I began to work out various stratagems, some childish but deadly in effect, to warn any would-be buyer that he might be purchasing a Pandora's box of legal troubles, and these I began to put into operation myself, as soon as I was discharged. But I wonder who else defied the County Court by printing on my white cottage walls in red letters, so bold that they cried out to be read by passengers on the top of buses over two hundred yards away, the ominous words "CAVEAT EMPTOR." [Let the buyer beware]

Through the kindness of a total stranger who gave us all house-room, I was allowed to be discharged to St. Ives, where I immediately fell ill with glandular fever. However, I recovered in time to go with Peggy to a phone-box near the Wharf, at tea-time on the day of the auction, to call the Penzance auctioneers, and learn our fate.

There had only been one bid for Windswept, at the reserve price of £500, and the hammer had gone down like greased lightning a few seconds after. It was on mother's behalf. She had bought our home back for us. For all the things, for all the multitude of kindnesses I have had from her for over fifty years, for her loyalty to me, and the love she poured out to help me fight sickness, for her stubborn strength in times of trouble, I hope I am abundantly grateful, and that she knows it. But the greatest debt of gratitude and love I owe her is for saving Windswept for us all.[2]

It was Peter Lanyon who insisted on taking us all back home one radiant September morning, when the air was clean, and the croft was crystal with dew. He brought a token gift of coal and kindling, and laid it down on our hearth. In vastly different ways, Peter and I have served the same gods, Lares et Panates, the household gods of hearth and home.

1> Patrick Heron — see biographies

2> In September 2003, 'Windswept' was on the market for considerably more than £500!

XX
A Quasi-Carnival

IF THERE IS ONE quality, above all others except loyalty, that delights me in a man or a woman, it is gusto. Gusto, the rich delight in living, and in doing, the sheer love of this world's shining array of diversity, that glowed, for instance, through every word and deed of F.E. Smith, the great Lord Birkenhead. "He galloped ventre-a-terre through his brief life," records his son. It is the quality that Alexandre Dumas shared with Winston Churchill; have you ever thought, as I do, that echoes of D'Artagnan resound through the pages of My Early Life?

Gusto is being slowly suppressed in this present decade. The silly snobberies of the gossip columnist change the suburbs into futile forcing-houses of social emulation, based on no value but the urge to imitate. A Social Column is for a closed society; a Morticians' Social Column, for example, might spread joy among the wives of morticians, if it circulated in a closed circle of corpse-conductors. A Social Column in a mass circulation newspaper is a waste of good paper and ink.

Gusto is damped down by the titter and the sneer. All titters are trivial; most sneers are anaemic. You cannot titter or sneer with gusto. You may mock with it, on a Homeric scale, as Swift and Voltaire mocked. They put whole hearts into their mockeries. I suppose that is the test; if you can put your whole heart into a thing, if you can heighten your zest to a white-heat, then you can do it with gusto.

Several years ago, I came across a case of heightened zest at the Tinner's Arms at Zennor. It was at my expense, but I valued it the more for that. The Brewers who own this pleasant tavern, once sported a red hop-leaf as an emblem. This clashed with the grey of the Norman Church, and the general understatement of the village. Could not someone have risen to the very heights of imagination, and designed a green leaf for Zennor? In time, I am sure, the country folk would have grown used to it.

The Landlord of the Tinner's Arms is Andrew Waterworth, the Eminence Grise of Westcountry Licensed Victuallers. I once dared to publish a lampoon on him, and escaped with nothing worse than a free John Haig.

The Perils of Zennor

(Dedicated, without any warning, to Andrew Waterworth)

Mad mermaids haunt the Tinner's Arms,
They lie on bars and flaunt moist charms,
But Andrew's no Trewhella.
This stately landlord cannot swim,
So when they flap their tails at him
He scuttles to his cellar.

The liquid virgins scream with grief;
Such chastity is past belief,
All Zennor hears them weeping.
And Andrew's just a bit to blame –
He bears a sea-bedworthy name
But won't risk ocean sleeping.

[*One Hundred Doors Are Open*]

Andrew's partner in the Tinner's Arms was once a cheerful soul named Roger Grace. Roger died too young, and his memory still brings people pleasure. Between Roger and myself, there was a resemblance that sometimes confused those who knew neither of us well, and was certainly strong enough for occasional confusion of us in the minds of casual acquaintances.

One year, Roger went and whooped it up at Helston Flora, while I, through reasons of genteel impoverishment, had to stay at home and drink strong tea, which gives you nothing but flatulence, and wonder, with the wistfulness of an alcoholic Cinderella, whether any of my friends were falling through the big Bass drum.

I met Roger a day or so after the Flora, and he told me a tale, with uproarious glee.

He had been carousing, and singing, and dancing, with disgraceful abandon, in that part of Helston's main street where the swing of the door of a pub on the right side is just strong enough to propel you right across the highway, and through the door of a pub on the left side. This sort of shuttle service is made for people like Roger. Well, in the middle of one of these crossings, Roger had been stopped short by a hefty sergeant of police, who put his hand on Roger's shoulder in a fatherly way, and admonished him thus:

"Arthur Caddick, my handsome, I been watching you, I have. And I'm telling you straight, Arthur Caddick, that someone had better pipe down! Now, Mr. Caddick, I've warned you, less carrying on, if you please, Sir!"

"It's a good thing your recognised me, officer," replied Roger, shaking the sergeant's hand warmly (and, I imagine with tears in his traitorous eyes). "Yes, officer, a very good thing. You've done your duty, and thanks for the tip!"

"Only looking after your safety, Mr. Caddick, Sir!" replied the sergeant, overcome with fifty thousand volts of Roger's fabulous charm.

Off went Roger, dancing, singing, carousing, in my name behaving more noisily than ever until closing-time fell on him like an axe, and watched over, now and then, by a benevolent sergeant, who was heard to explain Roger away with the words: "It's only that mad Arthur Caddick — and thank God he comes just once a year!"

Roger finished his tale and beamed on me with devilish delight. I couldn't help what I did. I laughed so hard that I got hiccups. That's what I call living with gusto. And that's what comes of compulsory virtue; all the sins in the Duchy are heaped on you like live coals; and Jolly Rogers get drunk on someone else's bad name.

My ruminations on gusto welled forth from my memories of our chastened exile in St. Ives, while we were absent from Windswept; it was contrast that let loose the flood, not likeness. The native gaiety of St. Ives townsfolk, or some of them, beats in vain against the bulwarks of municipal melancholy.

They had a civic carnival there in 1959. I was asked by Malcolm Haylett, the Carnival's Artistic Co-ordinator, if I would write them a one-page Foreword for their Official Programme. I agreed to do this, and sent him my text. I had taken great care to include what I considered the most valuable aspects of the town as a tourist centre, tried to bring out some of the vivid things in its' long history, and especially pointed out the beauty of the countryside that contains it to three points of the compass.

A Foreword full of candy-floss, however prettily served, can never be so appetising at Carnival-time, as one that has a spice of mild humour in it. Moreover, big-wigs who can take, and laugh at, harmless jests about themselves are usually much more popular than the big-wigs who want nothing but obsequious tributes to their own virtues. So, in my middle paragraph, I poked a little kindly fun at the contrast between the new invasion of young painters, and the old strait-laced traditions of the borough. I included the words, similar to words I used in this book: "The City Fathers say 'no' to most things on principle." The yearly attempts of some traders to sell a few postcards on Sunday in St. Ives invariably becomes national news. They are invariably defeated; there is clearly a corruption in this type of trade that totally eludes the eyes of the innocent. In other words, the City Fathers say "no" to the selling of Sunday postcards, on principle, which must be based on occult knowledge.

Malcolm Haylett wrote back to say that my Foreword was excellent, and then went on to mention a verse prologue to the *Carnival*, which it had been suggested I might write and speak at the opening. He was enthusiastic, and said: "A Prologue here would be perfect." I started to get a text ready, which would be easy and rhythmic to speak, and would also give pleasure to the children, who would form the bulk, and the great attraction, of the procession on the last day of the Carnival. Malcolm Haylett was making marvellous masks of legendary creatures for the parade through the streets; and, in my Foreword, I had mentioned "the doings of drolls, the frolics of piskeys and the felonies of giants." I was looking forward to the whole thing immensely.

A month passed, and one day, I idly asked at the Guildhall if there was any chance of seeing an advance copy of my Foreword, in the Programme. There was a great deal of evasion and dithering. This prompted me to pay a call on the printer, where I found that the Mayor had, without any sanction from myself, taken upon himself the task of censoring my Foreword, and had struck out two clauses, including the one I quoted about City Fathers. There are some things I will not stand; I said that if there was to be any alteration I would do it myself, otherwise the whole Foreword would have to come out. I then suggested this amendment: "Its' municipal maps give Teetotal Street as a recommended by-pass. The City Fathers agree with most things, provided they are agreeable, and this is the direct route to Queer Street." At this, I stuck; they could have my original, which Malcolm Haylett had liked, or they could have the amendment by me. What they did was to send out the Programmes already printed with cellotape stuck over my Foreword. This made the public eager to read it, so they dropped it altogether in the next printing. What a way to run a postcard stall!

I then had a letter of apology from the Committee for the alterations attempted to be made without my consent.

The next casualty, of course, was my Prologue. They wrote that they were "regretfully unable to accept the offer." When Peggy and I went to join the scatterings of people who spared their half hour to listen to the desultory oratory at the opening from the Guildhall balcony, I was hilariously gratified to find that a Police Inspector had been detailed to see that I did not try to read a Prologue uninvited. What sort of people are they? What do they think poets are? Are they confusing verse-speaking and vitriol-throwing; or, what are they confusing?

If ever a true Carnival were held in St. Ives, I should like to stand on top of one of their unspeakable public conveniences, and declaim a little Prologue, that might well run something like this:

Let Carnival mean Carnival!

As timid as a monkey shot through Space,
I am the Fool who grovels for your grace
Before Your Worships, all assembled here
In this exalted Guildhall stratosphere.

Your Worships ... yes, indeed! ... But for how long?
At Carnival, the Saints themselves go wrong,
All black turns white, all truths are changed to lies,
All husbands tremble when the cuckoo cries.

O GREAT GOD PAN, stride down through Street-an-Pol,
And bid each Councillor embrace his moll!
Let Preachers make sweet love on Tren Crom Hill
To civic concubines who have the Pill!

Swirl through the Stennack with your wanton tread,
And drive uncoupled couples into bed,
For Carnival frees flesh from guilt and sin,
And love brings out what lust once locked within!

Then, O GREAT BACCHUS MIGHTY GOD OF GRAPE,
Do you descend to soothe this rage of rape,
Turn dustcarts into chariots filled with crates
Of vintage clarets paid for by the Rates,

Make all St. Ives drink long then fall asleep
Along the Wharf in one fraternal heap,
Purged for one night of brother's hate for brother! –
Morning's the time to swindle one another.[1]

Autumn, the year we went out of the cottage and back in again, was tranquil and golden, or, maybe, these were the qualities we saw everywhere on our return home. Somebody had very cordially raided our garden during our absence; all Peggy's special roses were gone and many small conifers. We found a large macrocarpa half out of its' soil base, as if the thief had been disturbed. We soon forgot these things, and Simba resumed his rounds along the habitual tracks dogs seem to make for themselves, and keep to.

In December of that year, the Royal Literary Fund very decently made me a Grant which saved our ship. To obtain a Grant from this old Fund, dating from the eighteenth century, and a Hanoverian King who was well disposed toward writers, you have first to submit your published works, which are scrutinised by a Court. If they are adjudicated as of merit, you then have to prove that you are in distress through no act of your own, and find impeccable referees as to the facts you put forward in support of your application. I was granted a sum for the two years from December 1958. This enabled us, in some measure, to pull together the threads of purpose so recently snapped.

In 1959, in an attempt to add a further source of income for my family, and also because it was a cause I was profoundly interested in, I began to work on a scheme to get an organization into being that might help Cornish Craftsmen to sell their wares outside Cornwall, during the bleak months, from September to April, when there is so much depression in Cornish trade, and so much local unemployment. I had the idea of selling by post through the medium of a well produced, illustrated, Catalogue, supported by selective advertising, particularly at Christmas. It appeared that Mr. Greville Howard, M.P. for the St. Ives Division, had been simultaneously thinking on much the same lines, and when we met and talked things over, he suggested I enlist the active help of Mr. Norman Shipton, of the Cornish Stone Company. I was pleased at this, as Norman and I have been friends ever since 1950, when he blew into the County Court to learn all about Mead. After circularising craftsmen, and announcing our intention in local papers, I eventually got Mr. Howard's promise to take the Chair at a Public Meeting at Lelant, to bring an organization into being.

When it is considered what the full success of such a project might have meant to Craftsmen in Cornwall, the sparse attendance at the meeting was staggering. The smaller potteries were hardly represented at all; it was the potters from the more successful potteries, already on the way up, who came to hear what was proposed. Although the meeting did bring into being the Guild of Cornish Craftsmen, I began there and then to suspect that there was no Guild-sentiment at all in Cornwall, and that most craftsmen, like most writers, were cats who walked alone, and liked it better that way.

However, we got going, and I was elected Secretary, and given the commission to write and see through the Press a Catalogue, and organize a Christmas Sales campaign. The Catalogue, with photographs, was ready in the late autumn of 1959, and sent off in large numbers by post as a trade circular. We conducted the Christmas campaign in the columns of the *Sunday Times, Observer*, and *Daily Telegraph*. The results were not spectacular; yet they did prove that we were working on the right lines. Peterborough, of the *Daily Telegraph*, gave us a great boost when he quoted my write-up from the Catalogue in his column. However, I realised that the prospect of their needing a paid Secretary for more than the month in the year which covered the Christmas effort was so remote as to be nebulous. I lost interest, as, I believe, the Members did. I have heard no more about the Guild.

I think it is a mistake to confine it to craftsmen, and that a general Catalogue of trades, skills, and crafts, peculiar to Cornwall, or particularly thriving there, would have been much more successful. There would have been more money available for a bigger, coloured, Catalogue. I am still convinced that Cornwall does not make nearly enough use of the post for selling. One hears talk of the shrinking of distances in the age of super-travel, but it is still a long and tiring journey to Cornwall from most of the larger industrial centres.

[1]> *See also* "Lets Have A Carnival Instead Of A Festival"; Broadsides from Bohemia.

XXI

Broadsides from Bohemia[1]

YOU WILL REALISE THAT I have just set out the profound opinions of an abysmal commercial failure; everything I touch turns to cupro-nickel, except cupro-nickel; that turns to substitute cupro-nickel compound (7d off two packets, this week, in Euphoria-Emporia Stores).

This explains why, at sporadic periods throughout my life, I have decided, again and again, that the only serious interest I am really devoted to is comic verse.

Although I have broadcast on sound radio quite a number of times, I have never read any of my own poems on it; half-a-dozen of my poems have, however, been broadcast on sound in programmes chosen by other poets.

I was very interested, therefore, two years or so ago, when a BBC producer from their Mobile Television Unit came up to Windswept one morning, and gradually broke it to me that the Unit itself would be arriving after lunch to make a series of four short films of myself speaking my own poems.

In younger and vainer days I used to imagine that, when I was declaiming, I might even sound a little like, say, Sir John Martin-Harvey gone to seed. I got a rude shock when, for the first time, I listened to a recorded broadcast by myself on the BBC. With staccato pangs of an anguish that tore to shreds the last tatters of my self-esteem, I sat and listened to a bull-moose at bay, endowed with a supersonic boom. I had the wit to realize that my voice was so heavy for speaking light verse that, unless I practised volume control and variation of pitch, even what I thought of as my best comic poems were going to fall as flat as "The Death of Nelson" at a French Naval Reunion. I started to study singing seriously, for some years when I was young, but abandoned it at once when I got asthma; I did not want to risk giving a rendering of Mozart's "Within these sacred bowers" that sounded like *The Pipes of Pan*. You cannot sing with your mouth almost closed; you can speak poetry like that, however; it conceals asthmatic wheezes, and disguises my hereditary short-tonguedness. This makes you clip the ends off words. Peter Howard, the Moral Re-Armament Leader who recently died, once put this fault of mine much more extravagantly when he reviewed a speech of mine in *Isis*. His stark comment on my delivery was "He must not eat the last half of his sentences." This is a much heavier meal than the ends of words, and I took notice of his criticism, and, I hope, soon eradicated these overtones of gluttony.

The Producer who arrived in advance of the Unit was Michael Charlton, a friendly and helpful man. We picked out four poems he thought would be suitable, and representative (myself tacitly selecting them on the principle that the BBC pay by length), and then Michael Charlton dealt me a devastating blow.

"I'll speak these," I said. "I don't need a text."

"Oh, no!" he exclaimed. "Speaking poetry is not right for Television. It looks unnatural. I'd much prefer you to read them."

He was experienced, and I assumed he must be right, while tucking away in my brain a small thought that he was wrong.

When the Mobile Unit came up our uncouth lane, with the cameramen, the script-secretary, the lighting man, and the driver, I felt so important that I was tempted to have a look to see if Richard Dimbleby was in the boot of the Producer's car. It seemed on the small side, so I didn't.

They decided they would film me on the croft. There was a fitful sun, a high cloud ceiling, and a fresh west wind, which exhilarated me. I think the cameramen decided they had reached the North Pole as soon as they got on the croft. They lugged their heavy equipment into a clump of gorse, and then learnt that one of the poems I was going to give was written round this piece of croft. It was called "The kingdom of the snake", all about adders. This shook their technical poise considerably. They recovered very quickly, and one of them came up with a very bright idea. He asked me to find an adder to film as a background shot. When I explained that the only time I ever saw adders was when I was not on my guard, and not watching for them, he changed his request, and asked me to find him a dead adder to film. I had to tell him that, on that particular afternoon, I had run out of dead adders. I added that there was probably a live one lurking in the clump where he was standing. He leapt skywards and looked at me reproachfully, and was never quite at ease thereafter.

I did three comic poems, one short, two longish, and then they proceeded to do "The kingdom of the snake," taking infinite pains over camera shots, moving over granite boulders, bracken, gorse, and massive walls, as I spoke. I looked forward to seeing this very much, but this was the only one that didn't turn out right, and they never broadcast it.

The other three, all satires, irked me when I saw them on Television, for the very reason I had instinctively pounced on, when the Producer talked about reading them, not speaking them without a text. The films all showed me walking, fairly naturally into a grass stretch of croft, looking quite clean-living because my hair was flopping all over in the wind. Then I had to stop, produce a book, and stand there reading from it. It seemed all-wrong to me. You cannot throw your voice out if you are supposed to be poring over a book. If you are not really reading at all, you have to pretend to be, and looking up and down jerks your tone all over. However, they all seemed pleased, and amused by the verses, and we all crowded back home for tea and biscuits. They were easy men to get on with, and fascinating to talk to, and it was a pleasant hour.

As they were leaving, the Producer said he would send me advance notice of the dates of showing, so that I could watch. I forgot all about tact, and manners, and social poise, and blurted out "I haven't got a set. I hate TV!"

There was a moment of petrified silence. Then they all laughed heartily, and the proceedings ended on this happy note. I have often wondered, since, whether the reason they were not offended was that they thought I was making a good joke. I wasn't. I just forgot, and blurted out the truth, which they must have found so wild and far-fetched as to be totally incredible. The reason babies are born, today, is so that they can grow up and watch TV, and keep the audience rating statistics rising, rising, rising.[2]

The best of the three films was *Druids' Whoopee*, which is given earlier in this book. It was illustrated by weird and wonderful still cartoons of Druids at Stonehenge, and it was shown, very topically, on Midsummer Day.

The other two were poems I had published in my short series, *Broadsides from Bohemia.*

My first satire in this series was on the ukase by Mr. Phil Rogers, Landlord of the Sloop Inn, St.Ives, to the effect that persons falling below decent standards of dress and appearance, decided by himself, would not in future be served in his tavern. This caused a certain amount of chaos in the Sloop, and one or two international celebrities found themselves being bustled into the cold outer world, before the Code was finally settled. Even then, it continued to cause some resentment.

Top Person Talking

Put out my pink plastic bow, dear,
And wipe off those splashes of soup,
And spray me with Gentleman's Eau, dear –
I wish to take wine at the Sloop.

Their patrons are utterly tops, dear,
All Mayfair plonked down in the West,
Not tradesmen who keep little shops, dear,
Just Debrett and Who's Who and the Best.

By Gad! How it heartens a fella
To find finger-bowls out on the bar,
And a pedigree cat in the cellar,
And CD on the cellarman's car!

You'd like to trot down for a drink, dear?
Yes! ... But do please wash both feet,
And sling on that bra trimmed with Mink, dear,
You never know who you may meet.

The aristocrats down at the Sloop, dear,
Would never wear anything brash,
They jump through an autocrat's hoop, dear,
Like Gentry at Bath under Nash.

By Gad! This will shake the Tregenna!
I bet British Railways will droop —
And, darling, please lend me a Tenner,
They're always so flush at the Sloop.

The second in this serious of Broadsides was the short poem they filmed for TV.

Parasites in Paradise

"Happy days!" trilled a flea to his sweet little flea-male,
"Our Beatnik has solved us the problem of living!
We have boarded a beard in Chelsea and itch-iked
Way down to St. Ives for a summer of spivving!"

"How true!" piped a voice from the Beatnik's left temple,
"This world is a dream passed in mild Cornish weather!"
Then he grabbed at his love in a passionate rapture,
Singing: "Nit one and purl one and nit two together!"

"Alas!" sighed a creature whose name I daren't mention,
"I view all my future with grave discomposure!
I jumped on a Cubist and booked for the season,
But now he's turned Nudist — I die of exposure!"

The last of my St. Ives poems I shall quote in this book caused, or so I am told, by far the most amusement. It was written in 1961, but it may rationally be regarded as the end-product of a chain of lunatic logic which started in 1952.

I wrote, further back, a short account of the accident I had in 1952, when following my true vocation as a Bus-Bar Isolator. It was assumed by myself, and the doctor, that the matter was ended, medically, when the plaster was removed towards the end of that year. In 1959, however, alarming things began to happen to my right hand, and to my right arm up to the elbow. All the muscles started to wither; the sensation in three fingers began to disappear, and my right hand, which I write with, started to resemble a claw, with the fingers turned inwards to the palm. It flashed across my mind, of course, that there might be a new career open to me in Horror Films, as Dracula II, but I put temptation aside and went to the doctor. Doctor Slack took it very seriously, and examined my arm thoroughly. He always does examine thoroughly. One of the benefits of living near St. Ives is that you can have all the care, courtesy, and kindness of the traditional family doctor, if you are sensible enough to get on Dr. Roger Slack's list. How many Health Service doctors nowadays, after giving a patient an anaesthetic for the extraction of obsolete teeth, would wait until he came round, and take him home by car, three miles out of his morning round? Or take a patient four miles by car to a Hospital, to make certain that the feckless fellow did see a specialist from whom he had foolishly dodged by getting dressed and peremptorily discharged himself? I have to confess that I did this in 1950, when I was sent to Hospital after a minor nervous collapse, with some suspicion of cardiac symptoms, no doubt brought on by serving subpoenas on Bishops.

The trouble was that I did not really feel well enough to be ill in the Public Ward I was admitted to. It radiated good-humoured uproar, and children were admitted to visit, and skidded down the polished floors, and a blacksmith opposite me, just operated on for rupture, ate so many Cornish Pasties brought to him for comfort by his friends that his stitches burst and he had to be rushed away to be sewn up again. But the nights brought my neurotic disquiets to a climax; the patient next to me, another rupture patient, was, like myself, suffering from insomnia. So he often whispered to me across the night intimate details of his professional life, from which he was on holiday when he ruptured himself. He was a Cancer Radiologist. My flesh crept till every dawn, until the day I jumped out of bed, found my clothes, dressed, and told successive seniorities of Nurses that I was discharging myself. Their last hope was to call the doctor, an Irishman. He looked at me quizzically, and said I could go if I promised not to have more than two pints on the way home, and called Dr. Slack when I arrived. All this I faithfully did — I had not enough cash for more than two pints — and Dr. Slack was very tolerant and forgiving, and, I am sure, sensed that my panic to get away was part of the claustrophobia that often goes with asthma. He has done Peggy, myself, and all my children all sorts of kindnesses, and I still marvel at the speed he often arrives at when we call him. Part of the reason is, I hope, that he relies on me not to send for him unless I feel it is essential. I try very hard not to; when I fail, it is due to sheer ignorance.

Dr. Slack sent me to a Specialist, who repeated his own fears that an examination in hospital of my central nervous system might be necessary. This terrified me; it sounded as if they were calling in the F.B.I. So I became so earnest and eloquent about my conviction that the old Electric accident was the cause, that I persuaded the Specialist to let me see the Orthopaedic Specialist, before they packed me off to have my reflexes catalogued. I did not fancy that at all.

Fortunately, against all probability, and the long space of time that had elapsed, I was right. Old X-Rays, by the side of new X-Rays, told the full story. I had a carpal tunnel syndrome, which they decongested at Truro Hospital Infirmary, in February 1961.

If you are wondering where the lunatic logic leading to my poem comes in, it will leap out at you in a moment; unless we get side-tracked to chase another grasshopper.

As my first accident was an Industrial Injury, I became entitled to a Lump Sum for my Palsy, a beautiful mediaeval word that reminds me of King's Evil, and the Hunchback of Notre Dame, and — no! Definitely not Palsy-Walsy. I went before a Board and got an interim sum before they sent me to be decongested. This sum entailed the discovery that the Ministry's idea of a Lump Sum is a Morsel, a crumb you take with a lump in your throat. After I had been purged of my carpal tunnel syndrome, I went before another Board, to be assessed for a Final Sum.

This is where my poem begins as an airy nothing, and then assumes a local habitation and a name (I believe my thoughts are running along the same lines as Shakespeare's.)

The Ministry unconscionably tarried over my settlement, and I became aggrieved. So I went to St. Ives, and got some soothing mixture on tick from an off-licence, to make the delay a bit more palatable. There was a further Ministerial torpidity. One morning, some time after the soothing-mixture, I had a letter from the Wine Merchant about it, and by the same post my cheque from the Ministry. I went into St. Ives at once, and cashed the cheque, and paid what I owed at the off-licence.

Then, I believe, I spent a shilling or two, or three, or perhaps a little more, on strong drink, for, at five o'clock, a policeman found me sitting in the Digey in my winter overcoat and a state of profound abstraction. He gently suggested that I might care to join him in a walk to the Police Station, which I did, still enveloped in my melancholy silence. At the Police Station, the Station Sergeant chased my blues away, by sending me home in a police car, driven by our village constable, who assured me that he expected this would be the end of the matter. I was delighted. The police car had saved me ten shillings for a taxi.

About three weeks later, I got a Summons for my alleged Offence. It was at the sight of the particulars on this Summons that an irritation began to rise in me that culminated in my poem. The Summons was authorised against me by a Magistrate who was also the Wine-Merchant (though his brother held the Off-Licence) to whom I had paid my account on the morning of my alleged Offence, and from whom that morning I had received the letter about my account which took me to his place of business. Clearly, palpably, there was no suspicion at all of any dishonourable motive whatever. The Magistrate stood to gain or lose nothing, and he was known all over Cornwall as a man of the highest conscientious scruples.

Nevertheless, it was as constitutionally untidy and objectionable as if a Judge, in a Civil Case, had invited the Defendant to sit next to him on the Bench while the Plaintiff presented his case. When a Magistrate is on the Bench, his function is purely judicial when he is trying a person accused of a criminal offence. But he has other functions. Some of these are administrative; others are quasi-judicial. The granting of a Summons is not an administrative act, it is a quasi-judicial act, and all the ancient safeguards of our Constitutional Law come at once into operation and must be scrupulously observed. Clearly, a Magistrate must declare any interest; must reveal anything that may make him a parti pris; must follow the rule that justice must not only be done but seen to be done; must refuse to act at all if he has any prior knowledge, in his way of business, of any matter that it is to come before any Court as a dispute, criminal or civil.

Consider what was done in my case. The Magistrate was authorising a Summons against me for drunkenness. What do Wine Merchants sell? Drunkenness. Was I a customer of his in this trade? Yes. When did I last deal with him? On the day of the alleged Offence. You will observe that he is going to sit on the Bench to try a charge of Drunkenness, having effectively removed from the Defendant the possibility of two quite legitimate Defences: (a) that the Defendant was not at the place stated in the Charge when the alleged Offence took place, and (b) that the Defendant was an habitual Temperance Worker, and personally a total abstainer.

I went to the Guildhall for this case seething with Constitutional indignation, but in no way angry with the Magistrate involved. I knew and liked him. I thought he had gone on just doing one of those things that everybody does in Cornwall, and nobody else does in the kingdom.

When I was asked to plead, I asked leave to put a point of law first. To my horror, the Clerk to the Court, for whom I felt a very real regard, started shushing at me, and admonishing me to plead, in the nicest, and most irritating way possible, for nobody would stop talking and just listen for the space of a brief submission in Law. They kept telling me I could make all the points of Law I wanted, after I had pleaded. If they had no jurisdiction to try me, why must I plead at all? Well, I shrugged my shoulders and pleaded not guilty. At the end of the evidence, the Magistrates retired, save for the Wine Merchant, the Chairman having announced that he would not adjudicate in this case at all. The Bench stayed out for an appreciable time, and then came back and fined me ten shillings [50 pence, perhaps £15 today]. I decided to call it a day.

Some days later, Peggy and I were coming out of the pictures, when a poem started popping up in my brain. I went to the Castle Inn and completed it over two Stouts and a rum. The last stanza refers to a fairly recent episode in the history of St. Ives, when a civic visit was made to one of H.M. Frigates, at anchor in the bay. The visit ended as a catastrophic nation-wide sensation, for His then Worship the Mayor put the Ward Room's Silver Cigarette Box in his pocket, and made off with it, and a Lady Councillor fell into the sea. Perhaps she just dived, mistaking herself for a dolphin. Anyhow, there was the father-and-mother of municipal schemmozzles. Happily, the former Mayor was cleared of all felonious intent at a subsequent trial.

Never Sit Down In The Digey

Seated alone in the Digey,
Dumb in a doorway at dusk,
My breath full of blessings from Bacchus,
My stomach as empty as husk.

I pondered, at peace in the twilight,
But the Vice Squad had sounded alarm,
And a constable marked for promotion
Came up and exerted his charm.

He bowed, and his shoulders were azure,
I bowed, but my outlook was black.
He told me his favourite Sergeant
Was dying to meet me, way back.

I consented. We strolled off politely,
Exchanging opinions on Art,
No dancing, no singing, no swearing –
I insisted on this from the start.

I would have lodged at the Station with pleasure
But the Staff was not really prepared —
The Cook was off duty and courting,
The beds for the guests were not aired.

Nor could they make use of their Cooler,
A burglar had stolen the ice.
So they drove me straight home without charging,
I thanked them and said they'd been nice.

But then — O constabular cunning! —
Just fourteen days after my call,
They gave me a Ticket for Christmas,
Which said I'd been tight after all.

O never sit down in the Digey!
Its' cobbles may lead to the clink.
Box clever and look for a frigate!
At worst, you will land in the drink.

The St. Ives Times printed this in the middle of its' front page the next week. A few days later I was Guest Speaker at a St. Ives Round Table Dinner. They presented me with a framed ten shilling note, with the inscription beneath: "Presented to Arthur Caddick, Esq; for having sat down in the Digey."

The frame at the moment hangs empty; the engraving in crisp salmon-red has been put on temporary loan.

[1]> Broadsides from Bohemia *(1973). The distinctive cover has* broadsides from bohemia *in lower case. The subtitle,* In praise of Painters, Publicans and other Cornish Saints *in upper case. Throughout when referring to* Broadsides, *I have used upper case*

[2]> *David Caddick told me that in his later years Caddick became quite a keen television fan.*

XXII

La Dolce (far niente) Vita

ATMOSPHERE, IN URBANISED ENGLAND, means nowadays – except when industrial pollution is specifically indicated – the social climate people live in, not the air they breathe.

The atmosphere of the Land's End peninsula is its' social climate, for the weather may vary as freakishly from day to day as it might if a barometric quick-change artist were controlling it from behind celestial scenes. In unpredictable succession, Cornishmen round here imperturbably face languorous swathes of mist that drape their hillside homesteads in layers of aerial cotton-wool; unheralded visitations of torrential rain lashed shorewards by a sou'-wester; swift visions of skies of flawless blue from which the light of a brilliant sun scintillates through air as clear as crystal; perhaps a Christmas Day far warmer than a May Day in London; all the infinite variations that winds veering round the four points of the compass may bring to a land rimmed on three sides by the sea.

There is no escape from the atmosphere here. It is always on top of you. This is a very salutary thing for the human spirit. It brings home to you that there are forces than man does not control, and ills for a remedy for which he cannot run round to his M.P.'s political surgery. It tends to make men grumble less at trifles. For non-Cornishmen, it makes the taking up of life in West Penwith an intricate and, often, exasperating labour.

When writers and painters come down here from great cities and other environments uncongenial to the solitary creator, this atmosphere starts working on them. It starts by calming them down, so that they become less edgy, first, and then more reflective. Then it leads to introspection. There is a timelessness about West Penwith that puts the twentieth century into perspective. The antiquity evidenced by Celtic stones is so remote that it gives you none of the sense of contact with warm history that you get, for instance, from looking at the ancient splendours of York Minster. These hills are an immense neolithic graveyard of Ancient Britons, but none of their legacies are in daily use today, like many of the legacies of the Romans and the Anglo-Saxons. A man comes here from a metropolis, and finds himself face to face with the silent, unrelenting, scrutiny of the eternal elements. In the few outlying cottages still available to the artist, he may have to get used to humouring oil-lamps when he needs to have light after dusk; he will have to learn to turn a mine-shaft into a garbage bin for his empty tins and bottles, for there are still areas here where the dustman cometh not. All these things are the elements in a calmative compound far more valuable than the psychiatrist's couch. The artist who comes here, and stays, becomes simpler, and stronger, and deeper. The glibness of galleries disappear, with the silly sophistications of half-understood smart conversation.

This is the real gold that creators come down to Cornwall to find, and many have found it, and been enriched. But you can stay too long. Behind the quick scene-changes of weather is the backcloth of a mild, gentle, indolent climate. The soft West wind is the real breath of West Cornwall, and the mists are the maps on which the Cornishman traces the nebulous contours of impracticable dreams.

On the rare occasions when anyone asks my advice about anything, a strange thing is liable to happen to me. I quite likely become level-headed, clear-eyed, far-sighted.

Now, young man, it is time for you to leave Cornwall. The place you should be in is elsewhere, which is not in the Cornish Directory. And the time to go is now. If you leave it too late, you will slowly change over from creating to brooding over why you are not creating. You will become naturalised, and the mists will enshroud your mind. You will end up supremely happy, but indolent for ever, the lethargic prey of the moody and tempestuous West.

Had I been capable of prudence, I suppose that this is the advice I should have given myself when we were driven into an aviary by the parson's ghost. I should have sat down, and drafted an advert, and set about claiming my rightful place in this gloriously sinful world.

SITUATION DEMANDED

GENTLEMAN with contracting liver desires Managing Directorship of expanding organization. Must be computerised. Willing to learn decimals. Wife would help with dusting. 2 ½ day week essential. No references.

Box XYZ. *Cornishman* Newspaper, Penzance. Box 123. *The Times*. Box Clever. *St. Ives Times*. Etc. Ad lib.

What may I not have missed by not putting this at once in all the Top Papers? Instead of being still on the Land's End Peninsula, on the borders of Penzance, and the outskirts of penury, we might all have been bankrupt in a basement at World's End. Thank heaven fasting for a good man's improvidence.

I had celebrated my recovery from pneumonia, in 1958, by publishing, in a limited edition of one hundred copies, a fairly long satirical poem in heroic couplets, entitled *Argument from Design*. This laudable but quite uncommercial venture was made possible by Nancy Wynn-Jones, who lent me the money to pay the St. Ives printer. I still owe her for it, as she well knew I would when I borrowed it. Nancy has such a large fund of kindness that I should imagine she finds it impossible to get angry even with herself. Her studio used to be that military apparition on the Island at St. Ives which was erected to stop the Germans landing, and keep Dr. Goebels from access to St. Ives Public Library. How the doctor's wicked eyes would have gleamed had he caught sight of the proudest possession of the Reading Room there, Lloyd's Register of Shipping, 1917! The year of the U-Boat!

Nancy now has half of one of West Cornwall's stately homes, Trevaylor, where you can find grapes in the greenhouse, and Tony O'Malley in the woodshed. The other half is owned by the Redgraves. William Redgrave and his wife and family used to live at Island Road, St. Ives, which, in a few short years, became almost a rival institution to the Arts Council, a free-lance clearing house for ideas, and a main-line junction for painters from all over the world. It was here that Bill's wife — whom everyone in the Westcountry calls Boots, though her name is Mary — used to run Dauber's Café, and dispensed good food to the comfortable, and coffee and good advice, and very often more tangible help, to the uncomfortable, struggling artist. Boots helped everybody but the phonies. It was here, also, that William Redgrave lived when he and Peter Lanyon founded, in partnership, the St. Peter's Loft School of Art, which they ran nearby in the old workshop which now stands, transmogrified by the Gulbenkian Foundation, into the Penwith Society's Gallery. I believe Terry Frost later became a partner in the School as well, but of this I am not quite certain. I know he taught for a long time there and so did Bryan Wynter. In my own opinion, it was the splendid teaching work done at this School, over a period of time which was brief but brilliant, that finally sealed the reputation St. Ives acquired and, amazingly, still enjoys, as an international art centre.

Argument from Design was printed, as I have said, in an edition of one hundred copies only. After family copies, copies for friends, review copies, had been set aside, the commercial bulk of this publication could be contained, and was contained, in one large tattered envelope, which someone pilfered from me in a pub.

Since the days when Joe Martin adorned its' staff shortly after the end of the war, I have always had the friendliest relations with The Cornishman, which, although it is incorporeal, I always think of as a person, disembodied, yet benevolent, and always at hand in Parade Street, Penzance. There is a Dickensian air about its' premises, and I hope they never get modernised.

John Page, the present Editor of the Cornishman, achieved the minor miracle of persuading the Proprietors of The Cornishman to pay me hard cash for my poetry, that is to say, a cheque which Bolitho's Bank readily turned into money for me, at the end of the quarter, for which I got paid in arrears. This is always the hardest part, for poets, about newspaper cash, the waiting.

So I agreed with John Page to write a series of comic verses for *The Cornishman*, in the form of an *Alphabet of West Cornwall*[1], which appeared during 1963, in twenty-seven instalments. Yes! Twenty-seven. The week before John Page went off on his summer holidays, they had published *Q is for Queues*. The next week they were due to bring out *R is for Railways*. [2] This was the only poem in the series of which I had sent in John Page a second version, which I thought tightened up and improved the first. I was relieved, therefore, to see the corrected version in print. I had asked them to destroy the first one. The next week, however, *R is for Railways* came out again, this time in the text I thought had been destroyed for ever. I had a strange feeling of relief mixed with chagrin, when I learnt the effect on my devoted public; not a soul seemed to have noticed the error at all. Everybody was always assuring me they were enjoying my "Alphabet"; nobody could have been studying it very hard.

I published the *Alphabet* as a booklet, in December 1963. This was made possible through the help of Gerald Whitmarsh, a great friend of John Page, who financed the printing. Gerald Whitmarsh stood as the Liberal Candidate for St. Ives at the last two General Elections, not successfully, but with a sharp increase in the Liberal poll. He is not contesting this seat next time.

Here is *W is for Western Hunt*:

Hunting-Song

I need not wish you luck, Good Sirs,
And Huntsmen, One and All,
You take the field with mighty odds
Against a thing so small,

A hunted harried hounded thing,
Not much for you to take,
A living creature's universe,
Its' everything at stake.

You viewed near here one New Year's Day,
And made our peaceful lane
An atavistic cavalcade
Of fear and noise and pain,

As if the Stone Age, dressed to kill,
In ritual rebirth,

Had come to make a sacrifice
On twentieth century earth.

And were there echoes in your horn
Of Goering out with Hess?
I think that Belsen started with
A zoo in fancy dress.

And this was lettered out in blood
When decencies began —
While boys still murder beasts for fun,
Then man will murder man.

My heart is with the hunted ones,
The fox, the hare, the deer,
The birds, the beasts, that bullies kill,
The brotherhood of fear.

And as for all the women folk,
Whom death gives such a kick,
God Bless their tender hunting hearts —
If God's not being sick.

In 1963, also, the Fortune Press brought out a short story of mine in volume form, as a novella. This book, *The Tilting of the Scale*, contains, though I may be biased, some of my best writing. When I last enquired how it was going, the score for Cornwall ran: five good reviews — two sales.

I also wrote a Children's Book that year, and I see from a rough record in my drawer that I had one Children's Book rejected that year. I am not surprised. I have lived so long with and so close to children that I realise that there are no children left, nowadays. There is nobody but Teenagers, up the chimney, and under the bed, round every corner, down every street, in every restaurant, behind every comic strip, alongside every record player, on top of every situation, on top of everybody, Teenagers are the Tops, the Tops, Tops, Tops, with their God-forsaken Pops. O for an hour of glorious deafness!

Peggy and I have been volunteer victims of Teenage persecution for over thirteen years. Egos have been ruthlessly developed and nurtured by the energy automatically released by sitting on fuddy-duddies, and squashing dreary old squares. The fuddy-duddies and squares are the Head of the Family, me, and the Father-Figure's wife, Peggy. I have often wondered whether they will decide one day to chop off our heads and shrink them. Clearly, we look like neolithic shrunk-heads, to the curious eyes of Teenagers. I wonder how soon the day will come when all British fathers have to call their sons "Sir", and mothers address their daughters as "Madam." My vindictive consolation is that nature will soon turn my Teenagers into square-headed fuddy-duddies themselves, and it will be their turn to wilt and shrink and grow faint before flesh-and-blood noise-boxes. And their fate will be worse than ours. Each generation of Teenagers is more pandemonic than its' predecessor.

All the same, I should have hated to miss my own private Teenagers. They have preserved me from putrefaction, and, after all, they are infinitely, vastly, immeasurably superior to anybody else's Teenagers. That is why I love them.

Last New Year's Eve, for the first time since Anne was born in 1940, Peggy and I realised that we would be alone at home to let the New Year in, unless we decided, also for the first time on a New Year's Eve, to go out somewhere together. All our children were hilariously planning to scatter themselves, that night, at parties, and dances, and places where only the young foregather.

Fortunately, we had an invitation to go out. We went to a glorious, Bacchanalian, bust-up, given at Trevaylor by William Redgrave and his wife. Not long after midnight, a young and ravishing woman swooned up to me and gave me a passionate kiss.

Thirty years fell from my shoulders and thudded to the floor. Then my Cleopatra ruined everything by saying "Happy New Year, Daddykins!" Then she rushed off to jive with a boy with bobbed hair. I realised she was not ravishing. She had a stupid profile; the bad light had tricked my eyes.

I sagged, and fingered my asthma-cure. Then, for the hell of it, I went up to a pretty young thing, and gave her, with much less conviction, a perfunctory peck on the lips that made her giggle. Does Sex Appeal in masterful males provoke giggles? I very much doubt it.

Peggy had watched these proceedings with some amusement. She came up to me, and I kissed her guiltily, for she dislikes indiscriminate necking.

"It's your age, dear," she said. "Fifties are the foolish years for men, you know."

I totally disagree. From birth, through adolescence, all through my prime, until now, when I stand teetering before the prospect of becoming a juvenile delinquent in my second childhood, my folly has remained constant, invariable, enormous, at the bedrock of my being. I am a fool. I am also a Fool, in cap-and-bells, and motley.

I used up all the wisdom I ever had when I made the decision to make Windswept Cottage our family home.

Finis

1> *See appendix IX*

Appendix I

THIS IS A TRANSCRIPT of a letter Caddick wrote to his daughter Diana's husband, Ken. I reproduce it here both as a record of Arthur and Peggy's courtship — if it can be called that! And as it is an example of the sort of letter he could write to celebrate family occasions. The original is handwritten and not — in parts — easy to decipher! — even with Diana's help!!

It is the speech he made on the celebration of his and Peggy's Ruby Anniversary celebrations held at Ken and Diana's home.

Ken — as we shall see was unable to be present.

My dear Ken,

May I reconstruct for you as far as I can accurately recall it, the speech I made at your home on the anniversary of our Ruby Wedding. Here it is.

"My family and friends, the great Francis Bacon, the Lord Chancellor who was dismissed by James I for taking bribes, began one of his celebrated essays with these words: "He that hath wife and children hath given hostages to fortune."[1] As everybody here tonight can see, I have been fortunate in my hostage.

Wife and children let me describe, in an old fashioned word, the virtues of long courtship. 40 years and 4 weeks ago today, I saw Peggy for the first time. She was seated at the bar of a to me respectable tavern, the Holland Arms, with a bore I knew slightly whose conversation had the rapidity of creeping paralysis. I saw this elegant girl, with deep-set eyes, and decided that it was my duty to rescue her. So I went up to them. I am by nature a silent man, but I got the better of nature and in ten minutes flat, drove him away, so that a threesome became a twosome.

Peggy was elegant. In those days women wore high-heeled shoes, so that by natural progression, a man's gaze travelled upwards — to the face of course. Nowadays they have low cleavages, so that the gaze travels downwards, of course to the ground. This is progress in a sordid form.

Well I talked to Peggy for 20 minutes, and then asked her to marry me. To my astonishment, she refused, but smiled faintly as she did so. I rushed out to the Boltons, to the Earl's Court Tavern, to the Courtfield, to the Persdale, to drown my sorrows and ended up in the Goat in Boots. All the same I woke remembering that gentle smile and those deepest innocent eyes.

For 6 days I looked for her in vain. 40 years and 3 weeks ago, today, I found her. She was with a young girl who had a flat in Peggy's genteel establishment for Young Ladies. I talked to Peggy for 2 hours, and then we went out in the glorious night of September 1938, with a waxing moon. And something happened to us both I took her to her genteel doorstep (?) had trod (...?) and kissed her and proposed to her again. She accepted. This time I was not at all astonished. She had told me that she had just qualified at the London Academy of Beauty Culture, in Sackville Street. Clearly my profile was exactly that which her education had qualified her to worship.

Forty years ago today, we were married and have since spent 4 decades together. Not a cross word. Not a sullen look. Not a door banged in anger. Not a cup thrown to the ground in temper. It was like that line in Tennyson. "The coo of doves is immemorial..." — and then the children arrived, "the murmuring of innumerable little bees." [2]

Wife and children how moved and how touched, and how proud are Peggy and myself, tonight when we realize the love and care and generosity they have expended in arranging this celebration for us both. Five of our flesh and blood, and four who are equally our children by marriage.

Then, I must strike a sad note. I hope Diana, my middle daughter, will not sue her tottering father under the Sex Discrimination act, if I reveal that the true Lord and Master of this house is absent tonight, by the iron force of circumstance, Ken became the innocent victim of the financial shenanigans between two global mining companies. This week is his first full week in a splendid appointment, where he is to meet the Heads of all Departments. So he cannot be with us. But this is his home. I therefore ( ) out this sheet of drawing paper, headed with our thanks to him, and my best wishes in his new career. Will you all be so kind as to sign it?

Finally, I have one more thing to say. You will all remember the music of Stephen Foster now part of America's historical folk story 3*. When he died in a freezing winter, bankrupt, emaciated, shunned by his friends who had sponged upon him in his hey-day, they found in his threadbare clothes two remarkable things — a stub of pencil with a carefully sharpened point, and a sheet of paper. On this he had written the first words, and the first bars of a song which death peremptorily cut short. The words were "kind friend and Comrades too." The first abiding happiness of my life has been the companionship of my friends. The only virtues of which I can boast is that I have always been loyal to them and so have they been to me.*

I now order all my friends to stop drinking, and I ask the Windswept Society for Total Temperance to join me in this toast. To our dear friends here tonight, and to them, alas, who are no longer with us.

Our Friends!

For Ken with love from Dad — I am afraid that the family was too overcome with emotion to organize the signatures of those present. Still, you have them symbolically.

Dad

[1]> *Francis Bacon 1561-1626*

"He... Fortune; for they are impediments to great enterprises either of virtue or mischief"

Of Marriage and Single Life

[2]> *Alfred, Lord, Tennyson 1809-1892. Poet Laureate 1850.*

"The moan of doves in immemorial elms,

And murmuring of innumerable bees."

The Princess Song 3 *(1847)*

[3]> *Stephen Collins Foster 1826-64*
American song-writer — best known for — among others:
The Old Folks at Home, Camptown Races, Jeannie with the Light Brown Hair *Despite great success he died in poverty and obscurity.*

Appendix II

Arthur Caddick as Poet Laureate?

THE FIRST POET LAUREATE in the modern sense is regarded as Ben Jonson who was appointed in 1616 during the reign of James I. The title became established with the appointment of John Dryden in 1668 during the reign of Charles II. An eminent poet was appointed as a salaried member of the British Royal Household

The Poet Laureate was formerly expected to write poems for state occasions, but since Victorian times the post has carried no specific duties. The title is largely honorific to mark a leading poet.

Caddick had the ability to write 'to order' birthdays etc.

On the death of John Betjeman 1984 there was a suggestion that Caddick could be considered for the post of Poet Laureate.

Hirth suggests one member of the art colony in West Cornwall declined to support Caddick on the grounds that it would be inappropriate to suggest a well known frequenter of saloon bars as a candidate for the position of Queen's poet. Others thought him too left wing.

When Wordsworth accepted the Laureate it led Robert Browning to write:

> *"Just for a handful of silver he left us,*
> *Just for a riband to stick in his coat"*

Robert Browning 1812-1889; *The Lost Leader* 1845

He considered Wordsworth had abandoned his radical principles by accepting the post.

Would Caddick have compromised some of his views, e.g. his thoughts on hunting?

In the event Philip Larkin was the original choice but when he declined, Ted Hughes (1984-1999) was appointed.[1]

Today's holder of the post is Andrew Motion. (1999 to date) Here's an extract from his poem, *A Song for Jonny* which celebrates England's Rugby Team, after their World Cup victory 2003 and of course their match winning No. 10.

"Oh Jonny the power of your boot,
And the accurate heart stopping route,
Is a triumph we gladly salute."

Or, we have this from Scottish Laureate, Edwin Morgan. He wrote a poem called *We Got'Im*, and is about the capture of Saddam Hussein and his subsequent medical examination. It ends:

"Some say he only got what he deserved
Some say the cause of justice was at last served.
I say there are decencies which were not observed"

Somehow I feel Caddick would have made a somewhat better effort.

Interestingly the post holder received a butt of canary wine. . . but this was discontinued in 1790 when Laureate Henry James Pye decided he preferred the equivalent in money! It's nice to surmise that one old tradition could well have been revived with Caddick's appointment!

[1>] *Both Sir Walter Scott 1771 — 1832 and Thomas Gray 1716 — 1771 rejected the post of Laureate.*

Appendix III

A POEM DAVID CADDICK wrote shortly after the death of his father.

TO MY FATHER A POET

When Wife, Daughters, Sons
and Children's Children Wept
beneath a Cornish sky.

Surrounded by laurels, flowers and love
The Day was Crystal Clear
Tribute to a Poet we were all so near.

David Caddick. 1987

Appendix IV

Giants of Cornwall

NO, MY SWEET READER, this is not a drawing of Arsenal winning the Cup at Wembley.

These are Cornish Giants. They took umbrage, first. Now, in a fit of super spleen, they are taking Tren Crom away from Mount's Bay, and placing it where it now stands, by arrangement with the St. Ives Chamber of Commerce.

I am chronicling fact. This is a fact preserved by the Drolls, the Cornish equivalent of Troubadours, except that the Drolls weren't quite so potty about Love. The Drolls wandered from village to village, and told tales, to beguile the long, melancholy nights of winter. The tales they told were legends, and legends are folk-memory, preserving fact and embroidering it with fantasy. There were Giants in Cornwall. The Drolls said so and the angular groupings of jagged, massive granite confirm it. Who but Giants could have dropped such bricks? Who but pygmies could say otherwise?

[An example of Caddick's art from *Curiosities of Cornwall* (1957). A superb, surreal picture of the Fight on Trencrom]

Appendix V

CADDICK HAD HIS FIRST poem published in Punch magazine

January 6th 1937.

Orpheus and Eurydice

A GUY called Orpheus had a uke,
A real big shot he was, like Duke,
And played it swell and class,
This Orpheus though he'd like to splice
A hotcha dame called Eurydice,
And made a winning pass.
Now Eurydice went out one day
To pick some daisies by the way
A phoney thing to do.
A snake from under cover jerks
And gives young Eurydice the works;
The poor dumb dame was through.
Well, Orpheus went and cut up rough;
I guess he thought the deal was tough.
But he was kinda cute;
He aimed to travel down below
Where Grecian stiffs would always go.
And play his uke to Plute.
There must have been some graft down there,
For Orpheus doesn't get the air,
But Plute gives him a break.
He says to Orpheus, "Take your frail,
But don't look backwards on the trail
The only rule I make."
They hit the happy homeward track.
Then Orpheus, like a sap, looks back
To give his dame the eye.
Of course old Plute was kinda sore;

She had to join the stiffs once more
And leave him high and dry.
I don't think much to such a guy
Who'd lose his dame and go and try
To win her by a fluke.
It's no use muscling in below
Without the boys and guns in tow
With just a sissy uke.

Here is another Punch poem from January 21st 1959 — and coincidentally, another American theme!

Unhand Me, False Villain!

BLOSSOM K. VANDERBLOOM, widow from Texas
(Sum of her petal-weight two hundred pounds),
Lights upon London, cute daughter beside her,
Glory Gay Vanderbloom, doing the rounds.

Doors open smoothly to Oil's application,
Gush greeting gushers that bubble way back,
Blossom breathes deeply the incense of ushers,
Glory Gay glitters with Ice on her Sack.

Then to their innocent idyll of roses —
Sneaks, in a Daimler, a sinister snake —
The son of a Lord, yes, a Lord's only offspring —
Glory Gay doodles a crest for her cake.

Blossom K. Vanderbloom dreams of her status
Feudally changed when the old stiff-shirt drops —
A real Lady's Mamma and then a Lord's Grandma,
And one in the eye for that family of Pop's.

Then an old school-friend comes whispering smugly
An ugly and creeping, incredible, fact —
This Lord is a phony, a Government Issue,
Something brought in by a Life Peerage Act!

Straight via Boeing proud Blossom whisks Glory
Way back to the State where a Star shines above
A race of austere and republican daughters
Who cry scorn on titles and marry for love.

Other poems published in Punch include: *An Ultra-modern Sculptor* and *On a Certain Poet* — both are in *Quiet Lutes and Laughter (1955)*

Appendix VI

"WASSAIL!" is the toast

by Harry Hopkins

"DRINK HAIL!" is the correct reply. The drink is mead, the wine of the bees, called the nectar without a hangover. One man's faith has re-created it from the secret recipes of the medieval tipplers

LIEUT. COL. G. R. Gayre, MA., D.Sc., is an unusual man. He has a sense of the past, so over powering, so vivid, that he has actually been able to start a business in it — and make it pay.

When the bearded Vikings came storming up the Kent shore recently, they celebrated their invasion in beakers of mead. This ancient English drink was not just another pageant property. It came from the streamlined plant of Mead Makers Limited.

And it was being drunk at that moment not only by pseudo-Vikings in Broadstairs but by highly contemporary citizens of this jet-propelled world. It was, in fact, Colonel. Gayre's mead.

What turned the colonel's attention at the age of forty to this novel field of postwar enterprise? It is a long and colourful story strung upon two main strands. The first strand was his love of bees and bee-keeping; the second, his passionate interest in the old ways of life, background to the study of ethnography, the science of the races.

A soldier by profession, he spent his leaves among the bee-hives of his Sussex garden. He developed a theory about bees, as about most things.

It was a characteristic theory: that the foreign bees now so largely stocking British hives would never really habituate themselves to our weather.

The native bee was -the bee for us.

Unfortunately, the native bee was an angry fellow, a great stinger of beekeepers. The colonel decided that he would tame it. He would breed the wildness out of it, through Europe, studying the traditions, the old ways of life. Everywhere he found the aroma of mead.

According to the old Norse legends, draughts of mead served by beautiful maidens had been one of the rewards of the warrior on reaching Valhalla. From the Sanskrit *Rig-Vedas* of five thousand years ago to Chaucer and Shakespeare, the literature that came down from the past was full of the praise of mead, the drink of the gods.

Honey, the fruit of the bee. Honey brew the drink of the ancient peoples. In mead, Colonel Gayre's two interests came together.

He began to comb through old books for mead-making hints. They were plentiful and varied, but they were not, he felt, enough. For who, possessing the secret, would be fool enough to write it down?

Putting together his gleanings, helped by his early training as a biologist, he went to work himself with honey and water and yeast and spices. He became a nuisance in the kitchen. From the old books, .the colonel had developed a precise idea of the nature of true mead. Could he and his English bees not re-create the drink of the medieval Britons?

For ten years he tried to find the answer.

When the war came he was getting near. But even the war could not altogether stop the colonel's pursuit of his elixir. As he jolted around the East Anglian countryside between his anti-tank gun positions, his Kilner jars of honey and yeast rattled together in the back of the Army truck.

By a strange coincidence, his batman was a beekeeper also. When the two of them spied a wild bees' nest in a hollow tree they would stop the truck and chop the tree down to gather the honey: raw material for one more experiment.

It's Made Like A Wine

By VE-Day the colonel felt he held the secret.

Pondering over the product of his researches, he decided that what had been good enough for Chaucer and Shakespeare and the medieval drinkers was very definitely good enough for him and probably would be for a good many others.

Far from being a heavy sticky brew, mead could be made through all the delicate variations of good white wine.

And, though the alcoholic content of the wine of the bee was greater than that of the equivalent wine of the grape, it left no hangover.

Mead, the [...? Colonel?] discovered, had given way to wine not because of any inferiority but because, with an increase in population, grape cultivation could be easily extended, whereas honey became more and more scarce.

Today, he reflected, conditions had changed once again. Britain had miles of cultivated clover and around 150,000 bee-keepers. These men could be trusted to give an enthusiastic backing to a revived mead industry.

Moreover, there was a powerful nostalgic appeal, which the colonel was not the man to neglect. Sipping this old English nectar, men might escape for a moment from this drab hurrying age. The ancients had written of mead as a magic drink. Maybe it would have a magic for moderns, too.

The colonel found himself getting down to details. There would, for instance, be climatic requirements.

These would probably place the revived British wine industry in the southwest of the mild winters.

Search For A Site

Thus it came about that one morning in the spring of 1947 the town clerks of every town in the south-west found in their mail a letter making a somewhat unusual request. Were there, the writer wished to know, within their district, any vacant premises suitable for making mead.

With one exception, the town clerks do not appear to have treated this request very seriously. The exception was a businesslike letter, which drew attention to a certain disused flourmill in the hamlet of Gulval, twelve miles from Land's End.

As soon as he saw the old Gulval mill, tall and stoutly built of stone, the colonel knew that this was it. Here were 40,000 square feet of floor space. And Gulval was almost the most southerly parish in England.

On June 1st, 1947, Mead Makers Limited took possession. Mead making started the moment the company moved in. The great oak vats were mounted on the bare joists and the floors built in around them as the first batches of liquid honey began to ferment.

Sitting in his office in the Mead House, surrounded by old prints, heraldic designs and ancient weapons, the chief meadmaker told me the story of how he had grappled with the problem of reviving and marketing in the twentieth century a medieval product.

Gravity Does The Work

With future competition from low labour cost winemaking lands very much in mind, he designed a streamlined system in which gravity would do much of the work. As the wine matured, it descended through the oak vats from floor to floor.

I saw the honey-melting room, the honey extracting room, the immense honey-storage tanks ready to receive the products of the company's twelve apiaries, stocked now with native English bees duly tamed.

I went into the "Gruit" room where a score of different sorts of herbs from the company's two herb gardens are dried and mixed into a "gruit" according to a treasured formula.

There were sections, too, for the byproducts, yeast tonic, packed herbs, honey.

When it comes to marketing the product, Colonel Gayre abandons the twentieth century and makes a dive again into his beloved Middle Ages.

"We're old fashioned people here," he says. "We're not going to use modern methods to push mead. We're not going to cover the country with announcements. We believe it's the sort of thing that sells itself"

Bait For The Buyers

To assist his good article to make its virtues manifest, however, he has had the ingenious idea of constructing in a tumbledown corner of the old mill an exact replica of a medieval "Mead Hall," complete with cloisters, herb gardens, pigeons, bee garden, buttery, heraldic flags and stained — glass windows. Nothing if not versatile, the colonel made the stained — glass windows himself.

In this persuasive setting, foreign buyers and tourists alike can sit down to meals cooked according to medieval recipes and served with mead.

There is — or soon will be — a type of mead to accompany every course. *Cyser,* a sherry-like aperitif, *sack methaglin,* a herbalized liquor similar to vermouth, *mead,* a dry table wine, *sack mead,* a dessert mead described as not unlike Imperial Tokay. Later there will be sparkling mead and mead liqueurs.

All this, of course, is very much what the American tourist ordered. Already the trail-blazers have been down to Cornwall to drink their mead and eat their lunches cooked according to medieval recipes and, perhaps, even get a glimpse of the Worshipful Company of Meadmakers assembling round its long table.

The Worshipful Company, explains the colonel, is [missing text] properly restored medieval [. . . ?] registered with the appropriate [. . . ?] in this case the town council its members include directors, shareholders and workers duly qualified.

"Our troubles today," says the colonel, "arise from industry having cut itself off from the life of the neighborhood." To avoid this error, he has devised for the mead industry an annual ceremony to take place on St. Bartholomew's Day — St. Bartholomew being the patron saint of mead making and honey.

In June this year, the first Cornish-made mead began to flow into the slim long-necked bottles sealed with wax, embossed with the Worshipful Company's *fleur de lis.* (They hadn't any tin foil in the Middle Ages).

Demand from America has been impressive. When I visited the Mead House, a large order had just been received from Mexico. Other consignments were going to Switzerland, Brazil, and Australia.

Meanwhile, in the old silo [missing text] mill, carpenters are hammering [missing text] preparing the distillery. The [missing text] pot-still is already in position and next year mead brandy and mead liqueurs will be added to the Mead Makers' list.

Today, the colonel's faith in the judgment of the past is beginning to pay-off. But all is not yet clear ahead.

One obvious danger is that, as soon as the mead makers have built up a large and profitable market, imitators will cash in with a cut-price product.

Mapping Vintage Areas

"We shall give them a good run for their money," says the colonel, who studied strategy in the Army. He plans to identify mead as firmly as possible with Cornwall-just as the genuine bordeaux is identified with Bordeaux, cognac comes from Cognac and champagne from the old French province of Champagne.

He will issue maps of the "vintage area" with his bottles of mead. And he is comforted by the thought that there isn't so much room down there in England's toe.

The auguries are good. Between mid-June and mid-July, when the fanners pray for rain, the beemen are secretly hoping for drought. This, year the beemen got their way. Nineteen forty-nine's is a bumper honey harvest.

Already the Mead Hall is absorbing 250,000 pounds of honey a year — a concentrate, adds Colonel Gayre, equivalent to a million pounds of grape juice. Next year, when the distillery starts up, they'll need another hundred tons. In four years time they calculate to be getting through a million pounds of honey a year.

With the bee — the native bee — thus busier than ever and the wine of old England flowing once again from Cornwall to the ends of the world, the colonel snatches a moment from the re-creation of an industry to attend to the re-creation of the customer.

When drinking the drink of' the gods, he says, let us have no more shoddy, cheap, and vulgar "Cheerios" and "Here's Hows." The proper toast when drinking mead is "Wassail" and the correct reply is "Drink Hail."

— from *John Bull* magazine 1949

Appendix VII

THIS IS AN ILLUMINATED copy of Caddick's, *Madrigal of Mead*, which was "Designed and drawn for Cornish Mead Co. Ltd by Marsden Prophet, St Ives".

The reproduction here does not show effectively the plethora of detail as the original.

This measures 35cm x 29cm.

A MADRIGAL OF MEAD

"Minstrel from the past appearing
Through the dreams that haunt this room,
Tell me, tell me, what's the musick
That you make at Newlyn Coombe?"

"Sir, my lute and I are pilgrims
Wheresoever fancies lead
I come to bless a humble wedding
With my madrigal of mead.

Mead bodes well for holy wedlock!
If it starts the month of bliss
Every honeymoon tastes sweeter
Sweeter cupid, sweeter, sweeter!
When there's honey in each kiss!"

"Shepherd down the chine descending,
Piping on your oaten reed,
Tell me, tell me, what your tune is?"
Master, 'tis a song of mead!

I be altar pledged tomorrow
To a maid from Mousehole way —
Master, he who weds tomorrow
Seeks new strength from mead today!"

"Wise men praise it! ... If, at cockcrow,
All's a-buzzing in my head
Well then bees must quit my bonnet! —

Honest bees will quit my bonnet —
When the twilight bids us bed!"

Drain your true and ancient nectar!
Drink rich bounty while you can
Mead gives brides the bloom of Venus
Mead makes Hercules from man!

Hedgerows, herbs and furze and heather,
Stately gardens cottage flowers,
Give the harvest gathered only
By the bees in sun-blessed hours.

Honeybees store summer's treasure
For their elemental need,
Crystal days of cloudless sunshine —
Sea and sky made one by sunshine
Shine again in Cornish mead.

[Here is *A Song of Mead and Merriment,* originally in *Lyrics from Nancledra* (1950) and later *Call of the West* (1983). Does anyone know the tune? Interestingly in the acknowledgements for *Lyrics,* Caddick is grateful to Lt Col. G. R. Gayre for permission to include *A Song of Mead and Merriment*!]

A Song of Mead & Merriment

In the golden haze of summer
And the hey-day of the rose,
When the honey-suckle sweetly
Clings to every breeze that blows,
Bees will sip their ancient nectar,
Bondsmen to an age-old need,
And the rich and mellow Honey
Slowly, slowly, turns to Mead.
O when all the days are darkened
And the nights of winter long,
Let us drink and dream of sunlight
As the Mead evokes our song!

The Meadery
Land's End
Cornish Mead
Trade Emblem
A Madrigal of
"Minstrel, from the past appearing
Through the dreams that haunt this ro
Tell me, tell me, what's the musick
That you make at Newlyn Coombe?"
"Sir, my lute and I are pilgrims
Wheresoever fancies lead
I come to bless a humble wedding
With my madrigal of mead.
Mead bodes well for holy wedlock!
If it starts the month of bliss
Every honeymoon tastes sweeter
Sweeter Cupid, sweeter, sweeter!
When there's honey in each kiss!"
Drain your tru
Drink rich boun
Mead gives brid
Mead makes her
Hedgerows, herbs
Stately garden
Give the harves
By the bees in s
Honeybees store
For their elemen
Crystal days of
Sea and sky mad
Shine again in c
Mead
Artem
Designed & drawn
Cornish Mea
by Marsd

St Michael's Mount
MEAD
CORNWALL
Shakespeare
"Shepherd, down the chine descending,
piping on your oaten reed,
tell me, tell me, what your tune is?"
Master, 'tis a song of mead!
He be altar pledged tomorrow
to a maid from Mousehole way-
master, he who weds tomorrow
seeks new strength from mead today!
Wise men praise it!—if, at cockcrow,
all's a-buzzing in my head
well then bees must quit my bonnet-
honest bees will quit my bonnet!-
when the twilight bids us bed!"
Ruta
e and ancient nectar!
ty while you can
es the bloom of Venus
cules from man!
, and furze and heather,
s, cottage flowers,
t gathered only
un-blessed hours.
summer's treasure
tal need,
cloudless sunshine-
one by sunshine
ornish mead.
for
Co Ltd Newlyn Coombe Nr P.Z
Prophet. St. Ives
Mead

Chorus:
Mead it hath an ancient virtue
And it maketh laughter start –
Horas necon tristiores
Numerat sed laetos flores! –
And it taketh care apart.
Wassail! . . . Drink Hail! . . . Woe resigneth!
Wassail! . . . Drink Hail! . . . Mirth inclineth!
Wassail! . . . Drink Hail – from the heart!

Let the old in potions golden
Welcome what has come to pass,
Let the young see future pleasure
In the mirror of their glass.
Every man is full of folly,
Whatsoever his disguise,
Sometimes smiling, sometimes weeping,
But the bees are always wise.
All they do is garner honey,
As they serve a simple creed,
And the wisdom of their service
Live within a glass of Mead.

Chorus:
Mead it hath an ancient virtue
And it maketh laughter start –
Horas necnon tristiores
Numerat sed laetos flores! –
And it taketh care apart.
Wassail! . . . Drink Hail! . . . Woe resigneth!
Wassail! . . . Drink Hail! . . . Mirth inclineth!
Wassail! . . . Drink Hail – from the heart!

Appendix VIII

“I stands for Ives
(a Saint comes before)
Cornwall's New Athens
with genius galore;
The Ancient don't care;
for the influx of freak
But they think of the Rates
And strive hard to look Greek."

From *Lowdown on Uplift*, included in *Renaissance and St Ives, Both Sides of the Tamar*. See also *The Call of the West*, which includes these verses; *Z is for Zero* and *H is Henrico.*

Extracts from:

Lowdown on Uplift
(You, Too, Can Be A Highbrow)

Z is for Zero
(in Yorkshire spelt nowt)
which much highbrow chatter
is mostly about;
they fly round what’s simple
in cerebral rings
till centres aren’t middles
and objects aren’t things.

H is Henrico,
the poet, of course,
who writes all his sonnets
entirely in Morse;
an amateur station
transmits them at noon
and skippers of trawlers
translate them and swoon.

Appendix IX

COMPARE THE TWO VERSIONS and then you can decide which poem was actually published as Caddick wanted!

"R" IS FOR RAILWAYS

A LINE THEY CANNOT CLOSE
What differences there might have been
Upon the brooding Land's End scene!
This long peninsula was chopped
In half, when private interests stopped,
By lobbying and cut-and-thrust,
The railway planned to reach St. Just —
A Parliamentary murder which
Made richer the already rich.

For all their cutlasses and noise,
The old-time buccaneers were boys
Beside the mercenary troops
Of mid-Victorian pressure-groups.
No doubt, these pious pirates prayed
In earnest, but they still betrayed
The Cornish cause. The vital Lines
Were never laid to save the Mines.

Well, there are gruesome compensations
For never having had these stations!
The last express from Mousehole West
Might break the hearts that loved it best,
The signalman at Sennen Halt,
Despairing, might be on the malt,
With Catchall's Guard, redundant now,
With none to tell him why or how;

And somewhere near Lamorna Wink
Some doting widow's hopes might sink,
For he who drove the stopping-train

Would never let off steam again,
To make the fervour of its hiss,
The panting prelude to a kiss,
And then, with gift of gin, alight
At love's own siding for the night.

Trip no further, Doctor Beeching!
Railways end with pretty speeching.
The Land's End may disdain your arts,
As locomotives spurned these parts,
And who'd be metaphysically sad
At losing — what he'd never had?
I think no Cornish Einsteins speak
Of yesterdays to come next week.

"R" IS FOR RAILWAYS

THE LINE THEY CANNOT CLOSE
What differences there might have been
Upon the brooding Land's End scene!
This long peninsula was chopped
In half, when private interests stopped,
By lobbying, and cut-and-thrust,
The railway's ending at St. Just
(A Parliamentary murder which
Made wealthy persons still more rich).

For all their cutlasses and noise;
The old-time buccaneers were boys
Beside the mercenary troops
Of mid-Victorian pressure-groups.
No doubt the social pillars prayed
In earnest, but they still betrayed
The Cornish cause. These railway lines
Were never laid to save the mines.

Well, there are gruesome compensations
For never having had these stations.

The last express from Mousehole West
Might break the hearts that loved it best,
The signalman at Morvah Halt,
Despairing, might be on the malt
With some staid Guard, redundant now,
With none to tell him why or how.

And — oh! — the Buffet at Pendeen
(Was it the Railway Temperance Queen
The year that Minoru was pipped?)
Would be For Sale, its counter stripped
Of urns which served metallic tea
To General Booth in '93,
And not one record left to tell.
That Wilkie Collins rang this bell.

Trip no further, Doctor Beeching!
Railways end with pretty speeching.
Land's End may disdain your arts,
As locomotives scorned these parts,
And who'd be metaphysically sad
At losing what he'd never had?
Einstein, perhaps, for he could speak
Of yesterdays to come next week.

[*The Cornishman* 1963, and *Alphabet of West Cornwall* 1963]

Appendix X

Toni's Poem

A POEM ARTHUR WROTE for Toni Savage of New Broom Press, it was Caddicks' response after seeing a colour photograph of Toni at a jazz club; drink in hand.

Toni, in your golden jumper,
Knocking back your hundredth bumper,
Your photo fills me with surprise
Somewhere, I have seen your statue.
Yes! . . . In marble, proving that you
Are ancient Bacchus in disguise.

Biographies

HERE ARE A FEW brief notes on some of the artists and writers who feature in Laughter From Land's End. These biographies do little credit to the people mentioned.

For further and more detailed information see my list for suggested reading.

Chapter V

Peter Lanyon (1918-1964): born in St Ives — the only modern member of the St. Ives Society of Arts born in Cornwall.

Apart from wartime service, he lived in Cornwall for most of his life. His war experience in the R.A.F. altered his attitude to art and he found increasing inspiration in the Cornish Landscape. He was elected a Bard of the Cornish Gorsedd for services to Cornish Art.

In 1959, he started gliding to re-explore the landscape. He died in 1964 after a gliding accident in Somerset.

Bryan Wynter (1915-1975): Born in London, he was a conscientious objector during the war. He moved to a cottage above Zennor in 1945.

He was one of the many who came to St. Ives after the war to enjoy the ambiance of art and artists, as well as the light, colour and beauty of the area.

He painted local landscapes, farms and mines, later producing abstract work. Some of his paintings are regarded as rather 'dark'.

Broadsides from Bohemia (1973) is dedicated, "To my friend Bryan Wynter, and to the memories of creative carousals we shared with such splendid others in St. Ives long, long, long ago".

Bernard Leach (1887-1979): Possibly Britain's most influential potter. Born in Hong Kong. After studying in Japan and China for 11 years, he returned to England in 1920 and established his pottery in St Ives. He produced stoneware and rakuware using local materials.

One of his aims was to provide sound hand made pots cheaply enough for daily use which everyone could afford.

The 17th century technique of English slip decoration was revived at St Ives.

He was also a painter and etcher. "He raised the work of craftsman-potter to an accepted art form" (Cross — *The Shining Sands*). A set of postage stamps were issued on the centenary of his birth commemorating 'Studio Pottery'.

He wrote a number of books, the best known perhaps, *A Potter's Book* 1940.

John Wells (1907 — 2001) Born in London, where he qualified as a doctor. He visited Cornwall frequently. After working for a time in a hospital, he was a G.P. on the Isles of Scilly 1936 — 1945.

He retired from the medical profession in 1945 to become a full time painter, living and working in Newlyn.

A lot of his work was influenced by his time on the Isles of Scilly.

Chapter VI

Hyman Segal (1914-2004): Born in London, served in Africa during World War II and moved to St. Ives in 1947.

In 1948, he took over No. 10 Porthmeor Studios where he worked until his death.

He was a cartoonist, author, sculptor especially a portraitist. He was well known for his black and white drawings of fishermen and others; and of course, cats. He was always very concerned with the welfare of animals.

He worked as an art therapist with individuals and groups at Tehidy Sanatorium, near Camborne. Good examples of his work are to be seen in the Sloop Inn, St. Ives.

David Caddick told me that Segal had dearly wanted to draw Arthur Caddick, but could never catch him for long enough! — A great pity.

Chapter VII

Denys Val Baker (1917- 1984): Born in Yorkshire of Welsh parents — was a conscientious objector during the war. He moved to Cornwall in 1948 after training as a journalist.

He wrote over 100 books, 400 short stories, many magazine articles and also worked for radio. Between 1949 — 1952 and 1966 — 1974, he edited and published the *Cornish Review*. He was also a very keen sailor.

A memorial bench on the coastpath between Zennor and Gurnard's Head has the following inscription:

In Memory of Denys Val Baker 1917 — 1984
Author, Editor and Seafarer

Chapter XII

Morton Nance (1873-1959) Born in Cardiff, of Cornish parents, an artist, a keen student of pottery and the history of ships and sailing, writing several books on both subjects. After many visits to Cornwall, by 1906 he was living Nancledra.

He was a friend of Bernard Leach, (qv) his son Dicon marrying Leach's daughter, Eleanor.

In 1919, he founded the first Old Cornwall Society in St. Ives.

He was President of the Federation of Old Cornwall Societies and editor of it's journal *Old Cornwall.*

He wrote several plays in Cornish; and a number of pamphlets.

He evolved a unified system of spelling for Cornish creating, between 1936 and 1938, the first Cornish dictionary. With Welshman A.S.D. Smith, they translated St. Mark's Gospel into Cornish.

Chapter XIII

Karl Weschke: (1925-2005) Born in Germany, he had some art training which was interrupted by War Service. He was a prisoner of war in Britain from 1945-1948.

He continued his art training during this period and carried out a variety of jobs in the United Kingdom and abroad, at one stage working as a lion feeder's assistant.

As a result of a meeting with Bryan Wynter (qv) he moved to Zennor, where he met W.S Graham (qv).

In 1960, he moved to the wild, rugged beauty of Cape Cornwall where with one break, he lived until his death.

His paintings have a close Cornish connection, especially those of Cape Cornwall, where his work reflects the landscape and climate of that area.

Chapter XIII

Winston Graham (1911-2003): Born in Manchester, moved to Cornwall after his schooling.

He wrote over 30 novels, several of which were made into films. *Marnie* (1964), was directed by Alfred Hitchcock, starring Sean Connery. He is also remembered for his series of 12 Poldark novels.

The first, *Ross Poldark*, was written in 1945. The last, *Bella Poldark* came out in 2002 shortly before his death. They were the basis for a very popular 1970's television series.

Charles Causley (1917-2003): Born in Launceston, where he lived and taught for most of his life. He served in the Royal Navy during World War II, returning home to teach.

His Royal Navy experiences inspired *Farewell Aggie Weston* (1951). A very popular writer, whose work is enjoyed by children and adults alike. *Figgie Hobbin* (1970) was written for children and I think every school has a copy of *Timothy Winters*.

His work appears in many anthologies and there are several volumes of his collective works.

William Sydney Graham (1918-1986): Born in Scotland, moved to Cornwall in 1943. Lived in London and abroad during the late 1940's and early 1950's but returned to live in Penwith.

He was a fisherman at Mevagissey for a while and later an Auxiliary Coastguard at Gurnard's Head.

It was here he found inspiration for one of his best known poems, *The Night Fishermen* (1955). He also wrote poems as memorials for friends such as, 'Dear Bryan Wynter'. His reading tours of the U.S.A. were very popular especially in the Universities.

Despite ill health, he and his wife, Nessie were able to attend Arthur and Peggy's Ruby Wedding anniversary celebrations described in appendix 1 where he read a poem that he had composed for the occasion.

Alfred Wallis (1855-1942): Born in Devonport. Had no real education, self taught to read and write. He went to sea at the age of 9. He later joined the fishing fleet at Penzance.

In 1890 he moved to St. Ives and worked as a scrap metal merchant.

He retired to No. 3 Back Road West, St. Ives (commemorated, today, by a plaque). He began painting at the age of 70 after the death of his wife, Susan. He painted the sea, boats and scenes from his life at sea. He used marine paints on any scraps of paper to hand or cardboard, and even household objects such as mugs, or on one occasion, a pair of bellows.

He was 'discovered' by Ben Nicholson and Christopher Wood in the 1920's.

A sad, lonely man in his old age, he died in Madron Workhouse. His grave in Barnoon Cemetry, St Ives, is decorated with tiles made by Bernard Leach (qv). Today, his pictures sell for up to £100,000.

The Alfred Wallis Appreciation Group celebrate the memory of Arthur Wallis and his life in St Ives. Membership is small and by invitation. Meetings are occasional, informal and light-hearted. The toast to his memory, drunk in Cornish brewed ale, reflects the nature of the man, "Alfred Wallis; Mariner, Scrap Dealer, Ice Cream Seller and Artist".

Chapter XV

A.S. Neill (1883-1973): Alexander Sutherland Neill — educationalist and Author.

In 1927, he founded the co-ed Summerhill School in Leiston, Suffolk. It was regarded as being very progressive providing an education free of any authority.

His ideas and methods were revered abroad as well as in Britain.

See 'Neill! Neill! Orange Peel!' (1973)

Chapter XIX

Patrick Heron (1920 — 1999) Born in Leeds, moved to Cornwall in 1925. As a 14 year old created designs for Cresta Silks, his father's textile firm. After a period in London, he moved to Zennor in 1955 and to the Porthmeor Studion in 1958. The Tate St. Ives has in it's entrance hall, his magnificent stained glass window which strikes the eye as soon as you enter.

Guido Morris: a brief biography

[Kindly contributed by Michael Bridge]

BORN IN ESSEX IN 1910, Morris was the son of an Anglican clergyman. Most of his childhood was to be spent in Devon where his father held a living. Admitted to Edinburgh University in 1929 to study medicine he failed his exams. With a strong interest in natural history, 1932 saw him working as an assistant to Professor Zuckermann first at London Zoo and then Oxford. In 1934 he moved to a post at Bristol Zoo.

During his stay in Oxford Morris dabbled in printing: having acquired a small, wooden handpress. Proud mention was made of producing bookplates. Undoubtedly he was attracted to the possibility of opening a Private Press at which he would use fine paper, quality ink, with skilful use of type to print small quantities of worthy, if not necessarily commercially viable, texts. The opportunity arose whilst he was working at Bristol Zoo. The management agreed to publish a monthly magazine and were persuaded by Morris to allow him to undertake the work.

A vintage 1843 Columbian Press handpress, weighing one and a half tons and needing major repair, was purchased from a newspaper office in Weston-Super-Mare. In the spring of 1935 Morris and the handpress took up residence in a cottage and outhouse (the Columbian being too large to fit into the living room) provided by a female friend in the village of Langford, Somerset, some twelve miles from Bristol. The first two editions of the broadsheet were printed and sold at the price of 1d. Each.

It was at this time that Morris made two decisions that were to mark his press for the future. Firstly, having been christened Douglas, he now adopted the name "Guido". Secondly he chose "Bembo" typeface for his work. The third issue (August 1935) of the Bristol Zoo Broadsheet records that it is, "printed this month in Bembo, a type cast by The Monotype Corporation (London). The Roman of this type was originally designed by Francesco Giffo da Bologna: for Aldus

Manutius, most celebrated Printer-Publisher of all time; and in the great age of the Venetians it was first used to print the De Aetna of Pietro Bembo, then a youth, & sometime Cardinal of the Holy Roman Church. (Anno 1495)".

The four page Zoo Broadsheet, was not a public success. By the third issue, the editor was announcing there would be a 100% price increase for the following edition and publication would then cease, "unless a sufficient number of people have by then subscribed their names as willing definitely to buy the magazine". The September edition was indeed the last. Other printings appeared from Langford (since joined by more reliable, somewhat smaller 1856 Albion handpress in the living room) both to order from the public and as speculative ventures by the proprietor. In March 1936 Guido printed a notice announcing, "the immediate intention of his Press and a Latin edition of Ecclesiastes". The intentions were twofold: "first, to acquaint you that a well printed edition of Ecclesiastes in the Latin version of the Vulgate will shortly be available at the price of five shillings; secondly, to solicit your patronage for a series of mediaeval Latin reprints". The reasoning behind the name Latin Press becomes self-evident. These initiatives, like the Zoo Broadsheet, did not prove to be financially viable. In June of 1937 the Latin Press went into voluntary liquidation.

Guido had been confronted with some inescapable facts involved in owning a Press. To be a Job Printer, producing work to the order of customers, required skill, organisation and application. The Private Printer should preferably to be independently wealthy so as to absorb the overheads, ignore the need for profits, and simply indulge his fancy as to the items printed. If personal wealth was not an option, the aspiring Private Printer should acquire a patron who was prepared to underwrite the project (to be fair, Guido did pursue this particular path with great energy if singular lack of success). It is just conceivable that even without private means or a rich patron the aspiring Private Printer could achieve success: but he would need exceptionally well developed financial acumen together with consistent organising abilities and time-management skills.

Having no private means; no rich patron; a lack of financial awareness and lamentable time-management skills lead to predictable results: for the next few years The Latin Press had a chequered career. It reopened in London (1937), returned to the Langford area (1938), reopened in London (1939), and came to rest in Northampton (1940). In that year World War Two gathered Guido into the Royal Army Medical Corps where he served in the ranks, in England, for the duration. Demobilised in 1945 Guido faced the austerity of post-war Britain with an undiminished desire to be a Private Printer. The Albion Press moved back south to a basement in Central London. Yet again financial problems remained to the fore exacerbated by an unreliability to produce work on time. Where to next?

In November 1945, Guido arrived in St Ives, Cornwall. With the help of the artist and writer, Sven Berlin he rented a one-room, granite building (a former fisherman's netloft) perched on rocks overlooking St Ives Bay. This was to be the seventh home of The Latin Press. The press and equipment arrived in April 1946 and there followed a highly productive eight years. Usually working alone, Guido produced headed notepaper, posters, notices, invitations, exhibition catalogues for clients both local and further afield. In the early 1950s he published a series of verse booklets, The Crescendo Poetry, on his own account. He also first printed then later typeset several books for other publishers. His Achilles heel of time and money management persisted: financial insecurity was ever present. In the summer of 1953 his creditors lost patience: bailiffs visited the netloft and removed the presses. On this occasion friends could not be persuaded to provide the money to rescue his equipment. This time there was to be no phoenix-like rebirth.

Guido left St Ives that autumn. Work in a London bookshop and as a specialist reader for the Cambridge University Press were to be followed by employment with London Underground. For a brief period in the early 1970s The Latin Press, located in Holborn, London flowered into life on a part-time basis. There was no longer a majestic Albion press merely a table-top Adana. By 1973 printing ended for the last time. Guido Morris died, in poverty, in London, in 1980.

Despite his all too evident weaknesses as a businessman, Guido was a fine printer. Items produced at The Latin Press are becoming increasingly collectable and this is reflected in the prices that are asked. Those who would like to own a representative item at reasonable cost should look out for one of the booklets (600 of each were printed) in the Crescendo Poetry series (1951-52). Issue No. 1, *The Speech of Phantoms* by Arthur Caddick is already scarce: reflecting his popularity when published and into the present day.

For further reading:

- The period to 1969: *The Quest for Guido* by Anthony Baker printed in the Winter 1969 edition of The Private Library, published by the Private Libraries Association. This includes a 'tentative' list of items produced by The Latin Press until 1953.
- The period 1970 to 1973: *Guido Morris, Fine Printer: The Last Chapter?* by David Wilkinson, published as a Book Gallery Monograph in 1995. Contains a comprehensive list of items produced 1970-73.
- The Latin Press in St Ives (1946-53): Exhibition Catalogue *Telling the Town*, Tremayne Applied Arts, St Ives, September 2003, by Michael Bridge.

Attention is also drawn to material held at the St Ives Archive Study Centre.

The Published Works of Arthur Caddick

THE PUBLISHED WORK OF Arthur Caddick. — all now out of print.

Respectable Persons — a novel; Hutchinson 1940

Lyrics from Nancledra; Fortune Press 1950

The Speech of Phantoms; Latin Press of Guido Morris 1951

Quiet Lutes and Laughter; Fortune Press 1955

One Hundred Doors Are Open — A Guide too 100 Cornish Inns; Pendragon Press 1956

One Hundred Doors Are Open — (Revised); Arthur Caddick Publications 1957

Curiosities of Cornwall — (subtitle: *A Miscellany to Divert the Tourist* — illustrated by the Author); Arthur Caddick Publications (1957) [For example of Caddick's art work see Appendix IV]

Lowdown on Uplift; Arthur Caddick Publications (1957)

This was:

"A complete guide to modern culture in the form of an Alphabet, written backwards, Z-A of twenty six verses... A novel feature was that the booklet was printed on both sides on one long strip of paper, folded in 'Concertina' fashion." See Appendix VIII and Chapter XVIII

Winding Ways to Carn and Cove; Arthur Caddick Publications 1958

Argument From Design — A Satire; Westwind Press — 1957
A limited edition of 100 copies, "a fairly long satirical poem in heroic couplets".

Admiral Benbow Ballads; Roland Morris — Mainsail Haul Press — 1957

The Tilting of the Scale — a novella; Fortune Press 1962

Alphabet of West Cornwall; Arthur Caddick Publications 1963

A Croft in Cornwall; Wordens of Cornwall 1968

Broadsides From Bohemia; Bossiney Books 1973

The Ballad of Michael Joseph; Headlands 1977

The Call of the West; Bossiney Books 1983

As far as I know, Caddick's poetry appears in only one anthology, and that very recently.

The Dreamt Sea : An Anthology of Anglo-Cornish Poetry 1928 – 2004; Edited by Alan M. Kent.

This has five of his poems including, *The Ballad of Michael Joseph, The Captain of Cornwall (1497).*

Portrait of Nancledra appears in *Cornish Review No. 20* — Spring 1972
Also published as *Nancledra,* in *My Cornwall* – edited Michael Williams; Bossiney Books 1973

A superb piece Renaissance and St Ives appears in *Both Sides of the Tamar* — edited Michael Williams; Bossiney Books 1975

It includes the poem: "*I stands for Ives,* from *Lowdown on Uplift* a pamphlet of mine, which pulled out like a concertina, and has sunk without a trace!" See Appendix VIII and also Chapter XVIII

The Cornish Review

Caddick had poetry and prose published in Denys Val Baker's *Cornish Review. The Cornish Review* had a run of 2 series. Series 1 1949 — 1952. Series 2 1966 — 1974.

His work can be found in the following editions.

Series 1: No. 2 - Summer 1949; *The Lighthouse;* No. 4 – Spring 1950 *The Worshipful Makers of Woad — Removed*! [see Chapter VII]; No. 5 – Summer 1950, *Ode On Becoming Respectable;* No.8 — Summer 1951, *A Sequence of Three Poems;* No. 10 — Summer 1952, *Funeral Lines.*

Series 2: No.1 Spring 1966, *The Second Launching (a poem); Laughter At Land's End — "From an autobiographical work in progress;"* No. 6 Summer 1967, *More Laughter At Land's End — "Further extracts from an autobiographical work in progress;"* No. 10 Winter 1968, *Lesverbyon Kernow* (Stepsons Of Cornwall), *Report of Inaugural Think-Out Held At Ding-Dong (Disguised As A Sing-Song) At Moonrise On The Feast Of ST. TREBOGUS, 1968.*

No. 20 Spring 1972, *Portrait of Nancledra;* No 22 Winter 1972, *Marks of Royal Favour*. [Described by Val Baker as being an amusing extract from *Laughter at Land's End*]

Caddick's work was reviewed locally and nationally. The following reviews appeared in the *Cornish Review*.

Lyrics from Nancledra (by Denys Val Baker), No. 6 Winter 1950; *Speech of Phantoms* (by George Manning-Sanders), No.9 Winter 1951

Also No. 10 Summer 1952 (by W. J. Strachan).

Series 2: *A Croft in Cornwall* (by Frances Bellerby), No. 9 Summer 1968.

He had a large number of poems published in newspapers and magazines before their publication in book or broadsheet form. As well as the *Cornishman*, and the *St Ives Times and Echo*, he had work in — among others — *Country Life; Punch* — see appendix 4; *The Scotsman; Daily Telegraph* and the *Daily Express; Sunday Times* and *John O'London's*. Some now, sadly, defunct.

The late Toni Savage's New Broom Press of Leicester published a number of beautifully produced broadsheets of Arthur Caddick's poetry.

The Phoenix Broadsheets are generally single sheets of varying sizes, usually in runs of 100.

They are delicately illustrated and, in my opinion quite exquisite.

Savage would get some of the broadsheets illustrated by major artists eg.

Phoenix Broadsheet 149; "there are days. . . " has three tiny black and white vignettes by Rigby Graham.

Broadsheet 280, *An end to love* and *Broadsheet 290*, *Italy 1929* both have illustrations by John Piper.

As well as individual poems he published such items as: *A fifty year span* — a booklet of 2 poems: *Italy 1929* and *Tend Your Roses Gently*; illustrated again by Rigby Graham in an edition of 120 copies — 1979.

Also,

The Day I Swam the Hellespont; this is described by St Ives book and art dealer David Wilkinson thus:

"Small 8vo. Sewn card covers. Eight hand sewn pages including self covers. Crosssed besom – broom emblem to rear cover." (New Broom Press!) "Hand set and printed at 78, Cambridge Street, Leicester, in an edition of 100 copies taken from typescript dated 26 VIII '82."

For a poetical description of Savage by Caddick see Appendix X

As well as published work he wrote poetry for friends and family for birthdays, anniversaries etc.

He broadcast on radio and television and produced a cassette of his poetry — The Sentinel Series, *Poets in Cornwall* — Now available on c.d. See advert!

He also wrote a number of plays for amateur production. e.g. *A Potted Pantomime* entitled *Cornubia and the Prince of Pops* — printed in the *Cornishman* Boxing Day 1963. A number of his plays are in the University of Exeter library, Special Collections.

The notes on Caddick in 'Contributers' in the *Cornish Review* — first series — number four, spring 1950 a reference is made to the fact that, "Twenty four lines of one of his unpublished war poems are embalmed in the columns of Hansard."

Well here they are!

They were included in a speech made by independent M.P. Mr. W. Brown 20/5/1942 during a war situation debate.

It was Brown's second 'maiden' speech.

> *"Finally, I say you must have a people with hope. Members of Parliament get a mixed lot of stuff sent to them at one time or another. I had something sent to me yesterday, and found it singularly moving. It is a poem by someone I never heard of, but it gets right to the roots of the situation in Britain and to the need for the postulation of positive aims of a better world after the war. It is not only a question of economics. The dominant emotion in Britain on this subject is not a demand for equality of wealth. It is a demand for a state of society, which does less violence to a man's social conscience, and less indignity to his worth as a*

human being, than our present state. I will quote a few verses of what this man wrote to me:

'Costers have died that culture shall remain;
And country lads for freedom on the seas,
Who saw no ships before they went to fight,
And derelicts have died for decencies,
And outcast men have perished to maintain
The Christian faith against the powers of might.
****

Oh that the nation with one voice could say
This time the land you save shall be your own.
This time, at last, the good rich English soil
Shall yield to those whose hands have made it pay
Yourselves shall profit by what you have grown
And harvests shall belong to those who toil'.
****

Say this and see the land electrified
By one galvanic, splendid, human spark.
Add to the hate of all that Hitler holds
Of degradation and of loathsome, dark
Duress, the hope that victory unfolds
Of decency, equality and pride.
****

Say this, and see the men of England rise,
Strong in the prizing of their future's worth
To give back justice to the weak again,
To scour the bully from the seas and earth
Hurl down the Devil's night-hawks from the skies
And prove to God, He made not man in vain.

I do not know whether that moves Hon. Members, but it moves me".

Hansard Vol 380 — full speech, columns 292-300.
Poem — columns 298-299

Peggy has the complete poem which is called *Visions Singular*

I think one has to consider the period it was written before comparing it to his later work.

Bibliography

The Dark Monarch
Sven Berlin; The Gallery Press 1962

The Coat of Many Colours
Sven Berlin; Radcliffe Press 1994

Virgo in Exile
Sven Berlin; Finishing Publishing 1996

I'll Raise the Wind Tomorrow
Diana Calvert (nee Caddick); No. 3 in the occasional series of Book Gallery Monographs; The Book Gallery, St Ives 1994

Wassail! In Mazers of Mead
G.R.Gayre; Phillimore & Co. Ltd. 1948

Never Sit Down in the Digey!
Eric Hirth; Turnstone Publications 1992

Everyone Was Working
Alison Oldham; Tate St. Ives/Falmouth College of Arts Research Series 2002

Cornish Studies – Second Series No. 7
Edited by Philip Payton ; University of Exeter Press
Chapter 8 — Cornish Identity and
Landscape in the Work of Arthur Caddick
Catherine Brace (University of Exeter)

A Popular Dictionary of Cornish Place Names.
O.J. Padel; Alison Hodge 1998

An Index to the Cornish Review
Phoebe M. Procter; Institute of Cornish Studies 1978

The Cornish World of Denys Val Baker
Tim Scott; Ex Libris Press 1994

Britain's Art Colony By the Sea
Denys Val Baker; George Ronald 1959
New Edition, Sansom & Co. Ltd 2000

A View from Land's End
Denys Val Baker; William Kimber and Co. Ltd 1982

The Spirit of Cornwall
Denys Val Baker; A Star Book; W.H. Allen & Co. Ltd 1980

Cornish Place Names and Language
Craig Weatherhill; Sigma Leisure 1995

Curiosities of Cornwall
Michael Williams; Bossiney Books (1983)

Hansard — Volume 380 Columns 292-300

St Ives Times and Echo
17/4/1987 Obituary of Arthur Caddick.
Author at present unknown.

St Ives Times and Echo
19/6/1992 Review of Eric Hirth's *Never Sit Down in the Digey*! by Toni Carver

Squib: 'The magazine of Comedy Allsorts'
No.1 January 1992/January 1993
Article *Giles* by Will Adams

Various editions of the *Cornishman*, *West Briton*, *Western Morning News* and *Punch Magazine*.

General Oxford Companion to English Literature
O.U.P.; 2nd Edition — reprint with corrections April 1940

The Concise Oxford Dictionary
6th Edition 1976 13th impression 1982

The Oxford Dictionary of Quotations
3rd Edition 1979

Chambers Biographical Dictionary
Editor Magnus Magnusson; 5th Edition 1996

Simon Hoggart's Diary
Guardian 2004 (exact date unknown)

Who Was Who Volume X 1996 – 2000
A.C. Black 2001

Twelve Boxes of Caddick's Papers are held at:
The University of Exeter
Special Collections
Old Library
University of Exeter
Prince of Wales Road
Exeter, EX4 4SB
Ref: EUL MS 124

Full details in:
Modern Literary Papers in the University of Exeter Library: A Guide
Jessica Gardner and Ian Mortimer
University of Exeter Library and Information Service 2003

I found everyone at the University very helpful both during my visits and on the telephone

Suggested Further Reading

BOOKS ABOUT CORNWALL ARE legion, some serious, some not so!

Tor Mark Press produce a wide range of easily obtained titles which give a very good introduction to the county.

For a good general history, I suggest:

Cornwall For Ever! Kernow Bys Vyken!
St Ives, Roche Ltd, 2000

A book published to mark the millennium and given to every young person aged 18 and under in Education in Cornwall.

For more detail:

A History of Cornwall
F E Halliday; Gerald Duckworth & Co. Ltd. 1959; 2nd Edition 2000

Cornwall, A History
Philip Payton; Cornish Editions Ltd., 2004

For St. Ives

The Book of St. Ives
Cyril Noall; Barracuda Books Ltd. 1977; 2nd Edition 1984; 3rd impression Baron Buckingham 2000

The Story of St. Ives
Cyril Noall; Tor Mark Press 1994; Fourth edition 2002 – reprinted 2004

For the Cornish Language and place names:

The Story of The Cornish Language
Peter Berresford-Ellis; Tor Mark Press 1998

The Cornish Dialect and the Cornish Language (leaflet)
Pol Hodge; The Cornish Language Board 1997

The Art History of St. Ives and Cornwall is covered very thoroughly. You may like to try these:

Painting the Warmth of the Sun: St. Ives Artists 1939-1975
Tom Cross; Halsgrave 1984
Revised 1995 – West Country Books in Association Lutterworth Press.

The Shining Sands. Arts in Newlyn and St. Ives. 1880 – 1930
Tom Cross; Halsgrave 1994 – Reprinted 1999

St Ives Revisited – Innovators and Followers
Peter Davies; Old Bakehouse Publications 1994

St Ives 1883 – 1993. Portrait of an Art Colony.
Marion Whybrow; The Antique Collector's Club Ltd. 1994
Revised 2002

For Alfred Wallis

The Innocent Eye
Marion Whybrow; Sansom & Company 1999.

Alfred Wallis: Artist & Mariner
Robert Jones; Halsgrove 2001.

As for Giles!

His later annuals are usually available in charity or second-hand bookshops.

Pedigree Books produce annuals reproducing his earlier work. For his work and life, I recommend:

The Ultimate Giles
Peter Tory; Headline Book Publishing 1995

If you want to follow in the footsteps of Caddick, a la *Winding Ways to Carns & Coves* you will do little better than to use the following by Bob Acton.

Around Land's End

A View From Trencrom

Exploring Cornish Mines – Vols. 3, 4, and 5. These cover the Penwith area more than adequately. Landfall Publications – all readily available at local bookshops.

FURTHER COPIES OF *Laughter From Land's End* may be obtained from the editor at a cost of £12 including post and packing.

Caddick made a number of radio broadcasts and also appeared on television but never recorded any of his work until 1977. Sentinel Records of Paul, near Penzance issued a series of cassettes featuring the work of Frank Ruhrmund, John Barber and Arthur Caddick.

The tapes were released in December 1977, but sales were disappointing. The tape is now available on C.D., called *Illusive hour*. It takes it's name from the title of Peggy's favourite poem. It comprises of 28 poems. It's an excellent recording; as his daughter Diana said: "It's as if he is in the room".

A few copies are still available from the editor £6.00 including postage and packing.

Rod Humphries
1 Wesley Passage
St Ives
TR26 1SQ

Finally

IF YOU ARE EVER in St Ives or Penzance go to Nancledra and make your way to the old power station. A discreet glance at Windswept – please don't disturb any residents with headlights or noise.

The power station is about two hundred yards off the B330 – Explorer O.S Map 102 grid ref. 494 353.

Be careful! – it is a mud track and has ditches on both sides. There is no parking in the lane leading to the Power Station.

Park carefully on the road and explore on foot. Preferably you should go on a really wet and windy day – or better still, at night! You really need to be there in total darkness! Then, declaim to the four winds one of his poems – Any one, your choice!

After, make your way to the Engine Inn in Cripplesease or The Castle in St Ives or perhaps The Dock in Penzance, or any of the hundred and while there raise a glass to Arthur Bruce Caddick, the Poet Laureate of Penwith.

Cheers Arthur!

